Cloud Foundry:
The Definitive Guide
Develop, Deploy, and Scale

Duncan C. E. Winn

Beijing · Boston · Farnham · Sebastopol · Tokyo

Cloud Foundry: The Definitive Guide

by Duncan C. E. Winn

Printed in the United States of America.

Published by O'Reilly Media, Inc. , 1005 Gravenstein Highway North, Sebastopol, CA 95472.

O'Reilly books may be purchased for educational, business, or sales promotional use. Online editions are also available for most titles (*http://oreilly.com/safari*). For more information, contact our corporate/institutional sales department: 800-998-9938 or *corporate@oreilly.com*.

Editors: Brian Anderson and Virginia Wilson	**Indexer:** Judy McConville
Production Editor: Melanie Yarbrough	**Interior Designer:** David Futato
Copyeditor: Octal Publishing, Inc.	**Cover Designer:** Karen Montgomery
Proofreader: Christina Edwards	**Illustrator:** Rebecca Demarest

May 2017:   First Edition

Revision History for the First Edition
2017-05-22:   First Release

978-1-491-93243-8

[LSI]

To my daughters, Maya and Eva.
Dream BIG. The world awaits you...

Table of Contents

Foreword

When we think of transformative innovation, it's easy for our minds to grasp the tangible and overt technologies—the television, the personal computer, the smartphone. These inventions are visible, material commodities that serve a physical purpose in our lives. These technologies start small and then eventually gain widespread adoption, at which point they change the way we interact and engage with the technology —and often with the world around us. When we talk about strides in technology to most people, these are the gadgets they envision: separate objects that can be picked up, plugged in, and turned off.

But for those of us who are quietly enabling digital transformation across multiple industries, we know what innovation can look like. It can be invisible and intangible —the velocity behind a high dive into the pool. The operators and developers of the world no longer reside in the technology aisle. You are leading the change at every kind of company across every industry. It's one thing to demonstrate how a printing press increases the pace of printing papers exponentially. It's another thing entirely to explain how a platform that is not visible has the ability to transform a company's ability to compete in a quickly changing marketplace. This book is a resource for you as you lead the digital revolution within your organization.

This is undoubtedly a technical book devoted to the underlying concepts of Cloud Foundry and how it works, but it is emblematic of something larger at play. The author, Duncan Winn, has spent a career helping customers achieve more with technology. Most recently, at Pivotal, he helped customers implement, deploy, and get apps up and running on Cloud Foundry. He saw such incredible results that he took it upon himself to begin the project of cataloging, explaining, and evangelizing the technology. Duncan saw the monumental benefit of Cloud Foundry to everyone, from the business itself right down to the developer. He saw how cloud-native application, architecture, and development are driving and accelerating digital innovation, and that Cloud Foundry was the invisible platform that could take this process from days to minutes.

Cloud Foundry is dedicated to improving the ability of developers to code and deploy new applications. The collaborative nature of this open source project facilitates cooperative, interactive creation, driving innovation. A platform that expedites the deployment of applications does so with the understanding that an iterative approach to development enables a user-first mentality. Cloud Foundry's support of continuous delivery empowers developers to iterate applications based on user feedback, eliminating the need for late-night adjustments during limited change windows. It minimizes risk around release failure because incremental change is easier to perform and less drastic. In short, Cloud Foundry makes a developer's job faster and easier.

Cloud Foundry is the standard for application platforms with the noble vision of unifying the market for enterprise software. *Cloud Foundry: The Definitive Guide* is an integral rulebook for building the software of the future and maintaining the momentum of digital transformation across industries. The power of open source is self-evident in the potency of Cloud Foundry, with a commitment to sharing and continuous innovation.

It is my hope that you use this book as your digital transformation encyclopedia. Read it, revisit it, learn from it, and challenge it. Cloud Foundry is for you.

— Abby Kearns
Executive Director of
Cloud Foundry Foundation

Preface

Cloud Foundry is a platform that helps you develop and deploy applications and tasks with velocity. Velocity, as a vector quantity, is different from raw speed because it is direction aware. In our case, direction is based on user feedback. Application velocity allows you to adopt an iterative approach to development through repeatedly gaining fast feedback from end users. Ultimately, this approach allows you to align your products, user requirements, and expectations. This book covers Cloud Foundry's technical concepts, providing a breakdown of the various platform components and how they interrelate. It also will walk you through a typical setup of BOSH (a release-engineering tool chain) and Cloud Foundry, and unpack the broader considerations of adopting Cloud Foundry for enterprise workloads.

Like all distributed systems, Cloud Foundry involves various levels of complexity. Complexity is fine if it is well defined. Cloud Foundry does an excellent job defining its internal complexity by providing explicit boundaries between each of its components. For the most part, this removes the need for the platform operator to deal with Cloud Foundry's internal complexity. However, there are still many other factors to consider when running Cloud Foundry; for example, choosing your underlying infrastructure, defining your networking architecture, and establishing your resiliency requirements. These concerns are environmental, relating to the ecosystem in which Cloud Foundry resides. Getting these concerns right is essential for reliably handling business critical workloads. *Cloud Foundry: The Definitive Guide* aims to tackle these environmental considerations and decision points that are required for configuring and running Cloud Foundry at scale.

In addition to unpacking the various considerations required for running the technology, this book also explores the concepts surrounding Cloud Foundry. My goal is to provide the necessary content for understanding the following:

- Cloud Foundry's underlying concepts

- How Cloud Foundry works, including the flow of communication between the distributed components
- How to begin deploying BOSH and Cloud Foundry, including the key configuration decision points

An understanding of how Cloud Foundry works is vital if you are running business-critical applications, services, and workloads on the platform. Understanding the role of each component along with the flow of communication is vital for troubleshooting platform issues.

Who Should Read This Book

My hope is that you are reading this book because you already believe Cloud Foundry will enable you to deliver software with higher velocity. If you are unfamiliar with the high-level concepts of Cloud Foundry and what it enables you to achieve, I suggest (shameless plug, I know) that you begin by reading *Cloud Foundry: The Cloud-Native Platform*. The purpose of that book is to provide an understanding of why you should care about using a platform to achieve application velocity.

This book is primarily aimed at Cloud Foundry operators who are responsible for installing, configuring, and operating Cloud Foundry. Cloud Foundry significantly simplifies the operational concerns of running applications and services. For example, imagine not having to provision infrastructure for every new project, and systematically repaving all your deployed machines via rolling upgrades with zero downtime. Empowering developers to deliver software with significantly less complexity and overhead is powerful. However, configuring and running Cloud Foundry itself can involve some complexity.

The team responsible for operating Cloud Foundry is often known as the platform operations team. This team's responsibility includes deploying and operating Cloud Foundry so that application developers can take advantage of its capabilities.

Typical expertise required for the platform operations team is very broad. A list of required roles and skills is discussed at length in "Team Structure: Platform Operations for the Enterprise" on page 44. The list is diverse because Cloud Foundry leverages different technology layers across your infrastructure. Many platform operators have expertise with a subset of these disciplines. The challenge of adopting technology that touches so many varied layers is understanding each layer and how it should be configured to interact with the others. An additional objective of this book is therefore to enable platform operators to quickly expand their areas of expertise, and to gain understanding of the salient points of any unfamiliar territory.

The approaches in this text come from real experience with numerous companies from many different industries. The companies I have worked with all have embarked on a journey toward establishing Cloud Foundry at scale. If you are looking for a way of introducing Cloud Foundry into your development and deployment pipeline, this book is for you.

Cloud Foundry also makes developers' lives easier, abstracting away the middleware, OS, and infrastructure concerns so that they can focus on just their application and desired backing services. Using Cloud Foundry is straightforward and sufficiently covered in the Cloud Foundry documentation. Therefore, developer usage of Cloud Foundry is not a focus of this book. With that said, many developers I have worked with find Cloud Foundry's technology interesting and often desire a deeper understanding of the operational aspects detailed in this book.

This is a technically focused book intended for platform operators. Therefore, you should have some of the following basic system administrative skills:

- Know how to open a terminal window in your OS of choice
- Know how to install software tools such as command-line interfaces (CLIs)
- Know how to use secure shell (SSH) and work with virtual machines (VMs)
- Know how to work with source code from GitHub (*http://github.com*) by both downloading and installing it (Mac users—Homebrew should be your go-to tool of choice here)

When I talk about specific Cloud Foundry tools such as BOSH, I will link you to an appropriate download location (often a GitHub repository). You can then follow the instructions in the linked repositories. For Mac users, you can also install most Cloud Foundry tools via Homebrew.

Why I Wrote This Book

As a platform architect for Pivotal, I have worked with numerous companies from various industries to help them install and configure Cloud Foundry. Like most platform operators, I began with knowledge of a subset of the technology; everything else I learned on the job. In my early days with Cloud Foundry, there are two key things that would have helped me:

- An understanding of the critical configuration considerations for both the platform and the underlying distributed infrastructure
- A reference architecture detailing the rationale and trade-offs for all implementation decisions

To address the first point, Cloud Foundry has forged a fantastic collaborative community from numerous companies and industries. I have been fortunate to work alongside an incredibly talented team with a diverse skill set, both within Pivotal and from other companies within the Cloud Foundry community. The reason I wrote this book is to document the best practices and considerations I have learned through working with Cloud Foundry.

Regarding the second point, as a consultant working across numerous industries, I see the same issues and questions coming up with every new engagement. It is therefore my hope that this book will explain the basic reference architecture for Cloud Foundry deployments, including detailing the rationale and trade-offs for all implementation decisions.

A Word on Cloud-Native Platforms

Cloud Foundry is a cloud-native platform. Such platforms are designed to do more for you so that you can focus on what is important: delivering applications that directly affect your business. Specifically, cloud-native platforms are designed to do more (including reliably and predictably running and scaling applications) on top of potentially unreliable cloud-based infrastructure. If you are unfamiliar with the high-level concepts of Cloud Foundry and what it enables you to achieve, you should begin by reading *Cloud Foundry: The Cloud-Native Platform*.

Online Resources

There are some great online references that you should familiarize yourself with as you embark on your Cloud Foundry journey:

- The Cloud Foundry Foundation (*https://www.cloudfoundry.org*)
- Bosh.io (*http://bosh.io*)
- The cf-deployment GitHub repository (*https://github.com/cloudfoundry/cf-deployment*)
- Cloud Foundry's continuous integration tool Concourse (*http://concourse.ci*)

Conventions Used in This Book

The following typographical conventions are used in this book:

Italics
    Indicates new terms, URLs, email addresses, filenames, and file extensions.

`Constant width`
    Used for program listings, as well as within paragraphs to refer to program elements such as variable or function names, databases, data types, environment variables, statements, and keywords.

Constant width bold
> Shows commands or other text that should be typed verbatim by the user.

Constant width italics
> Shows text that should be replaced with user-supplied values or by values determined by context.

 This icon signifies a tip, suggestion, or general note.

 This icon indicates a warning or caution.

 This icon indicates a item to take note of.

Sidebar

Sidebars are used to provide some additional context to the main text.

Command prompts always start with $, for example:

```
$ cf push
```

O'Reilly Safari

 *Safari* (formerly Safari Books Online) is a membership-based training and reference platform for enterprise, government, educators, and individuals.

Members have access to thousands of books, training videos, Learning Paths, interactive tutorials, and curated playlists from over 250 publishers, including O'Reilly Media, Harvard Business Review, Prentice Hall Professional, Addison-Wesley Professional, Microsoft Press, Sams, Que, Peachpit Press, Adobe, Focal Press, Cisco Press, John Wiley & Sons, Syngress, Morgan Kaufmann, IBM Redbooks, Packt,

Adobe Press, FT Press, Apress, Manning, New Riders, McGraw-Hill, Jones & Bartlett, and Course Technology, among others.

For more information, please visit *http://oreilly.com/safari.*

How to Contact Us

Please address comments and questions concerning this book to the publisher:

O'Reilly Media, Inc.
1005 Gravenstein Highway North
Sebastopol, CA 95472
800-998-9938 (in the United States or Canada)
707-829-0515 (international or local)
707-829-0104 (fax)

To comment or ask technical questions about this book, send email to *bookques-tions@oreilly.com.*

For more information about our books, courses, conferences, and news, see our website at *http://www.oreilly.com.*

Find us on Facebook: *http://facebook.com/oreilly*

Follow us on Twitter: *http://twitter.com/oreillymedia*

Watch us on YouTube: *http://www.youtube.com/oreillymedia*

Acknowledgments

One of the things I love about Cloud Foundry is its community. It is genuinely collaborative, and many people within the community have invested both time and expertise helping to shape the content and accuracy of this book. A brief section is not enough to encapsulate the extent to which my friends, family, and colleagues have helped me, but I will most certainly mention their names. Due to the breadth of support and the time it took to write this book, I have a sinking feeling that I've missed someone really important, in which case I apologize.

Various product managers and subject matter experts were incredibly generous with their time, both upfront to go deep on specific topics, and later on reviewing the relevant sections at length. In chapter order, I would like to thank: David Sabeti and Evan Farrar on Chapter 5; Eric Malm and Brandon Shroyer on Diego; Shannon Coen on Routing; Will Pragnell, Glyn Normington, and Julian Friedman on Containers; Ben Hale on Buildpacks; Dmitriy Kalinin on BOSH; Dan Higham on Debugging; Allen Duet and Mark Alston on Logging; Sree Tummidi and Filip Hanik on UAA; Haydon Ryan and Sean Keery on HA and DR; and Dieu Cao on the final Summary.

Numerous colleagues provided incredibly valuable input and tech reviews, including Matthew Stine, James Bayer, Onsi Fakhouri, Robert Mee, Graham Winn, Amit Gupta, Ramiro Salas, Ford Donald, Merlin Glynn, Shaozhen Ding, John Calabrese, Caleb Washburn, Ian Zink, Keith Strini, Shawn Neal, Rohit Kelapure, Dave Wallraff, David Malone, Christopher Umbel, Rick Farmer, Stu Radnidge, Stuart Charlton, and Jim Park, Alex Ley, Daniel Jones, and Dr Nick Williams—along with many folks at Stark and Wayne.

Most of the material in this book was derived from experiences in the trenches, and there are many people who have toughed it out in those trenches alongside me. Several of the people already mentioned belong in this category, but in addition, I would like to thank Raghvender Arni, Mark Ruesink, Dino Cicciarelli, Joe Fitzgerald, and Matt Russell for their superb guidance and for establishing excellent teams in which I had the good fortune to work.

Thanks also to my good friend Vinodini Murugesan for her excellent editing. Special thanks to my mother, who always invested in my education, and to my father, who provided tireless coaching and feedback throughout my career; you both inspired me to do what I love to the best of my ability. And, finally, and most importantly, thanks to my wonderful wife, Tanya Winn, for her endless understanding and support in all my endeavors.

## CHAPTER 1

The Cloud-Native Platform

Cloud Foundry is a platform for running applications, tasks, and services. Its purpose is to change the way applications, tasks, and services are deployed and run by significantly reducing the *develop-to-deployment* cycle time.

As a cloud-native platform, Cloud Foundry directly uses cloud-based infrastructure so that applications running on the platform can be infrastructure unaware. Cloud Foundry provides a contract between itself and your cloud-native apps to run them predictably and reliably, even in the face of unreliable infrastructure.

If you need a brief summary of the benefits of the Cloud Foundry platform, this chapter is for you. Otherwise, feel free to jump ahead to Chapter 2.

Why You Need a Cloud-Native Platform

To understand the business reasons for using Cloud Foundry, I suggest that you begin by reading *Cloud Foundry: The Cloud-Native Platform* (*http://pivotal.io/cloud-foundry-the-cloud-native-platform*), which discusses the value of Cloud Foundry and explores its overall purpose from a business perspective.

Cloud Foundry is an "opinionated" (more on this later in the chapter), structured platform that imposes a strict contract between the following:

- The infrastructure layer underpinning it
- The applications and services it supports

Cloud-native platforms do far more than provide developers self-service resources through abstracting infrastructure. Chapter 2 discusses at length their inbuilt features, such as resiliency, log aggregation, user management, and security. Figure 1-1 shows a progression from traditional infrastructure to Infrastructure as a Service

(IaaS) and on to cloud-native platforms. Through each phase of evolution, the value line rises due to increased abstraction. Your responsibility and requirement to configure various pieces of the software, middleware, and infrastructure stack in support of your application code diminish as the value line rises. The key is that cloud-native platforms are designed to do more for you so that you can focus on delivering applications with business value.

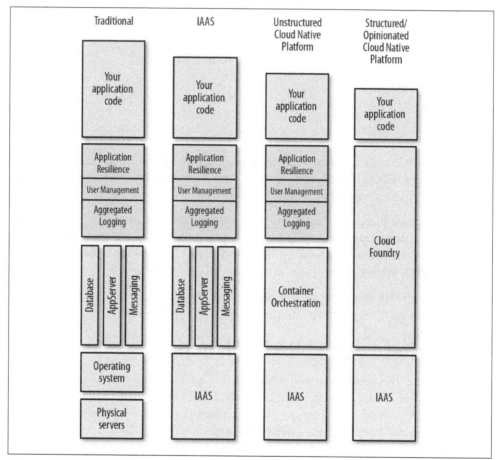

Figure 1-1. Cloud-native platform evolution

Cloud-Native Platform Concepts

In the Preface, I pointed out that Cloud Foundry's focus is not so much what a platform is or what it does, but rather what it enables you to achieve. It has the potential to make the software build, test, deploy, and scale cycle significantly faster. It removes many of the hurdles involved in deploying software, making it possible for you to release software at will.

Specifically, here's what the Cloud Foundry platform offers:

Services as a higher level of abstraction above infrastructure
Cloud Foundry provides a self-service mechanism for the on-demand deployment of applications bound to an array of provisioned middleware and routing services. This benefit removes the management overhead of both the middleware and infrastructure layer from the developer, significantly reducing the development-to-deployment time.

Containers
Cloud Foundry runs all deployed applications in containers. You can deploy applications as container images or as standalone apps containerized by Cloud Foundry. This provides flexibility. Companies already established with Docker can deploy existing Docker images to Cloud Foundry. However, containerizing applications on the user's behalf offers additional productivity and operational benefits because the resulting container image is built from known and vetted platform components. This approach allows you to run your vulnerability scans against your trusted artifacts once per update. From this point, only the application source code requires additional vulnerability scanning on a per deployment basis. Essentially, there is less to check on a per deployment basis because all of your supporting artifacts have already been vetted.

Agile and automation
You can use Cloud Foundry as part of a CI/CD pipeline to provision environments and services on demand as the application moves through the pipeline to a production-ready state. This helps satisfy the key Agile requirement of getting code into the hands of end users when required.

Cultural shift to DevOps
Cross-cutting concerns is a well-understood concept by developers. Adopting Cloud Foundry is ideally accompanied by a cultural shift to DevOps, meaning that you need to break down traditional walls, team silos, and ticket-based hand-offs to get the most benefit from it.

Microservices support
Cloud Foundry supports microservices through providing mechanisms for integrating and coordinating loosely coupled services. To realize the benefits of microservices, a platform is required to provide additional supporting capabilities; for example, Cloud Foundry provides applications with capabilities such as built-in resilience, application authentication, and aggregated logging.

Cloud-native application support
Cloud Foundry provides a contract against which applications can be developed. This contract makes doing the right thing simple and will result in better application performance, management, and resilience.

Not all cloud-native platforms are the same. Some are self-built and pieced together from various components; others are black-boxed and completely proprietary. The Cloud Foundry cloud-native platform has three defining characteristics: it is structured, opinionated, and open. I'll examine each of these traits in the following sections.

The Structured Platform

Within the platform space, two distinct architectural patterns have emerged: structured and unstructured:

- Structured platforms provide built-in capabilities and integration points for key concerns such as enterprise-wide user management, security, and compliance. With these kinds of platforms, everything you need to run your applications should be provided in a repeatable way, regardless of what infrastructure you run on. Cloud Foundry is a perfect example of a structured platform.

- Unstructured platforms have the flexibility to define a bespoke solution at a granular level. An example of an unstructured platform would involve a *"build your own platform"* approach with a mix of cloud-provided services and home-grown tools, assembled for an individual company.

Structured platforms focus on simplifying the overall operational model. Rather than integrating, operating, and maintaining numerous individual components, the platform operator just deals with the one platform. Structured platforms remove all the undifferentiated heavy lifting: tasks that must be done—for example, service discovery or application placement—but that are not directly related to revenue-generating software.

Although structured platforms are often used for building new cloud-native applications, they also support legacy application integration where it makes sense to do so, allowing for a broader mix of workloads than traditionally anticipated. The structured approach provides a much faster "getting started" experience with lower overall effort required to operate and maintain the environment.

The Opinionated Platform

When you look at successful software, the greatest and most widely adopted technologies are incredibly opinionated. What this means is that they are built on, and adhere to, a set of well-defined principles employing best practices. They are proven to work in a practical way and reflect how things can and should be done when not constrained by the baggage of technical debt. Opinions produce contracts to ensure applications are constrained to do the right thing.

Platforms are opinionated because they make specific assumptions and optimizations to remove complexity and pain from the user. Opinionated platforms are designed to be consistent across environments, with every feature working as designed out of the box. For example, the Cloud Foundry platform provides the same user experience when deployed over different IaaS layers and the same developer experience regardless of the application language. Opinionated platforms such as Cloud Foundry can still be configurable and extended, but not to the extent that the nature of the platform changes. Platforms should have opinions on how your software is deployed, run, and scaled, but not where an application is deployed; this means that, with respect to infrastructure choice, applications should run anywhere.

The Open Platform

Cloud Foundry is an open platform. It is open on three axes:

- It allows a choice of IaaS layer to underpin it (Google Cloud Platform [GCP], Amazon Web Services [AWS], Microsoft Azure, VMware vSphere, OpenStack, etc.).
- It allows for a number of different developer frameworks, polyglot languages, and application services (Ruby, Go, Spring, etc.).
- It is open-sourced under an Apache 2 license and governed by a multi-organization foundation.

Closed platforms can be proprietary and often focus on a specific problem. They might support only a single infrastructure, language, or use case. Open platforms offer choice where it matters.

Summary

Cloud Foundry is an opinionated, structured, and open platform. As such, it is:

- built on, and adheres to, a set of well-defined principles employing best practices.
- constrained to do the right thing for your application, based on defined contracts.
- consistent across different infrastructure/cloud environments.
- configurable and extendable, but not to the degree that the nature of the platform changes.

For the developer, Cloud Foundry provides a fast "on rails" development and deployment experience. For the operator, it reduces operational effort through providing built-in capabilities and integration points for key enterprise concerns such as user management, security, and self-healing.

Now you understand the nature of Cloud Foundry. Chapter 2 focuses on explaining Cloud Foundry's underlying concepts.

Concepts

This chapter explains the core concepts underpinning Cloud Foundry. Understanding these concepts paints a complete picture of why and how you should use the platform. These concepts include the need to *deal with undifferentiated heavy lifting* and why *cloud-based operating systems* are essential in protecting your cloud investment. This chapter also touches on the philosophical perspectives behind Cloud Foundry with its opinionated *do more* approach. Operational aspects, including release engineering through BOSH, and built-in resilience and fault tolerance are also introduced. Finally, some of the core capabilities of the platform beyond container orchestration are introduced, including the aggregated streaming of logs and metrics and the user access and authentication (UAA) management.

Undifferentiated Heavy Lifting

Cloud Foundry is a platform for running applications and one-off tasks. The essence of Cloud Foundry is to provide companies with the speed, simplicity, and control they need to develop and deploy applications. It achieves this by undertaking many of the burdensome boilerplate responsibilities associated with delivering software. These types of responsibilities are referred to as undifferentiated heavy lifting, tasks that must be done—for example, container orchestration or application placement—but that are not directly related to the development of revenue-generating software. The following are some examples of undifferentiated heavy lifting:

- Provisioning VMs, OSs, middleware, and databases
- Application runtime configuration and memory tuning
- User management and SSO integration
- Load balancing and traffic routing

- Centralized log aggregation
- Scaling
- Security auditing
- Providing fault tolerance and resilience
- Service discovery
- Application placement and container creation and orchestration
- Blue/green deployments with the use of canaries

If you do not have a platform to abstract the underlying infrastructure and provide the aforementioned capabilities, this additional burden of responsibility remains yours. If you are spending significant time and effort building bespoke environments for shipping software, refocusing investment back into your core business will provide a huge payoff. Cloud Foundry allows enterprises to refocus effort back into the business by removing as much of the undifferentiated heavy lifting as possible.

The Cloud Operating System

As an application platform, Cloud Foundry is infrastructure-agnostic, sitting on top of your infrastructure of choice. As depicted in Figure 2-1, Cloud Foundry is effectively a cloud-based operating system that utilizes cloud-based resources, which are hidden and abstracted away from the end user. As discussed in Chapter 1, in the same way that the OS on your phone, tablet, or laptop abstracts the underlying physical compute resource, Cloud Foundry abstracts the infrastructure's compute resource (specifically virtual storage, networking, RAM, and CPU). The net effect is that Cloud Foundry serves both as a standard and efficient way to deploy applications and services across different cloud-computing environments. Conversely, if you are stuck with directly using IaaS–specific APIs, it requires knowledge of the developer patterns and operations specific to the underlying IaaS technology, frequently resulting in applications becoming tightly coupled to the underlying infrastructure.

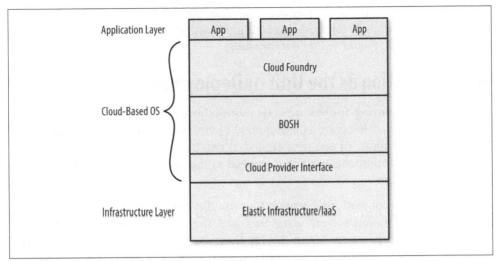

Figure 2-1. Cloud Foundry layers forming a cloud-based OS

Do More

Historically the long pole of application delivery, the part on the critical path that blocks progress, has been the IT department. This results in a concept I call server hugging, whereby developers hold on to (and hug) a plethora of VMs just in case they need them again someday.

Nowadays, businesses no longer need to be constrained by lengthy IT processes or organizational silos. Cloud Foundry provides a contractual promise to allow businesses to move with velocity and establish a developer–feedback loop so that they can tightly align products to user expectations. With Cloud Foundry, product managers *get their business back* and IT engineers can focus on more interesting issues and *get to eat dinner at home.*

Platforms are concerned not only with providing environments and middleware for running applications. For example, Cloud Foundry takes on the responsibility of keeping applications up and running in the face of failures within the system. It also provides security, user administration, workload scheduling, and monitoring capabilities. Onsi Fakhouri, Pivotal's Vice President of Research and Development, famously tweeted this haiku:

> Here is my source code,
> run it on the cloud for me.
> I do not care how!

Onsi's quote captures the essence of Cloud Foundry's *do more* capability. Cloud Foundry is about doing more on behalf of both the developer and operator so that they can focus on what really differentiates the business. This characteristic is seen all throughout the Cloud Foundry ecosystem. You can take a similar approach with BOSH, Cloud Foundry's release-engineering system, and state, *"Here are my servers, make them a Cloud Foundry. I do not care how!"*

The Application as the Unit of Deployment

Traditionally, deploying application code required provisioning and deploying VMs, OSs, and middleware to create a development environment for the application to run in. After that environment was provisioned, it required patching and ongoing maintenance. New environments were then created as the application moved through the deployment pipeline.

Early incarnations of platforms centered on middleware: defining complex topology diagrams of application servers, databases, and messaging engines into which you could drop your application. When this topology diagram (or blueprint) was defined, you then specified some additional configuration such as IP addresses and ports to bring the defined topology and applications into existence. Although this was a step in the right direction, from a developer's perspective there was still a layer of complexity that you needed to configure for each deployment.

Cloud Foundry differs from traditional provisioning and orchestration engines in a fundamental way: it uses middleware and infrastructure directly, allowing streamlined development through self-service environments. Developers can build, deploy, run, and scale applications on Cloud Foundry without having to be mindful of the specific underlying infrastructure, middleware, and container implementation.

Cloud Foundry allows the *unit of deployment*, i.e., what you deploy to run your application, to be isolated to just the application itself. Even though there are some benefits to encapsulating both your application and dependencies as a precomposed container image, I still believe it is more secure and more efficient to keep just the application as the unit of deployment and allow the platform to handle the remaining concerns. The trade-offs between both approaches are discussed further in Chapter 9; however, the benefit of Cloud Foundry is that it supports both approaches. Buildpacks are discussed at length in that chapter, but for now, it is enough to know that buildpacks provide the framework and runtime support for your applications. A specific buildpack is used to package your application with all of its dependencies. The resulting *staged* application is referred to as a *droplet*.

On-boarding developers is easy; they can deploy applications to Cloud Foundry using existing tool chains with little to no code modification. It enables the developer to remove the cost and complexity of configuring infrastructure for their applications. Using a self-service model, developers can deploy and scale applications without being directly locked into the IaaS layer.

Because developers no longer need to concern themselves with, for example, which application container to use, which version of Java, and which memory settings or garbage-collection (GC) policy to employ, they can simply push their applications to Cloud Foundry, and the applications run. This allows developers to focus on delivering applications that offer business value. Applications can then be bound to a wide set of backing services that are available on demand.

Units of Deployment

The phrase "the application is the unit of deployment" is used liberally. Applications as the sole unit of currency has changed with the emergence of Diego, Cloud Foundry's new runtime. Cloud Foundry now supports both applications running as long running processes (LRPs) and discrete "run once" tasks such as Bash scripts and Cron-like jobs. Diego LRPs are also referred to as application instances, or AIs. What you deploy, be it an actual app or just a script, is not important. The key takeaway is the removal of the need for deploying additional layers of technology.

Using cf push Command to Deploy

Cloud Foundry provides several ways for a user to interact with it, but the principal avenue is through its CLI. The most renowned CLI command often referenced by the Cloud Foundry community is $ `cf push`.

You use the `cf push` command to deploy your application. It has demonstrably improved the deployment experience. From the time you run `cf push` to the point when the application is available, Cloud Foundry performs the following tasks:

- Uploads and stores application files
- Examines and stores application metadata
- Stages the application by using a buildpack to create a droplet
- Selects an appropriate execution environment in which to run the droplet
- Starts the AI and streams logs to the Loggregator

This workflow is explored in more depth in Chapter 6.

Staging

Although it is part of the `cf push` workflow, staging is a core Cloud Foundry concept. Cloud Foundry allows users to deploy a prebuilt Docker image or an application artifact (source code or binaries) that has not yet been containerized. When deploying an application artifact, Cloud Foundry will *stage* the application on a machine or

VM known as a *Cell*, using everything required to compile and run the apps locally, including the following:

- The OS stack on which the application runs
- A buildpack containing all languages, libraries, dependencies, and runtime services the app uses

The staging process results in a droplet that the Cell can unpack, compile, and run. You can then run the resulting droplet (as in the case of a Docker image) repeatedly over several Cells. The same droplet runs the same app instances over multiple Cells without incurring the cost of staging every time a new instance is run. This ability provides deployment speed and confidence that all running instances from the same droplet are identical.

Self-Service Application Life Cycle

In most traditional scenarios, the application developer and application operator typically perform the following:

- Develop an application
- Deploy application services
- Deploy an application and connect (bind) it to application services
- Scale an application, both up and down
- Monitor an application
- Upgrade an application

This application life cycle is in play until the application is decommissioned and taken offline. Cloud Foundry simplifies the application life cycle by offering self-service capabilities to the end user. Adopting a self-service approach removes hand-offs and potentially lengthy delays between teams. For example, the ability to deploy an application, provision and bind applications to services, scale, monitor, and upgrade are all offered by a simple call to the platform.

With Cloud Foundry, as mentioned earlier, the application or task itself becomes the single unit of deployment. Developers just push their applications to Cloud Foundry, and those applications run. If developers require multiple instances of an application to be running they can use cf scale to scale the application to *N* number of AIs. Cloud Foundry removes the cost and complexity of configuring infrastructure and middleware per application. Using a self-service model, users can do the following:

- Deploy applications

- Provision and bind additional services, such as messaging engines, caching solutions, and databases
- Scale applications
- Monitor application health and performance
- Update applications
- Delete applications

Deploying and scaling applications are completely independent operations. This provides the flexibility to scale at will, without the cost of having to redeploy the application every time. Users can simply scale an application with a self-service call to the platform. Through commercial products such as Pivotal Cloud Foundry, you can set up autoscaling policies for dynamic scaling of applications when they meet certain configurable thresholds.

Removing the infrastructure, OS, and middleware configuration concerns from developers allows them to focus all their effort on the application instead of deploying and configuring supporting technologies. This keeps the development focus where it needs to be, on the business logic that generates revenue.

The Twelve-Factor Contract

An architectural style known as cloud-native applications has been established to describe the design of applications specifically written to run in a cloud environment. These applications avoid some of the antipatterns that were established in the client-server era, such as writing data to the local filesystem. Those antipatterns do not work as well in a cloud environment because, for example, local storage is ephemeral given that VMs can move between different hosts. The Twelve-Factor App (*http://12factor.net*) explains the 12 principles underpinning cloud-native applications.

Platforms offer a set of contracts to the applications and services that run on them. These contracts ensure that applications are constrained to do the right thing. *Twelve Factor* can be thought of as the contract between an application and a cloud-native platform.

There are benefits to adhering to a contract that constrains things correctly. Twitter is a great example of a constrained platform. You can write only 140 characters, but that constraint becomes an extremely valuable feature of the platform. You can do a lot with 140 characters coupled with the rich features surrounding that contract. Similarly, platform contracts are born out of previously tried-and-tested constraints; they are enabling and make doing the right thing—good developer practices—easy for developers.

Release Engineering through BOSH

In addition to developer concerns, the platform provides responsive IT operations, with full visibility and control over the application life cycle, provisioning, deployment, upgrades, and security patches. Several other operational benefits exist, such as built-in resilience, security, centralized user management, and better insights through capabilities like aggregated metrics and logging.

Rather than integrating, operating, and maintaining numerous individual components, the platform operator deals only with the platform. Structured platforms handle all the aforementioned undifferentiated heavy lifting tasks.

The Cloud Foundry repository is structured for use with BOSH. BOSH is an open source tool chain for release-engineering, deployment, and life cycle management. Using a YAML (YAML Ain't Markup Language) deployment manifest, BOSH creates and deploys (virtual) machines[1] on top of the targeted computing infrastructure and then deploys and runs software (in our case Cloud Foundry and supporting services) on to those created machines. Many of the benefits to operators are provided through using BOSH to deploy and manage Cloud Foundry. BOSH is often overlooked as just another component of Cloud Foundry, but it is the bedrock of Cloud Foundry and a vital piece of the ecosystem. It performs monitoring, failure recovery, and software updates with zero-to-minimal downtime. Chapter 10 discusses BOSH at length.

Rather than utilizing a bespoke integration of a variety of tools and techniques that provide solutions to individual parts of the release-engineering goal, BOSH is designed to be a single tool covering the entire set of requirements of release engineering. BOSH enables software deployments to be:

- Automated
- Reproducible
- Scalable
- Monitored with self-healing failure recovery
- Updatable with zero-to-minimal downtime

BOSH translates intent into action via repeatability by always ensuring every provisioned release is identical and repeatable. This removes the challenge of configuration drift and removes the sprawl of snowflake servers (*http://martinfowler.com/bliki/ SnowflakeServer.html*).

---

1 The terms VM and machine are used interchangeably because BOSH can deploy to multiple infrastructure environments ranging from containers to VMs, right down to configuring physical servers.

BOSH configures infrastructure through code. By design, BOSH tries to abstract away the differences between infrastructure platforms (IaaS or physical servers) into a generalized, cross-platform description of your deployment. This provides the benefit of being infrastructure agnostic (as far as possible).

BOSH performs monitoring, failure recovery, software updates, and patching with zero-to-minimal downtime. Without such a release-engineering tool chain, all these concerns remain the responsibility of the operations team. A lack of automation exposes the developer to unnecessary risk.

Built-In Resilience and Fault Tolerance

A key feature of Cloud Foundry is its built-in resilience. Cloud Foundry provides built-in resilience and self-healing based on *control theory*. Control theory is a branch of engineering and mathematics that uses feedback loops to control and modify the behavior of a dynamic system. Resiliency is about ensuring that the actual system state (the number of running applications, for example) matches the desired state at all times, even in the event of failures. Resiliency is an essential but often costly component of business continuity.

Cloud Foundry automates the recovery of failed applications, components, and processes. This *self-healing* removes the recovery burden from the operator, ensuring speed of recovery. Cloud Foundry, underpinned by BOSH, achieves resiliency and self-healing through:

- Restarting failed system processes
- Recreating missing or unresponsive VMs
- Deployment of new AIs if an application crashes or becomes unresponsive
- Application striping across availability zones (AZs) to enforce separation of the underlying infrastructure
- Dynamic routing and load balancing

Cloud Foundry deals with application orchestration and placement focused on even distribution across the infrastructure. The user should not need to worry about how the underlying infrastructure runs the application beyond having equal distribution across different resources (known as availability zones). The fact that multiple copies of the application are running with built-in resiliency is what matters.

Cloud Foundry provides dynamic load balancing. Application consumers use a route to access an application; each route is directly bound to one or more applications in Cloud Foundry. When running multiple instances, it balances the load across the instances, dynamically updating its routing table. Dead application routes are automatically pruned from the routing table, with new routes added when they become available.

Without these capabilities, the operations team is required to continually monitor and respond to pager alerts from failed apps and invalid routes. By replacing manual interaction with automated, self-healing software, applications and system components are restored quickly with less risk and downtime. The resiliency concern is satisfied once, for all applications running on the platform, as opposed to developing customized monitoring and restart scripts per application. The platform removes the ongoing cost and associated maintenance of bespoke resiliency solutions.

Self-Healing Processes

Traditional *infrastructure as code* tools do not check whether provisioned services are up and running. BOSH has strong opinions on how to create your release, forcing you to create a monitor script for the process. If a BOSH-deployed component has a process that dies, the monitor script will try to restart it.

Self-Healing VMs

BOSH has a Health Monitor and Resurrector. The Health Monitor uses status and life cycle events to monitor the health of VMs. If the Health Monitor detects a problem with a VM, it can trigger an alert and invoke the Resurrector. The Resurrector automatically recreates VMs identified by the Health Monitor as missing or unresponsive.

Self-Healing Application Instance Count

Cloud Foundry runs the application transparently, taking care of the application life cycle. If an AI dies for any reason (e.g., because of a bug in the application) or a VM dies, Cloud Foundry can self-heal by restarting new instances so as to keep the desired capacity to run AIs. It achieves this by monitoring how many instances of each application are running. The Cell manages its AIs, tracks started instances, and broadcasts state messages. When Cloud Foundry detects a discrepancy between the actual number of running instances versus the desired number of available AIs, it takes corrective action and initiates the deployment of new AIs. To ensure resiliency and fault tolerance, you should run multiple AIs for a single application. The AIs will be distributed across multiple Cells for resiliency.

Resiliency Through Availability Zones

Finally, Cloud Foundry supports the use of *availability zones* (AZs). As depicted in Figure 2-2, you can use AZs to enforce separation of the underlying infrastructure. For example, when running on AWS, you can directly map Cloud Foundry AZs to different AWS AZs. When running on vCenter, you can map Cloud Foundry AZs to different vCenter Cluster and resource-pool combinations. Cloud Foundry can then deploy its components across the AZs. When you deploy multiple AIs, Cloud Foundry will distribute them evenly across the AZs. If, for example, a rack of servers fails and brings down an entire AZ, the AIs will still be up and serving traffic in the remaining AZs.

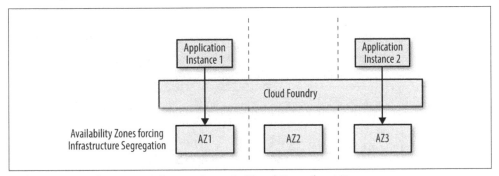

Figure 2-2. Application resiliency through Cloud Foundry AZs

Aggregated Streaming of Logs and Metrics

Cloud Foundry provides insight into both the application and the underlying platform through aggregated logging and metrics. The logging system within Cloud Foundry is known as the Loggregator. It is the inner voice of the system, telling the operator and developer what is happening. It is used to manage the performance, health, and scale of running applications and the platform itself, via the following:

- Logs provide visibility into behavior; for example, application logs can be used to trace through a specific call stack.
- Metrics provide visibility into health; for example, container metrics can include memory, CPU, and disk-per-app instance.

Insights are obtained through storing and analyzing a continuous stream of aggregated, time-ordered events from the output streams of all running processes and backing services. Application logs are aggregated and streamed to an endpoint via Cloud Foundry's Loggregator Firehose. Logs from the Cloud Foundry system components can also be made available and processed through a separate syslog drain. Cloud Foundry produces both the application and system logs to provide a holistic view to the end user.

Figure 2-3 illustrates how application logs and syslogs are separated as streams, in part to provide isolation and security between the two independent concerns, and in part due to consumer preferences. Generally speaking, app developers do not want to wade through component logs to resolve an app-specific issue. Developers can trace the log flow from the frontend router to the application code from a single log file.

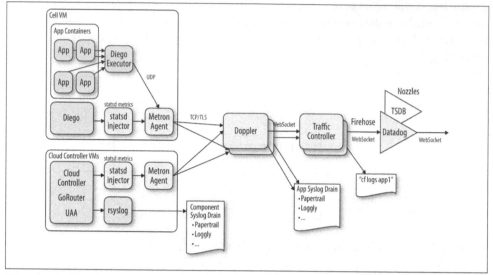

Figure 2-3. The Loggregator system architecture used for aggregating application logs and metrics

In addition to logs, metrics are gathered and streamed from system components. Operators can use metrics information to monitor an instance of Cloud Foundry. Furthermore, Cloud Foundry *events* show specific events such as when an application is started or stopped. The benefits of aggregated log, metric, and event streaming include the following:

- You can stream logs to a single endpoint.
- Streamed logs provide timestamped outputs per application.
- Both application logs and system-component logs are aggregated, simplifying their consumption.
- Metrics are gathered and streamed from system components.
- Operators can use metrics information to monitor an instance of Cloud Foundry.
- You can view logs from the command line or drain them into a log management service such as an ELK stack (Elasticsearch, Logstash, and Kibana), Splunk, or PCF Metrics.

- Viewing events is useful when debugging problems. For example, it is useful to be able to correlate an app instance event (like an app crash) to the container's specific metrics (high memory prior to crash).

The cost of implementing an aggregated log and metrics-streaming solution involves bespoke engineering to orchestrate and aggregate the streaming of both syslog and application logs from every component within a distributed system into a central server. Using a platform removes the ongoing cost and associated maintenance of bespoke logging solutions.

Security

For enterprises working with cloud-based infrastructure, security is a top concern. Usually the security teams have the strongest initial objections to Cloud Foundry because it works in a way that is generally unprecedented to established enterprise security teams. However, as soon as these teams understand the strength of Cloud Foundry's security posture, my experience is that they become one of your strongest champions.

Distributed System Security

Cloud Foundry offers significant security benefits over traditional approaches to deploying applications because it allows you to strengthen your security posture once, for all applications deployed to the platform. However, securing distributed systems involves inherent complexity. For example, think about these issues:

- How much effort is required to automatically establish and apply network traffic rules to isolate components?
- What policies should be applied to automatically limit resources in order to defend against denial-of-service (DoS) attacks?
- How do you implement role-based access controls (RBAC) with in-built auditing of system access and actions?
- How do you know which components are potentially affected by a specific vulnerability and require patching?
- How do you safely patch the underlying OS without incurring application downtime?

These issues are standard requirements for most systems running in corporate data centers. The more custom engineering you use, the more you need to secure and patch that system. Distributed systems increase the security burden because there are more moving parts, and with the advances in container technology, new challenges arise, such as "How do you dynamically apply microsegmentation at the container layer?" Additionally, when it comes to rolling out security patches to update the system, many distributed systems suffer from configuration drift—namely, the lack of consistency between supposedly identical environments. Therefore, when working with complex distributed systems (specifically any cloud-based infrastructure), environmental risk factors are intensified.

The Challenge of Configuration Drift

Deployment environments (such as staging, quality assurance, and production) are often complex and time-consuming to construct and administer, producing the ongoing challenge of trying to manage configuration drift to maintain consistency between environments and VMs. Reproducible consistency through release-engineering tool chains such as Cloud Foundry's BOSH addresses this challenge.

Environmental Risk Factors for Advanced Persistent Threats

Malware known as advanced persistent threats (APTs) needs three risk factors in order to thrive:

1. Time
2. Leaked or misused credentials
3. Misconfigured and/or unpatched software

Given enough time, APTs can observe, analyze, and learn what is occurring within your system, storing away key pieces of information at will. If APTs obtain credentials, they can then further access other systems and data such as important ingress points into your protected data layer. Finally, unpatched software vulnerabilities provide APTs the freedom to further exploit, compromise, and expose your system.

Challenge of Minimal Change

There has been a belief that if enterprises deliver software with velocity, the trade-off is they must reduce their security posture and increase risk. Therefore, traditionally, many enterprises have relied on a concept of minimal change to mitigate risk and reduce velocity. Security teams establish strict and restrictive policies in an attempt to minimize the injection of new vulnerabilities. This is evident by ticketing systems to make basic configuration changes to middleware and databases, long-lived transport layer security (TLS) credentials, static firewall rules, and numerous security policies to which applications must adhere.

Minimal change becomes compounded by complexity of the environment. Because machines are difficult to patch and maintain, environmental complexity introduces a significant lag between the time a vulnerability is discovered and the time a machine is patched, be it months, or worse, even years in some production enterprise environments.

The Three Rs of Enterprise Security

IThese combined risk factors provide a perfect ecosystem in which APTs can flourish, and minimal change creates an environment in which all three factors are likely to occur. Cloud Foundry inverts the traditional enterprise security model by focusing on the three Rs of enterprise security: rotate, repave, repair.[2]

1. Rotate the credentials frequently so that they are valid only for short periods of time.
2. Repave (rebuild) servers and applications from a known good state to cut down on the amount of time an attack can live.
3. Repair vulnerable software as soon as updates are available.

For the three Rs to be effective in minimizing the APT risk factors, you need to implement them repeatedly at high velocity. For example, data center credentials can be rotated hourly, servers and applications can be rebuilt several times a day, and complete vulnerability patching can be achieved within hours of patch availability. With this paradigm in mind, faster now equates to a safer and stronger security posture.

Additional Cloud Foundry Security

Cloud Foundry, along with BOSH and continuous integration (CI) tooling, provides tooling to make the three Rs' security posture a reality. Additionally, Cloud Foundry further protects you from security threats by automatically applying the following additional security controls to isolate applications and data:

- Manages software-release vulnerability by using new Cloud Foundry releases created with timely updates to address code issues
- Manages OS vulnerability by using a new OS created with the latest security patches

---

2 The three Rs of enterprise security is a phrase coined in an article by Justin Smith, a cloud identity and security expert. I strongly suggest that if you're interested in enterprise security, you read the full article titled The Three R's of Enterprise Security (*https://medium.com/built-to-adapt/the-three-r-s-of-enterprise-security-rotate-repave-and-repair-f64f6d6ba29d#.ntxh8g89z*).

- Implements RBACs, applying and enforcing roles and permissions to ensure that users of the platform can view and affect only the resources to which they have been granted access

- Secures both code and the configuration of an application within a multitenant environment

- Deploys each application within its own self-contained and isolated container-ized environment

- Prevents possible DoS attacks through resource starvation

- Provides an operator audit trail showing all operator actions applied to the plat-form

- Provides a user audit trail recording all relevant API invocations of an applica-tion

- Implements network traffic rules (security groups) to prevent system access to and from external networks, production services, and between internal compo-nents

BOSH and the underlying infrastructure expands the security posture further by han-dling data-at-rest encryption support through the infrastructure layer, usually by some device mechanism or filesystem-level support. For example, BOSH can use AWS EBS (Elastic Block Store) volume encryption for persistent disks.

Because every component within Cloud Foundry is created with the same OS image, Cloud Foundry eases the burden of rolling out these OS and software-release updates by using BOSH. BOSH redeploys updated VMs, component by component, to ensure zero-to-minimal downtime. This ultimately removes patching and updating concerns from the operator and provides a safer, more resilient way to update Cloud Foundry while keeping applications running. It is now totally possible to rebuild every VM in your data center from a known good state, as desired, with zero application down-time.

In addition, you can rebuild and redeploy the applications themselves from a known good release, upon request, with zero downtime. These rebuilding, repairing, and redeploying capabilities ensure that the patch turnaround time for the entire stack is as fast and as encompassing as possible, reaching every affected component across the stack with minimal human intervention. Cadence is limited only by the time it takes to run the pipeline and commit new code.

In addition to patching, if for any reason a component becomes compromised, you can instantly recreate it by using a known and clean software release and OS image, and move the compromised component into a quarantine area for further inspection.

There are additional detailed technical aspects that further improve security; for example, using namespaces for all containerized processes. I suggest reviewing the individual components for a more detailed understanding of how components such as Garden or the UAA help to further increase the security posture.

UAA Management

Role-based access defines who can use the platform and how. Cloud Foundry uses RBAC, with each role granting permissions to a specific environment the user is targeting. All collaborators target an environment with their individual user accounts associated with a role that governs what level and type of access the user has within that environment. Cloud Foundry's UAA is the central identity management service for both users and applications. It supports federated login, Lightweight Directory Access Protocol (LDAP), Security Assertion Markup Language (SAML), SSO, and multifactor authentication. UAA is a powerful component for strengthening your security posture for both user and application authentication. Chapter 15 looks at UAA in more detail.

Organizations and Spaces

Most developers are familiar with using VMs for development and deployment. Cloud Foundry is a virtualization layer (underpinned by containers) on top of a virtualization layer underpinned by VMs. Therefore, users do not have direct access to a specific machine or VM; rather, they simply access a logical partition of resources to deploy their apps.

To partition and allocate resources, Cloud Foundry uses logical boundaries known as Organizations (Orgs) and Spaces. Orgs contain one or more Spaces. Users can belong to any number of Orgs and/or Spaces, and users can have unique roles and permissions in each Org or Space to which they belong.

Orgs and Spaces provide the following:

- Logical separation and assignment of Cloud Foundry resources
- Isolation between different teams
- Logical isolation of development, test, staging, and production environments

For some enterprise customers with traditional silos, defining their required Orgs and Spaces can at first seem complex. Ideally, development teams should have autonomy to create and manage their own Spaces, as required. For development teams embracing microservices, the best approach is to organize teams by the big-A application—meaning a group of related (small-a) applications or services that can collectively and appropriately be grouped together, often referred to as *bulkheading*.

Ultimately, you know your business and how your developers work, so use these logical structures to provide meaningful working environments and pipelines for your developers.

Orgs

An *Org* is the top level of separation. A logical mapping could be to your business unit, a big-A application, or some other reasonable bounded context. When working with large enterprises that might have 200 developers in a business unit, I normally try to shift their thinking to the "Two-Pizza Team" model for application development. However, the actual number of developers within an Org or Space should not be a contentious point if it maps well to the physical organization and does not impede development or deployment.

Spaces

Every application and service is scoped to a Cloud Foundry *Space*. A Space provides a shared location that a set of users can access for application development, deployment, and maintenance. Every Space belongs to one Org. Each Org contains at least one Space but could contain several, and therefore can contain a broader set of collaborators than a single Space.

Environment Variables for Properties

The `cf push` command is the user saying to Cloud Foundry, "Here is my application artifact; run it on the cloud for me. I do not care how!"

The "I do not care how" needs explaining. There are properties you should care about, and these properties are configured by *environment variables*. Cloud Foundry uses environment variables to inform a deployed application about its environment. Environment variables include the following:

- How much memory to use
- What routes should be bound to the application
- How many instances of an application should be run
- Additional app-specific environment properties

The Cloud Foundry user can configure all of these properties.

Spaces are more of a developer concern. I believe there should be a limit to the amount of developers in a Space because there is a requirement for a level of trust due to the scope of shared resources and exposed environment variables that reside at the Space level. For the hyper security-conscious who have no trust between application teams, one Space per application is the only way forward. In reality, a Space for a big-A application might be more appropriate.

Colocation and Application Interactions

When considering the logical separations of your Cloud Foundry deployment, namely what Orgs and Spaces to construct, it is important to consider your application-to-application and application-to-services interactions. Although this consideration is more of a microservices consideration, an understanding of application and service boundaries is beneficial in understanding any colocation requirements. An example of this would be an application needing to access a corporate service in a specific data center or network. These concerns and their subsequent impacts become more noticeable at scale. You will need to design, understand, and document service discovery and app-to-app dependency, and additional frameworks such as Spring Cloud (*http://projects.spring.io/spring-cloud*) can significantly help here.

Resource Allocation

In addition to defining team structures, you can use Orgs and Spaces for assigning appropriate resources to each team.

Collaborators in an Org share the following:

- Resource quota
- Applications
- Services availability
- Custom domains

Domains Hosts and Routes

To enable traffic from external clients, applications require a specific URL known as a *route*. A route is a URL comprised of a domain and an optional host as a prefix. The host in this context is the portion of the URL referring to the application or applications, such as these:

my-app-name is the host prefix
my-business.com is the domain
my-app-name.my-business.com is the route

Route

Application consumers use a route to access an application. Each route is directly bound to one or more applications in Cloud Foundry. When running multiple instances, Cloud Foundry automatically load balances application traffic across multiple AIs through a component called the GoRouter. Because individual AIs can come and go for various reasons (scaling, app deletion, app crash), the GoRouter dynamically updates its routing table. Dead routes are automatically pruned from the routing table and new routes are added when they become available. Dynamic routing is a powerful feature. Traditional manual route table maintenance can be slow because it often requires submitting tickets to update or correct domain name server (DNS) or load balancer components. Chapter 7 discusses these various routing concepts further.

Domains

Domains provide a namespace from which to create routes. Cloud Foundry uses domains within routes to direct requests to specific applications. You can also register and use a custom domain, known as an *owned domain*. Domains are associated with Orgs and are not directly bound to applications. Domains can be shared, meaning that they are registered to multiple Orgs, or private, registered to only one Org. Owned domains are always private.

Context Path–Based Routing

A context path in a URL extends a top-level route with additional context so as to route the client to either specific application functionality or a different application. For example, *http://my-app-name.my-business.com* can be extended to *http://my-app-name.my-business.com/home* to direct a client to a homepage.

In the preceding example, your clients can reach the application via *my-app-name.my-business.com*. Therefore, if a client targets that route and uses a different context path, it will still reach only a single application. For example, *http://my-app-name.my-business.com/home* and *http://my-app-name.my-business.com/somewhereelse* will both be routed by GoRouter to your app *my-app-name*.

This approach works if all the functionality under the route *my-app-name.my-business.com* can be served by a single app. However, when using microservices, there is a need to have a unified top-level route that can be backed by a number of microservices. Each service uses the same top-level domain but can be individually reached by different paths in the URL. The microservices collectively serve all supported paths under the domain *my-app-name.my-business.com*. With context path–based routing, you can independently scale those portions of your app that are experiencing high/low traffic.

Rolling Upgrades and Blue/Green Deployments

As discussed in "Security" on page 19, both the applications running on the platform and the platform itself allow for rolling upgrades and zero-downtime deployment through a distributed consensus.

You can update applications running on the platform with zero downtime through a technique known as blue/green deployments (*https://docs.cloudfoundry.org/devguide/deploy-apps/blue-green.html*).

Summary

This chapter walked you through the principal concepts of Cloud Foundry. For example, you should now understand the meaning of a cloud OS, and the importance of the twelve-factor contract. The primary premise of Cloud Foundry is to enable the application development-to-deployment process to be as fast as possible. Cloud Foundry, underpinned by the BOSH release-engineering tool chain, achieves this by doing more on your behalf. Cloud Foundry provides the following:

- Built-in resiliency through automated recovery and self-healing of failed applications, components, and processes
- Built-in resiliency through striping applications across different resources
- Authentication and authorization for both users and applications, with the addition of RBAC for users
- Increased security posture with the ability to rotate credentials and repave and repair components
- The ability to update the platform with zero downtime via rolling upgrades across the system
- Speed in the deployment of apps with the ability to connect to a number of services via both platform-managed service brokers and services running in your existing IT infrastructure
- Built-in management and operation of services for your application, such as metrics and log aggregation, monitoring, autoscaling, and performance management

Now that you understand both the concepts and capabilities of Cloud Foundry, you are ready to learn about the individual components that comprise a Cloud Foundry deployment.

## CHAPTER 3

Components

This chapter explores the details of Cloud Foundry components. If you are keen to begin your journey by deploying Cloud Foundry, you are free to jump ahead to Chapter 4 and refer to this chapter at a later time.

Cloud Foundry is a distributed system involving several different components. Distributed systems balance their processing loads over multiple networked machines.[1] They are optimized between efficiency and resiliency against failures. Cloud Foundry is comprised of a modular distributed architecture with discrete components utilized for dedicated purposes.

Distributed Systems

As a distributed system, each Cloud Foundry component has a well-defined responsibility. The different components interact with one another to achieve a common goal. Distributed systems achieve component interaction through communicating via messages and using central data stores for system-wide state coordination. There are several benefits to using a distributed component model, such as the ability to scale a single component in isolation, or the ability to change one component without directly affecting another.

It is important for the operator to understand what comprises the Cloud Foundry distributed system. For example, some components are responsible for system state and you need to back them up. Other components are responsible for running your applications, and therefore you most probably want more than one instance of those

---

1 The terms VM and machine are used interchangeably because BOSH can leverage and deploy to multiple infrastructure environments ranging from containers, to VMs, right down to configuring physical servers.

components to remain running to ensure resiliency. Ultimately, understanding these components and where their boundaries of responsibility lie is vital when it comes to establishing concerns such as resiliency and disaster recovery.

In this chapter, you will learn about the following:

1. The core components, including their purpose and boundary of responsibility
2. The flow of communication and interaction between components
3. The components responsible for state[2]

Component Overview

The Cloud Foundry components are covered in detail in the Cloud Foundry documentation (*https://docs.cloudfoundry.org*). The Cloud Foundry code base is being rapidly developed by a growing open source team of around 250 developers. Any snapshot in time is going to change almost immediately. This book focuses not on the specific implementations that are subject to change, but on the purpose and function of each component. The implementation details change; the underlying patterns often remain.

We can group by function the components that make up Cloud Foundry into different layers. Table 3-1 lists these layers.

Table 3-1. Cloud Foundry component layers

Layer	Compoenents
Routing	GoRouter, TCPRouter, and external load balancer[a]
Authentication and user management	User Access and Authentication Management
Application life cycle and system state	Cloud Controller, Diego's core components (e.g., BBS and Brain)
App storage and execution	blobstore (including app artifacts/droplets and the Application Life-Cycle Binaries), Diego Cell (Garden, and runC)
Services	Service Broker, User Provided Service
Messaging	NATS (Network Address Translation) Messaging Bus
Metrics and logging	Loggregator (including Doppler and the Firehose)

[a] The external load balancer is not a Cloud Foundry component; it fronts the traffic coming into Cloud Foundry.

Figure 3-1 provides a visual representation of these components.

---

2 System state, along with configuration, is the most critical part of your environment; everything else is just wiring. Processes can come and go, but your system state and configuration must maintain integrity.

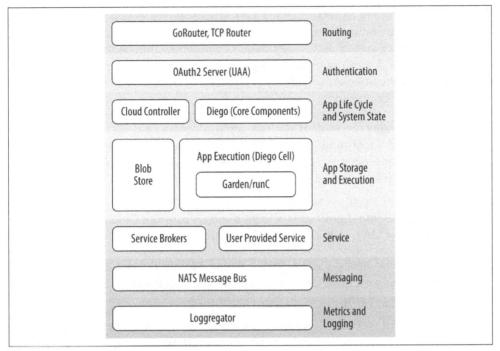

GoRouter, TCP Router	Routing
OAuth2 Server (UAA)	Authentication
Cloud Controller	Diego (Core Components)	App Life Cycle and System State
Blob Store	App Execution (Diego Cell) / Garden/runC	App Storage and Execution
Service Brokers	User Provided Service	Service
NATS Message Bus	Messaging
Loggregator	Metrics and Logging

Figure 3-1. Cloud Foundry component layers

To discuss the core components and their role within Cloud Foundry, we will take a top-down approach beginning with components that handle traffic coming into Cloud Foundry.

Routing via the Load Balancer and GoRouter

All HTTP-based traffic first enters Cloud Foundry from an external load balancer fronting Cloud Foundry. The load balancer is primarily used for routing traffic to the GoRouter.

Load Balancer Preference

The choice of load balancer is according to your preference. Infrastructure hosted on AWS often use Amazon's elastic load balancer (ELB). On-premises deployments such as those on vSphere or OpenStack take advantage of existing enterprise load balancers such as F5's BIG-IP.

The load balancer can either handle secure socket layer (SSL) decryption and then route traffic on to the GoRouter, or pass the SSL connection on to the GoRouter for SSL decryption.

The GoRouter receives all incoming HTTP traffic from the load balancer. The term "router" can be misleading to networking engineers who expect routers to implement specific networking standards. Conceptually, the router should be treated as a reverse proxy, responsible for centrally managing and routing all incoming HTTP(S) traffic to the appropriate component. Traffic will typically be passed on to either an application or the Cloud Controller:

- Application users target their desired applications via a dedicated domain. The GoRouter will route application traffic to the appropriate AI running on a Diego Cell. If multiple AIs are running, the GoRouter will round-robin traffic across the AIs to distribute the workload.[3]
- Cloud Foundry users address the Cloud Controller: Cloud Foundry's API known as the CAPI. Some client traffic will go directly from the GoRouter to the UAA; however, most UAA calls are initiated from the Cloud Controller.

The GoRouter periodically queries Diego, Cloud Foundry's container runtime system, for information on the location of the Cells and containers on which each application is currently running.

Applications require a route for external traffic to access them. The GoRouter uses a routing table to keep track of the available applications. Because applications can have multiple AIs, all with a single route, each route has an associated array of host:port entries. The host is the Diego Cell machine running the application. The GoRouter regularly recomputes new routing tables based on the Cell's IP addresses and the host-side port numbers for the Cell's containers.

Routing is an important part of Cloud Foundry. Chapter 7 discusses the GoRouter and routing in general in greater detail.

User Management and the UAA

As traffic enters Cloud Foundry, it needs to be authenticated. Cloud Foundry's UAA service is the central identity management service for managing:

- Cloud Foundry developers
- Application clients/end users
- Applications requiring application-to-application interactions

The UAA is an OAuth2 authorization server, that issues access tokens for client applications to use when they act on behalf of Cloud Foundry users; for example,

---

3 The GoRouter supports Sticky Session configuration if required.

when they request access to platform resources. The UAA is based on the most up-to-date security standards like OAuth, OpenID Connect, and System for Cross-domain Identity Management (SCIM). It authenticates platform users via their Cloud Foundry credentials. When users register an account with the Cloud Foundry platform, the UAA acts as the user identity store, retaining user passwords in the UAA database. The UAA can also act as a SSO service. It has endpoints for managing user accounts and registering OAuth2 clients as well as various other management functions. In addition, you can configure the UAA's user-identity store to either store user information internally or connect to an external user store through LDAP or SAML. Here are a couple of examples:

- Users can use LDAP credentials to gain access to the Cloud Foundry platform instead of registering a separate account.
- Operators can use SAML to connect to an external user store in order to enable SSO for users who want to access Cloud Foundry.

The UAA has its own database known as the UAADB. Like all databases responsible for system state, this is a critical component and you must make backups. Chapter 15 looks at the UAA in more detail.

The Cloud Controller

The Cloud Controller exposes Cloud Foundry's REST API. Users of Cloud Foundry target the Cloud Controller so that they can interact with the Cloud Foundry API (CAPI). Clients directly interact with the Cloud Controller for tasks such as these:

- Pushing, staging, running, updating, and retrieving applications
- Pushing, staging, and running discrete one-off tasks

You can interact with the Cloud Controller in the following three ways:

- A scriptable CLI
- Language bindings (currently Java)
- Integration with development tools (IDEs) to ease the deployment process

You can find a detailed overview of the API commands at API Docs (*https://apidocs.cloudfoundry.org/231/*). The V3 API extends the API to also include Tasks in addition to applications LRPs.

The Cloud Controller is responsible for the System State and the Application Life-Cycle Policy.

System State

The Cloud Controller uses two components for storing state: a blobstore and a database known as the CCDB.

The Cloud Controller blobstore

To store large binary files such as application artifacts and staged application droplets, Cloud Foundry's Cloud Controller uses a blobstore that holds different types of artifacts:

- Application code packages—unstaged files that represent an application
- Resource files
- Buildpacks
- Droplets and other container images

Resource files are uploaded to the Cloud Controller and then cached in the blobstore with a unique secure hash algorithm (SHA) so as to be reused without reuploading the file. Before uploading all the application files, the Cloud Foundry CLI issues a *resource match* request to the Cloud Controller to determine if any of the application files already exist in the resource cache. When the application files are uploaded, the Cloud Foundry CLI omits files that exist in the resource cache by supplying the result of the resource-match request. The uploaded application files are combined with the files from the resource cache to create the complete application package.

Droplets are the result of taking an app package and staging it via a processing buildpack to create an executable binary artifact. The blobstore uses FOG (*http://fog.io/*) so that it can use abstractions like Amazon Simple Storage Service (Amazon S3) or a mounted network file system (NFS) for storage.

The CCDB

The Cloud Controller, via its CCDB, also maintains records of the logical hierarchical structure including available orgs, spaces, apps, services, service instances, user roles, and more. It maintains users' information and how their roles map to orgs and spaces.

The Application Life-Cycle Policy

The Cloud Controller is responsible for the Application Life-Cycle Policy. Conceptually, the Cloud Controller is Cloud Foundry's CPU that drives the other components. For example, when you use the cf push command to push an application or task to Cloud Foundry, the Cloud Controller stores the raw application bits in its blobstore, creates a record to track the application metadata in its database, and directs the other system components to stage and run the application.

The Cloud Controller is application and task centric. It implements all of the object modeling around running applications (handling permissions, buildpack selection, service binding, etc.). The Cloud Controller is concerned with policy; for example, *"run two instances of my application,"* but the responsibility of orchestration and execution has been passed to Diego.

Continuous Delivery Pipelines

Many companies choose to interact with Cloud Foundry through a continuous delivery pipeline such as Concourse.ci that uses machines to utilize the CAPI. This approach reduces human error and offers deployment repeatability.

Application Execution

The components responsible for executing your applications and tasks include Diego, Garden (a container management API), and an Open Container Initiative (OCI)–compatible[4] backend container implementation (like runC).

Diego

Diego is the container runtime architecture for Cloud Foundry. Whereas the Cloud Controller is concerned with policy, it is Diego that provides the scheduling, orchestration, and placement of applications and tasks. Diego is designed to keep applications available by constantly monitoring their states and reconciling the actual system state with the expected state by starting and stopping processes as required. Chapter 6 covers Diego at length.

Garden and runC

Garden is a platform-agnostic Go API for container creation and management. Garden has pluggable backends for different platforms and runtimes, including Linux, Windows, and runC, an implementation of the OCI specification. Chapter 8 looks at containers in detail.

---

4 The OCI is an open governance structure for the express purpose of creating open industry standards around container formats and runtime. For more information, see *https://www.opencontainers.org/*.

Metrics and Logging

As discussed in "Aggregated Streaming of Logs and Metrics" on page 17, system logs and metrics are continually generated and streamed from every component. In addition, AIs should produce logs as a continual stream for each running AI. Cloud Foundry's logging system is known as the Loggregator. The Loggregator aggregates component metrics and application logs into a central location using a Metron agent.

Metron Agent

The Metron agent comes from the Loggregator subsystem and resides on every VM. It gathers a mix of metrics and log statistics from the Cloud Foundry components; for example, the Metron agent gathers application logs from the Cloud Foundry Diego hosts known as Cells. Operators can use the collected component logs and metrics to monitor a Cloud Foundry deployment. These metrics and logs can be forwarded by a syslog forwarder onto a syslog drain. It is possible to drain syslogs into multiple consumers. You can set up as many syslog "sinks" for an application as you want. Each sink will receive all messages.

Metron has the job of forwarding application logs and component metrics to the Loggregator subsystem by taking traffic from the various emitter sources (Cells in the case of apps) and routing that logging traffic to one or more Loggregator components. An instance of the Metron agent runs on each VM in a Cloud Foundry system and logs are therefore co-located on the emitter sources.

Loggregator

The Loggregator (log aggregator) system continually streams logging and metric information. The Loggregator's Firehose provides access to application logs, container metrics (memory, CPU, and disk-per-app instance), some component metrics, and component counter/HTTP events. If you want to see firsthand the output from the Loggregator, you can invoke the CF CLI command $ cf logs APP, as demonstrated in the following example:

```
2017-02-14T13:10:32.260-08:00 [RTR/0] [OUT] twicf-signup.cfapps.io -
[2017-02-14T21:10:32.250+0000] "GET /favicon.ico HTTP/1.1" 200 0 946
"https://twicf-signup.cfapps.io/"... "10.10.66.187:26208" "10.10.147
.77:60076" x_forwarded_for:"71.202.60.71" x_forwarded_proto:"https"
vcap_request_id:"2c28e2fe-54f7-48d7-5f0b-aaead5ab5c7c" response_time
:0.009104115 app_id:"ff073944-4d18-4c73-9441-f1a4c4bb4ca3" app_index:"0"
```

The Firehose does not provide component logs. Component logs are retrieved through an rsyslog drain.

Messaging

Most component machines communicate with one another internally through HTTP and HTTPS protocols. Temporary messages and data are captured in two locations:

- A Consul server stores the longer-lived control data such as component IP addresses and distributed locks that prevent components from duplicating actions.
- Diego's bulletin board system (BBS) stores a real-time view of the system, including the more frequently updated and disposable data such as Cell and application status, unallocated work, and heartbeat messages.

The Route-Emitter component still uses the NATS messaging system, a lightweight distributed publish–subscribe message queuing system, to broadcast the latest routing tables to the routers.

Additional Components

In addition to the aforementioned core system components, there are other components that comprise the Cloud Foundry ecosystem.

Stacks

A stack is a prebuilt root filesystem (rootfs). Stacks are used along with droplets (the output of buildpack staging). They provide the container filesystem used for running applications.

Cells can support more than one stack if configured correctly; however, a Cell must ensure buildpack and stack compatibility. For example, a Windows "stack" cannot run on Linux VMs. Therefore, to stage or run a Linux app, a Cell running a Linux stack must be available (and have free memory).

A Marketplace of On-Demand Services

Applications often depend on additional backing services such as databases, caches, messaging engines, or third-party APIs. Each Cloud Foundry deployment has the concept of a marketplace. The Cloud Foundry marketplace is a platform extension point. It exposes a set of services that are available for developers to use in support of running applications. Developers do not build applications in isolation. Applications often require additional middleware services such as data persistence, search, caching, graphing, messaging, API management, and more.

The platform operator exposes additional services to the marketplace through service brokers, route services, and user-provided services. The marketplace provides Cloud

Foundry users with the self-service, on-demand provisioning of additional service instances. The platform operator can expose different service plans to different Cloud Foundry Orgs. Developers are able to view and create service instances only for service plans that have been configured to be visible for their targeted Org and Space. You can make service plans public and visible to all, or private to limit service visibility.

A service can offer different service plans to provide varying levels of resources or features for the same service. An example service plan is a database service offering small, medium, or large plans with differing levels of concurrent connections and storage sizes. The provisioned service provides a unique set of credentials that can be used to bind and connect an application to the service.

Services not only enhance applications through providing middleware; they are concerned with all possible components to enable development teams to move quickly, including, for example, GitHub, Pivotal Tracker, CI services, and route services. For example, you can expose to the marketplace any application running on the platform that offers a service for others to consume. One advantage of this approach is that the service broker plans can prepopulate datastores with a specific schema or set of data (such as a sample customer set required for unit testing). Another example could be a service broker plan to provide specific preconfigured templates for apps.

Service brokers

Developers can provision service instances and then bind those instances to an application via a service broker responsible for providing the service instance.

A service broker interacts with the Cloud Controller to provision a service instance. Service brokers advertise a catalog of service offerings and service plans (e.g., a single-node MySQL plan or a clustered multinode MySQL plan). A service broker implements the CAPI to provide the user with the following:

- List service offerings
- Provision (create) and deprovision (delete) service instances
- Enable applications to bind to, and unbind from, the service instances

In general, *provision* reserves service resources (e.g., creates a new VM) and *bind* delivers the required information for accessing the resource to an application. The reserved resource is known, in Cloud Foundry parlance, as a *service instance*.

The service instance is governed by the broker author. What a service instance represents can vary not just by service, but also by plan. For example, an instance could be a container, a VM, or a new table and user in an existing database. Plans could offer a single database on a multitenant server, a dedicated datastore cluster, or simply an account and specific configuration on a running Cloud Foundry application. The key concern is that the broker implements the required API to interact with the Cloud Controller.

User-provided services

In addition to Cloud Foundry-managed service instances, operators can expose existing services via *user-provided services*. This allows established services such as a customer database to be bound to Cloud Foundry applications.

Buildpacks and Docker Images

How do you run applications inside Cloud Foundry? Applications can simply be *pushed* through the following CF CLI command:

```
$ cf push
```

There are currently two defined artifact types that you can `cf push`:

- A standalone application
- A prebuilt Docker image (that could contain additional runtime and middleware dependencies)

You can push standalone applications in both the form of a prebuild artifact such as a war/jar file or, in some cases, via raw source code such as a link to a Git remote.

Because a standalone application is not already part of a container image, when it is pushed to Cloud Foundry the buildpack process runs a compile phase. This involves compiling any source code and packaging the application and runtime dependencies into an executable container image. The buildpack process is also responsible for constructing the application runtime environment, deploying the application, and, finally, starting the required processes.

Buildpacks are a core link in the chain of the Cloud Foundry deployment process if you are deploying only an application artifact (e.g., JAR, WAR, Ruby, or Go source). The buildpack automates the following:

- The detection of an application framework
- The application compilation (known in Cloud Foundry terminology as *staging*)
- Running the application

The officially supported buildpacks are listed at *http://docs.cloudfoundry.org/build packs/index.html*. This list includes Ruby, Java (including other JVM-based languages), Go, Python, PHP, Node.js, and the binary and staticfile buildpacks.

Numerous additional community buildpacks exist. You can extend buildpacks or create new ones for specific language, framework, and runtime support. For example, the reason you might extend the Java buildpack (JBP) is to add support for additional application servers or a specific monitoring agent.

Buildpacks take your application artifact and containerize it into what Cloud Foundry calls a droplet. However, if you already have an OCI-compatible container image such as a Docker image, you can use `cf push` to move that directly to Cloud Foundry in order to run it. Containerization is the delivery mechanism for applications. This is true whether you push an application that Cloud Foundry containerizes into a droplet, or you push a prebuilt Docker image.

Infrastructure and the Cloud Provider Interface

Cloud Foundry relies on existing cloud-based infrastructure. The underlying infrastructure will have implementation-specific details. For example, vSphere's vCenter deals with clusters and resource pools, whereas AWS deals with regions and AZs. There are, however, some fundamental capabilities that need to be available and set up prior to installing Cloud Foundry:

- Networks and subnets (typically a /22 private network)
- VMs with specified CPU and memory requirements
- Storage for VMs
- File server or blobstore
- DNS, certificates, and wildcard domains
- Load balancer to pass traffic into the GoRouter
- NAT[5] for traffic flowing back to the load balancer

Cloud Foundry abstracts away infrastructure-specific implementations through the use of a cloud provider interface (CPI). Chapter 10 examines this topic further.

The Cloud Foundry GitHub Repository

Cloud Foundry uses the git system on GitHub to version-control all source code, documentation, and other resources such as buildpacks. Currently, the integrated Cloud Foundry code base can be located at cf-deployment (*https://github.com/cloud foundry/cf-deployment*). To check out Cloud Foundry code from GitHub, use the master branch because it points to the most recent stable final release.

---

5 NAT is only required if you are using nonroutable addresses.

Summary

By design, Cloud Foundry is a distributed system involving several components, grouped into the following functional layers:

- Routing for handling application and platform user traffic
- Authentication and user management
- Application life cycle and system state through the Cloud Controller and Diego's BBS
- Container runtime and app execution through Diego
- Services via the service marketplace
- Messaging
- Metrics and logging

Decoupling Cloud Foundry into a set of services allows each individual function to grow and evolve as required. Each Cloud Foundry component has a well-defined responsibility, and the different components interact with one another and share state in order to achieve a common goal. This loose coupling is advantageous:

- You can scale individual components in isolation
- You can swap and replace components to extend the platform capability
- You can promote a pattern of reuse

Now that you are aware of the components that comprise Cloud Foundry, you are ready to begin creating a Cloud Foundry instance. Chapter 4 defines the prerequisites for installing Cloud Foundry.

Preparing Your Cloud Foundry Environment

This chapter explores the steps you must perform prior to bootstrapping BOSH and deploying Cloud Foundry. Critically, Cloud Foundry is not a "one size fits all" technology, and therefore, you must make some decisions at the outset prior to installing the platform. It is important that you understand the key concerns and decision points that define your environment, including:

- Installation steps
- Non-technical considerations
- Cloud Foundry dependencies and integrations
- IaaS and infrastructure design
- Networking design and routing

This chapter assumes that you are familiar with the Cloud Foundry components discussed in Chapter 3.

Installation Steps

Following are general steps for deploying Cloud Foundry:

1. Create and configure your IaaS environment, including all the periphery infrastructure that Cloud Foundry requires, such as networks, security groups, blobstores, and load balancers.
2. Set up any additional external enterprise services such as LDAP, syslog endpoints or monitoring, and metrics dashboards.
3. Deploy the BOSH Director.

4. Create an IaaS/infrastructure-specific BOSH configuration such as cloud configuration.

5. Create a deployment manifest to deploy Cloud Foundry.

6. Integrate Cloud Foundry with the required enterprise services (via your deployment manifest).

7. Deploy Cloud Foundry.[1]

The rest of this chapter explores the necessary considerations for each step. Before we dive into those topics, let's address the non-technical considerations.

Non-technical Considerations

Before addressing the technical points, it is worth establishing two critical things:

- The team structure required for installing Cloud Foundry
- The required deployment topology of Cloud Foundry

These two concerns are especially pertinent when deploying Cloud Foundry for a large enterprise. Both concerns go hand in hand because the "where and how" of deploying Cloud Foundry should always be coupled with the team responsible for operating it.

Team Structure: Platform Operations for the Enterprise

Cloud Foundry is generally deployed either on a team-by-team basis with one installation per business unit, or via a central Platform Operations team who deploy and operate a centralized platform that other DevOps-centric teams can utilize.

 In my experience while working with companies helping them to install and run Cloud Foundry, I came across a decentralized deployment model only once. For that one company, it worked well; however, most enterprises choose to establish a centralized Platform Operations team.

Even with a cultural shift toward DevOps, organizations structure teams in a variety of different ways. Choose the team structure that works best for you. Whichever variant you choose, the Platform Operator's overall responsibility typically includes the following roles:

---

1 Deployment and configuration steps are significantly easier to manage if using a CI pipeline such as Concourse.ci.

- Networking administrator
- Storage administrator
- System administrator
- IaaS administrator
- Software development
- Security
- QA and performance testing
- Release management
- Project management

These are not necessarily nine exclusive roles; individuals might combine a number of the preceding capabilities. For example, an IaaS administrator might also have storage experience. Most of these roles—networking and security, for example—are more pertinent at the outset when you're setting up the platform and operational processes. It is often sufficient just to maintain a regular point of contact for ongoing expertise in these areas. A point of contact must still be responsive! If it takes a ticket and three days of waiting to get a network change, your operating model is broken.

If Cloud Foundry is deployed in your data center instead of on a hosted virtual infrastructure, the Platform Operations team will need to work closely with the teams responsible for the physical infrastructure. This is both to help facilitate capacity planning and because an understanding and appreciation of the hardware capabilities underpinning the IaaS layer is required to ensure a sufficient level of availability and scalability. If Cloud Foundry is deployed to a hosted virtual infrastructure such as GCP, Microsoft Azure, or AWS, your Platform Operations team still needs to work closely with the teams responsible for networking so as to establish a direct network connection between the cloud provider and your enterprise.

There is a software development role in the mix because it is necessary to define and understand the application requirements and best practices based on *Twelve-Factor* applications. Additionally, the Platform Operations team needs to appreciate the application services required to support the cloud-native applications running on the platform. Developers often have specific requirements for choosing a particular technology appropriate for their application. This need can be magnified in a world of microservices in which each service should be free to use an appropriate backing technology so that it can grow and evolve independently from other services. The Platform Operations team should work directly with other business-capability teams to ensure that they offer a rich and defined portfolio of platform services. You can host these services directly on the platform, where it makes sense to do so, instead of being operated and connected adjacent to the platform.

Deployment Topology

How many Cloud Foundry instances should you deploy? There are a number of factors to consider when addressing this question. For example, ask yourself the following:

- Do you need one instance for the entire company or one instance per organization?

- Should you have one instance for preproduction workloads and a separate instance for production apps?

- Do you need to isolate applications or data due to regulatory reasons such as PCI, NIST, or HIPAA compliance?

- Do you need high availability of Cloud Foundry itself (data center-level redundancy)?

There is no single answer; businesses have different requirements and companies adopt different approaches. However, the decision can be guided by the following considerations:

- A single instance, or set of instances (e.g., a sandbox; preproduction and production) for the entire company is a conservative and reasonable starting point. As you progress with your Cloud Foundry journey, an additional instance or set of instances per organization might be required if an organization mandates specific customizations (e.g., dedicated internal services that must be isolated from other departments at the network layer).

- Of primary importance, a sandbox environment is always essential for the Platform Operator to test out new releases without risking developer or production downtime.

- An instance for pre-production and a separate instance for production might be required if strict network segregation to backed services (such as a production database) is mandated.[2]

- Separate instances for non-regulated and regulated apps might be required if dealing with industry regulations such as PCI or HIPPA compliance. A new feature known as isolation segments might alleviate this requirement over time, as discussed further in "Isolation Segments" on page 285.

---

2 All companies I have worked with have adopted separate preproduction and production instances. From a technical standpoint, if you do not require strict networking segregation, and you size the environment for all workloads, then separate instances between preproduction and production are not required. However, the clean separation of concerns between the two environments is appealing for most companies, especially when considering additional concerns such as performance testing.

- Two instances, one in each data center, might be required to allow for data-center failover or active–active geodispersed application deployments.

Taking the aforementioned points into consideration, for a scenario in which Cloud Foundry is centrally managed, I tend to see five deployments for a company that has data centers in two locations (e.g., East and West regions):

- Two environments in a West data center—pre-production and production instances
- Two environments in an East data center—pre-production and production instances
- A sandbox environment for the Platform Operator

The importance of the sandbox environment should not be underestimated. Changes to the Cloud Foundry environment can occur from several aspects, such as the following:

- Changing or upgrading the network architecture
- Upgrading the IaaS and networking layer
- Upgrading Cloud Foundry
- Upgrading application services

When applying updates across the stack, there is always the potential, no matter how small, of breaking the underlying infrastructure, the platform itself, or the apps or services running on the platform. From the Platform Operator's perspective, both production and preproduction environments are essentially production systems requiring 100 percent uptime. Companies strive to avoid both application and developer downtime and there is a financial impact if any downtime occurs to either group. Therefore, it is vital for the Platform Operator to have a safe environment that can potentially be broken as new changes are tested, without taking developers or production applications offline. It is worth pointing out that although there is always a risk when updating software, Cloud Foundry and BOSH impose a unique set of factors, such as instance group canaries and rolling deployments, that all help mitigate risks and deliver exceptionally reliable updates.

Cloud Foundry Dependencies and Integrations

Before you can deploy and operate Cloud Foundry, you must ensure that all prerequisite dependencies are in place. These dependencies include concerns such as provisioning the IaaS and configuring a load balancer. Additionally, you can integrate Cloud Foundry with other enterprise services such as syslog endpoints, SSO solutions, and metrics dashboards.

Following are the minimum external dependencies:

- Configured IaaS and infrastructure environment with available administrator credentials
- Configured networking (subnets and security groups)
- Defined storage policy and an additional NFS- or Amazon S3–compatible blob-store (for both the BOSH blobstore and Cloud Foundry blobstore)
- External load balancers set up to point to GoRouter IP addresses
- DNS records set up, including defining appropriate *system*, *app*, and any other required wildcard domains along with SSL certificates

Additional integration considerations based on enterprise services may require the following:

- SAML, LDAP, or SSO configured for use with Cloud Foundry where required.
- A syslog endpoint such as Splunk or ELK (Elasticsearch, Logstash, and Kibana) is available to receive component syslog information.
- System monitoring and metrics dashboards such as DataDog set up to receive system metrics.
- An application performance management (APM) tool such as Dynatrace, New-Relic, or AppDynamics set up for receiving application metrics.

This section focuses only on the dependencies and integration points required for getting started with Cloud Foundry. However, before installing BOSH and Cloud Foundry, it is still worth considering any services and external dependencies with which Cloud Foundry might need to integrate. This is important because if, for example, Cloud Foundry requires access to an external production database, additional considerations such as network access and the latency of roundtrip requests might arise. Ultimately, where your vital backing services reside might be the key deciding factor in where you deploy Cloud Foundry.

IaaS and Infrastructure Design

Before installing Cloud Foundry, you must correctly configure the underpinning infrastructure.

The first technical decision to make is what IaaS or infrastructure you should use to underpin Cloud Foundry. Through the use of the BOSH release tool chain, Cloud Foundry is designed to run on any IaaS provider that has a supported CPI. Refer to the BOSH documentation (*http://bosh.io/docs*) for an up-to-date list of supported CPIs. As of this writing, there are BOSH CPIs for the following infrastructures:

- Google Compute Platform
- AWS
- Azure
- OpenStack
- vSphere's vCenter
- vSphere's vCloudAir
- Photon
- RackHD
- Your local machine (for deploying BOSH Lite)

Your infrastructure decision is often made based on the following three factors:

- Does your company desire to have an on-premises (vSphere or OpenStack) or a cloud-based (AWS, Azure, GCP) infrastructure? What on-premises infrastructure management exists today, and what is your desired future state?
- How long will it take to provision new infrastructure (if managed internally)?
- What is the long-term cost model (both capital and operational expenditure)?

With regard to the time to provision new infrastructure, public cloud providers such as AWS, GCP, or Azure become appealing for many companies because you can quickly spin up new infrastructure and then scale on demand. I have been on six-week engagements for which installing the hardware into the company's data centers required four weeks. Time lags such as these are painful; thus utilizing public clouds can accelerate your startup experience. Some companies choose to adopt both a public and private model to provide resiliency through dual deployments.[3]

From this point on, as a reference architecture, this chapter explores a Cloud Foundry installation on AWS. I selected AWS as the target IaaS for this book because it is accessible both to corporations and individuals who might not have access to other supported IaaS environments.

---

3 An example of such a deployment is documented at the Pivotal blog (*http://bit.ly/2q2Rear*).

BOSH Lite

If you would like to begin installing Cloud Foundry and using BOSH but do not want to incur the cost of running several VMs, I suggest using BOSH Lite (*https://github.com/cloudfoundry/bosh-lite*). BOSH Lite is a local development environment for BOSH using containers in a Vagrant box. The BOSH Director that comes with BOSH Lite uses a Garden CPI, which uses containers to emulate VMs. The usage of containers makes it an excellent choice for local development, testing, and general BOSH exploration because you can deploy the entire cf-deployment into containers all running on a single VM. This is a great environment to try Cloud Foundry, but be mindful that because everything is running in a single VM, it is suitable only for experimentation, not production workloads. BOSH Lite is discussed further in "BOSH Lite" on page 175.

Designing for Resilience

As discussed in "Built-In Resilience and Fault Tolerance" on page 15, Cloud Foundry promotes different levels of built-in resilience and fault tolerance. The lowest layer of resilience within a single installation is achieved through the use of AZs to drive anti-affinity of components and applications to physical servers.

Cloud Foundry AZs (assuming they have been configured correctly) ensure that multiple instances of Cloud Foundry components and the subsequent apps running on Cloud Foundry all end up on different physical hosts. An important point here is that if you desire to use AZs for high availability (HA), you will need a minimum of three AZs (due to the need to maintain quorum for components that are based on the Raft consensus algorithm). Chapter 16 offers more information on designing for resilience.

The Cloud Foundry deployment example discussed in Chapter 5 uses bosh-bootloader and cf-deployment. bosh-bootloader will configure the infrastructure on your behalf and will try and configure three AZs by default (assuming the IaaS you deploy to can support three distinct regions).

Sizing and Scoping the Infrastructure

Correctly sizing infrastructure for a specific Cloud Foundry installation can be challenging, especially if you cannot accurately forecast how many apps are going to be deployed to the platform. What's more, this challenge becomes compounded because a single application might require several instances due to a combination of the following:

- Running multiple instances for resilience

- Running multiple instances over different spaces throughout the application life cycle

- Running multiple instances for concurrency performance

For example, as depicted in Figure 4-1, a single AI can often require a minimum of seven instances when running in an active–active setting:

- Two instances in development (blue and green versions)

- One instance in the test or the CI/CD pipeline

- Four instances in production (two instances in each active–active data center)

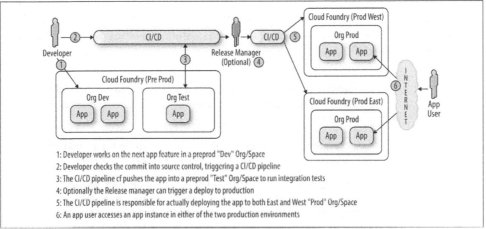

Figure 4-1. Typical multiregion, multi-instance deployment with user interaction flow

In addition, a typical application involves more than one process; for example, it might have a UI layer, controller/model layer, a service layer, and data layer. You can quickly begin to see that accurate upfront sizing can become complex as the number of running instances starts to scale.

Therefore, sizing and capacity planning is generally considered to be a "day two" concern that should be informed, driven, and actioned via metrics and real data, as opposed to hypothesis prior to deploying Cloud Foundry. A key advantage is that Cloud Foundry scales well at every layer, from deploying more AIs to deploying more Cloud Foundry resources, right down to upgrading the IaaS and the physical infrastructure underpinning the IaaS.

When sizing infrastructure for Cloud Foundry, I strongly suggest leaving sufficient headroom for growth. However, there is a danger that by doing this you can end up with an initial IaaS capacity that drastically exceeds what you actually require. For this reason, I tend to move away from explicit sizing and focus on general scoping. Scoping is based on a set of predefined concerns. Through scoping, it is possible to define the underlying infrastructure, and it becomes easier to be more explicit as to what resources will be required.

Scoping deployments on AWS is relatively straightforward because you can pick your desired AWS region, create and configure a new virtual private cloud (VPC) [along with subnets, security groups, etc.], and then map your Cloud Foundry AZs to the AWS region AZs. When deploying Cloud Foundry to physical infrastructure, you need to size your infrastructure in advance. For example, most vSphere customers have a minimum vSphere cluster configuration of three hosts. Two-host clusters are not ideal if 50% of the cluster is taken up via vCenter HA demands, and a single-host cluster is meaningless from a vSphere perspective. vSphere hosts sizes usually contain 256 GB, 384 GB, or 512 GB of RAM. Taking into account the requirement of three AZs based on three vSphere clusters, this implies that the total provisioned RAM is 2.25 to 4.5 TB, which is often drastically more than the initial requirement. The same logic holds true for CPU cores.

For an excellent reference point, the Pivotal Professional Services team has put together two fantastic resources to help structure and size your infrastructure:[4]

- For establishing the base architectural design, you can review the reference architecture (*http://bit.ly/2qEjZHs*).

- For sizing your base architecture for the required workload, there is a sizing tool—the PCF sizing tool (*https://pcfsizer.cfapps.io*)—based on some fundamental scoping questions.

After you define your architectural footprint and then size the infrastructure based on your anticipated workload, the next key requirement is to understand the implications of your applications operating under peak load. For example, a retail app on a critical sale day might require more instances to deal with concurrency concerns. Additional instances might require additional Cell resources. Throughput of traffic to the additional apps might require additional GoRouters to handle the extra concurrent connections. When designing your routing tier to handle the required load, you can review the Cloud Foundry routing performance page (*https://www.cloudfoundry.org/routing-performance/*).

---

4 These reference architectures and tooling are designed for Pivotal Cloud Foundry. The rationale behind these resources holds true for all Cloud Foundry deployments with the exception of AI Packs and the Ops Manager VM, which can be discounted if you are not using Pivotal Cloud Foundry.

Cell sizing

Cell sizing is of particular importance because Cells run your applications. This is where most of your expansion will be when your AIs begin to increase. Table 4-1 lists typical sizing for a Cell.

Table 4-1. Cloud Foundry example Cell configuration

Resource	Sizing
AI average RAM	1.5 GB
AI average storage	2 GB
Cell instance type	AWS m3.2xlarge (or vSphere eight, 4-core vCPUs)
Cell mem size	64 GB
Cell ephemeral storage size	64 GB

Overcommitting Memory

Overcommitting memory is configurable in BOSH. However, you need to have a crystal-clear profile of your workloads if you over-commit memory because you can run out of memory in cata-strophic ways if you calculate this wrong. Memory is relatively inexpensive, so it is best to avoid this.

A typical three-AZ deployment is often initially set up with six Cells in total: two Cells per AZ. You can always increase the size of your Cells or add additional Cells at a later date.

A key consideration when choosing Cell size is that if the Cells are too small and the average app size too high, you risk wasting space. For example, imagine an 8 GB Cell, with 2 GB apps. When you take into account headroom for the host OS, you will be able to fit only three 2 GB apps on a single Cell. This means that you are wasting well over 1 GB of RAM per Cell; as you replicate this pattern over several Cells, the wasted RAM begins to accumulate to a significant amount.

Conversely, if your Cells are too large, you risk unnecessary churn if a Cell fails. For example, imagine a 128 GB Cell hosting two hundred fifty-five 512 MB apps. Although the app density is great, if for some reason the Cell fails, Cloud Foundry[5] will need to subsequently replace 255 apps in one go, in addition to any other work-load coming onto the platform. Although this volume of replacement most likely will be fine, replicating this pattern across several concurrent Cell failures—for example, due to an AZ failure—can cause unnecessary churn. Even though Cloud Foundry can cope with a huge amount of churn in replacing applications, but if all of the Cells are

---

5 Diego is the subsystem responsible for app placement and the container life cycle.

running at maximum capacity (as in the scenario stated), rescheduling the apps will not work until you add additional Cells. However, Cloud Foundry is eventually consistent. Even for a situation in which Cloud Foundry fails to place the apps, it will eventually fix itself and reach a consistent state when additional resources are added.

Based on the preceding two illustrations, 32 GB to 64 GB Cells (for an average app size of between 512 MB and 2 GB) is a good sweet spot to work with.

 cf-deployment's manifest generation capability provides default Cell sizes that can be reconfigured after you generate the deployment manifest.

Instance group replication

HA requirements are discussed in detail in "High Availability Considerations" on page 263. For deployment of a single Cloud Foundry foundation, you are generally concerned with defining three AZs and removing single points of failure through instance group replication.

When using AZs, you can ensure that there are very few (or zero) single points of failure. In addition to running a multiple Cell instance group as previously described, you should also run multiple instances of the following:

- MySQL (for BBS, UAA, and CCDBs)
- NATS
- Diego (BBS, Brain, AccessVM, CC-Bridge, Cells)
- Routing (GoRouter, Consul, RouteEmitter)
- Cloud Controller (including the CC-Worker)
- UAA
- Doppler server and Loggregator traffic controller

 Strictly speaking, most of the aforementioned instance groups require only two AZs. Clustered components such as MySQL, Consul, and etcd require quorum and thus require three AZs. For simplicity, I recommend replicating all components across three AZs if you have enough IaaS capacity.

Therefore, a single Cloud Foundry deployment spanning three AZs should have at least two of the aforementioned components that do not require quorum. As discussed previously, any component that uses the Raft consensus algorithm (MySQL,

Consul, etcd) should have three instances to maintain a quorum. These instance groups always need an odd number of instances deployed, but you get no additional benefit from having more than three instances. For the other instance groups in the list, at least two instances are required to ensure HA and to allow for rolling upgrades. However, you might want a higher number of instances in order to handle additional capacity and concurrency.

For example, because the GoRouter is on the critical path for application traffic, it might be considered necessary to have two GoRouters per AZ to ensure that you can handle peak traffic if an AZ goes offline. Because the GoRouters load-balance between all the backend instances, the GoRouter is able to span AZs to reach the desired AI. Therefore, if two GoRouters can handle peak workload, adding an additional instance per AZ is not necessary.

Clock Global remains the only singleton. It is not a critical job. It is used for Cloud Controller cleanup and BOSH resurrection should be sufficient for this instance. Beyond that, the only single jobs remaining would be the internal NFS. The NFS can and should be replaced by an external blobstore such as Amazon S3. Additionally, the HAProxy and MySQL proxy are singletons by default. Again, you can and should use an enterprise load balancer, in which case the MySQL proxy can have multiple instances (e.g., one per AZ) when used in conjunction with an external load balancer. If you're using more than one Cloud Foundry AZ, any singleton instance group must be placed into a specific AZ. Other components that can run with several instances can and should be balanced across multiple AZs.

 bosh-bootloader will try to configure three AZs by default (assuming that the IaaS to which you deploy will support three distinct regions). cf-deployment will then deploy multiple instances of certain instance groups across the three AZs.

Setting Up an AWS VPC

Each IaaS that you use will have its own unique set of dependencies and configuration steps. For example, before setting up an AWS VPC, you will need the following:

- An AWS account that can accommodate the minimum resource requirements for a Cloud Foundry installation.
- The appropriate region selected within your AWS account (this example uses US-west).
- The AWS CLI installed on your operator machine, configured with user credentials that have administrative access to your AWS account.

- Sufficiently high instance limits (or no instance limits) on your AWS account. Installing Cloud Foundry might require more than the default 20 concurrent instances.

- A key-pair to use with your Cloud Foundry deployment. This key-pair allows you to configure SSH access to your instances. The key-pair name should be uploaded to the NAT instance upon VPC creation.[6]

- A certificate for your chosen default domain.

If you are deploying a highly distributed Cloud Foundry on AWS, built for HA, you will need to file a ticket with Amazon to ensure that your account can launch more than the default 20 instances. In the ticket, ask for a limit of 50 t2.micro instances and 20 c4.large instances in the region you are using. You can check the limits on your account by visiting the EC2 Dashboard on the AWS console; in the Navigation pane on the left, click Limits.

You can bootstrap VPC setup via bosh-bootloader, as described in "Installing Cloud Foundry" on page 67. Table 4-2 lists the external IaaS-related dependencies that you should take into consideration when manually setting up an AWS VPC.

Table 4-2. Cloud Foundry AWS VPC dependencies

Item
Access key ID
AWS secret key
VPC ID
AWS security group name
Region
Key-pair name (used for VM-to-VM communication and SSH)
DNS IP(s)
NTP IP(s)
SSH password (if applicable)
VPC to data center connection

If you are not using bosh-bootloader, there are some excellent instructions on setting up an AWS IaaS environment ready to install Cloud Foundry at prepare-aws (*http://bosh.io/docs/init-aws.html#prepare-aws*). Figure 4-2 presents an example of a typical direct VPC setup.

---

6 bosh-bootloader will create this key-pair for you.

Step 2: VPC with Public and Private Subnets

IP CIDR block:*	10.0.0.0/16	(65531 IP addresses available)
VPC name:	gswcf	
Public subnet:*	10.0.0.0/24	(251 IP addresses available)
Availability Zone:*	us-west-1b ⬍	
Public subnet name:	gswcf-Public-subnet	
Private subnet:*	10.0.16.0/20	(4091 IP addresses available)
Availability Zone:*	us-west-1b ⬍	
Private subnet name:	gswcf-Private-subnet	
	You can add more subnets after AWS creates the VPC.	

Specify the details of your NAT instance (Instance rates apply).

Instance type:*	t2.small ⬍	
Key pair name:	gswcf ⬍	

Service endpoints

Add Endpoint

Enable DNS hostnames:*	⦿ Yes ○ No
Hardware tenancy:*	Default ⬍

Figure 4-2. Setting up the VPC

 A strong word of caution. The Identity and Access Management (IAM) policy offered by BOSH.io is sufficient to get you started, but for corporate or production environments, it is highly recommended you set a very restrictive policy to limit unnecessary user access. In addition, when setting up the AWS security group (egress and ingress network rules), it is highly insecure to run any production environment with 0.0.0.0/0 as the source or to make any BOSH management ports publicly accessible.

Jumpbox

A jumpbox VM (or Bastian VM) provides layered security because it acts as a single access point for your control plane. It is the jumpbox that accesses the BOSH Director and subsequent deployed VMs. For operator resilience, there should be more than one jumpbox. Allowing access through the firewall only to the jumpboxes and disabling direct access to the other VMs is a common security measure.

Using a jumpbox from your VPC to deploy BOSH and Cloud Foundry can help navigate past network connectivity issues, given that most corporate networks will have firewall rules preventing SSH connections from a VPC to a local machine.

Instead of using SSH to connect to the jumpbox to run commands, newer CLIs respect the *SOCKS5* protocol. SOCKS5 routes packets between a server and a client using a proxy server. This means that you can set up an SSH tunnel from your laptop to the jumpbox, forwarded to a local port. By setting an environment variable prior to executing the CLI, the CLI will then run through the jumpbox on your workstation. This provides the advantage that you do not need to install anything on the jumpbox, but you have access to the jumpbox's network space.

You can create a jumpbox by using $bosh `create env`. There are also tools in the Cloud Foundry community to help manage, instantiate, and configure your jumpbox. One such tool is Jumpbox (*http://bit.ly/2pSlvbP*).

Networking Design and Routing

As with all networking, many configurations are possible. The key concern with networking is to design a network topology that suits your business while factoring in any specific security requirements. The most appropriate network configuration for Cloud Foundry is established by treating the Cloud Foundry ecosystem as a virtual appliance. Doing so establishes the expectation that all Cloud Foundry components are allowed to talk among themselves. Adopting this virtual appliance mindset will help articulate and shape the networking strategy that could stand in contrast to more traditional networking policies. Security and networking policies should be in place and adhered to for sound reasons, not because "that's the way we've always done it."

The principal networking best practice is to deploy Cloud Foundry to run on a trusted, isolated network, typically only accessible via an external SSL terminating load balancer that fronts Cloud Foundry. Although it is possible to run Cloud Foundry on any network—for example, where every deployed VM is accessible via its own IP—nearly all of the projects that I have worked on are deployed into a private network utilizing NAT for outbound traffic.

Before setting up your VPC, you need to consider the VPC-to-data center connection. If you are running your VPC in an isolated manner in which all external calls use NAT to reach out to your corporate network, the VPC to data center connection is not important. However, the VPC to data center connection becomes important if you are treating the VPC as an extension of your corporate network (through capabilities such as directconnect (*https://aws.amazon.com/directconnect*)) because the available network range can have a bearing on your VPC classless interdomain routings (CIDRs). The important concern in this scenario is to avoid IP collision with existing resources on the network by defining a portion of the existing network that is free and can be strictly reserved for Cloud Foundry. There are arguments for and against using NAT from the VPC because some companies desire the components within the Cloud Foundry network to remain explicitly routable. However, it is worth noting that if you consider the network as a single address space, you still can use NAT when required, but you cannot "unNAT" a VPC if your VPC has overlapping addresses with the corporate network.

For each AWS subnet used, you should gather and document the information listed in Table 4-3. You will use this information in your deployment manifest if you are creating it from scratch.

Table 4-3. Network dependencies

Network dependencies
AWS network name
VPC subnet ID
Subnet (CIDR range)
Excluded IP ranges
DNS IP(s)
Gateway

A best practice is to co-locate the services in a separate network from Cloud Foundry and allow a full range of communication (bidirectionally) between the two segments (the services and Cloud Foundry). You also might choose to have one network per service and do the same. However, white-listing ports can make the process very painful, and, for most companies, this extra precaution is regarded as unnecessary. The general recommendation is to allow full communication among all Cloud Foundry–managed components at the network-segment level. There is no reason to white-list ports if you trust all components. This approach is often regarded as entirely reasonable given that all of the components are under the same management domain.

For a simple installation, the Cloud Foundry documentation provides recommendations on basic security group egress and ingress rules.

Using Static IPs

The following Cloud Foundry components (referred to in BOSH parlance as instance groups) and IaaS components require static IPs or resolution via external DNS:

- Load balancer (static IP for HAProxy, VIP for F5, etc.)
- GoRouter (depending on the IaaS, some CPIs will resolve this for you)
- NATS

- Consul/etcd
- Database such as a MySQL cluster (relational databse service [RDS] referenced by DNS)

Static IPs are required for the aforementioned components because they are used by other downstream instance groups. For example, Consul and etcd, being apex instance groups, require static IPs; all other instance groups can then be resolved through external DNS, or internally through Consul's internal DNS resolution. For example, the following Cloud Foundry instance groups can have IP resolution via internal DNS:

- Diego components (BBS, Brain, etc.)
- Cloud Controller
- Cell
- GoRouter (depending on the IaaS, some CPIs will resolve this for you)
- Routing API
- Loggregator
- WebDAV, nfs_server (or S3 blobstore referenced by DNS)
- etcd

Subnets

Network design is dependent on a number of factors. As a minimum, it is recommended that you create one with a public and private subnet. With a public subnet, you get an internet GW with no NAT, thus every VM that needs internet access will require a public IP. With the private network, you can use an NAT gateway or NAT instance. By default, using bosh-bootloader will provision a management subnet and then a separate subnet per AZ. This is a basic configuration to get you started. However, there is a typical pattern of subnetting your network that has emerged as a common practice for production environments (see also Figure 4-3):

- A management subnet for the BOSH Director and or jumpbox
- A dedicated subnet for the core Cloud Foundry components (which also could contain the BOSH Director)
- A dedicated subnet for the Diego Cells (so as to scale independently as apps scale)
- A dedicated internet protocol security (IPsec) subnet for services that require the use of IPSec

---

- A dedicated subnet for services that do not use IPSec

The first three networks can be on an IPSec-enabled network if required, but it is important to ensure that you have a non-IPSec subnet for services that do not or cannot use IPSec.

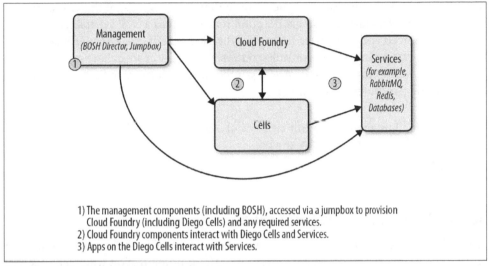

1) The management components (including BOSH), accessed via a jumpbox to provision Cloud Foundry (including Diego Cells) and any required services.
2) Cloud Foundry components interact with Diego Cells and Services.
3) Apps on the Diego Cells interact with Services.

Figure 4-3. Subnet architecture example

Security Groups

Security group requirements—with respect to egress and ingress rules—are defined in the Cloud Foundry documentation. It is worth noting that, when setting up the security group inbound rules, you will define SSH from your current IP. If you are on a corporate network, your IP will change as you hop on and off it. Therefore, if you are trying to use $ bosh create-env to update your environment, and you have a previously created security group policy, you might not have authority to connect to the Director VM as you try to establish a new connection. After the VM is fully set up, you can remove the "connect from MyIP" rules for SSH because they are no longer required.

bosh-bootloader will establish and configure the networking requirements (static IPs, subnets, security groups) on your behalf, across your VPC AZs.

Setting Up the Load Balancer

Application end users access applications via a generic domain such as myapp.com. A DNS is consulted as part of the path to the application; this is done to route traffic on to the correct Cloud Foundry installation.

Most Cloud Foundry deployments need more than one instance of the GoRouter for HA. However, DNS targets a single IP, often referred to as a VIP (virtual IP). Consequently, you need another device in front of the GoRouter to take requests on that IP and balance them across the available routers. In addition to balancing traffic, the load balancer (ELB in the case of AWS) can be used to terminate SSL or it can pass SSL on to the GoRouter for termination.

 bosh-bootloader will create your AWS elastic load balancer and subsequent security groups.

Setting Up Domains and Certificates

Regardless of the installation approach you choose, your Cloud Foundry installation will need a registered wildcard domain for its default domain. You will need this registered domain when configuring your SSL certificate and Cloud Controller. For more information, read the AWS documentation on Creating a Server Certificate (*http://amzn.to/2q2vrzC*).

When setting up a single Cloud Foundry deployment, it is recommended that you have at least two default wildcard domains: a system domain and a separate application domain, as demonstrated here:

- *.system.cf.com
- *.apps.cf.com

The system domain allows Cloud Foundry to know about its internal components because Cloud Foundry itself runs some of its components as applications; for example, the UAA. Developers use the application domain to access their applications.

If Cloud Foundry had only one combined system and app domain, there would be no separation of concerns. A developer could register an app domain name that infers it was a potential system component. This can cause confusion to the Cloud Foundry operator as to what are system applications and what are developer-deployed applications. Even worse, if an app is mapped to an existing system-component route such as api.mycf.com, the Cloud Foundry environment can become unusable. This is discussed in "Scenario Five: Route Collision" on page 241. By enforcing a separation of system and app domains, it is far more likely that you will avoid this scenario. Therefore, it is recommended that you always have at least one default system and default app domain per environment.

It is also recommended that you use unique system and application domain as opposed to deploying Cloud Foundry with a system domain that is in the app's domain list. For instance, you should use the preceding example; do not use the following:

- *.system.apps.cf.com
- *.apps.cf.com

You will need an SSL certificate for your Cloud Foundry domains. This can be a self-signed certificate, but you should use a self-signed certificate only for testing and development. A certificate should be obtained from a certificate authority (CA) for use in production.

A quick and effective way to get started is the AWS Certificate Manager (*https:// aws.amazon.com/certificate-manager/*). This allows you to create SSL certificates (multidomain storage-area network [SAN], wildcard, etc.) for free if you are using the AWS ELB. This makes it very easy to get the "green padlock" for Cloud Foundry on AWS environments. After it is authorized, a certificate will be issued and stored on the AWS ELB, allowing for secure HTTPS connections to your ELB.

You can use bosh-bootloader to generate and upload your AWS key and certificate. Alternatively, if you want to generate your certificate manually, you can use openssl as follows:

```
$ openssl req -sha256 -new -key <YOUR_KEY.pem> -out <YOUR_KEY_csr.pem>
$ openssl x509 -req -days 365 -in <YOUR_KEY_csr.pem> \
    -signkey <YOUR_KEY.pem> -out <YOUR_CERT.pem>
```

If you are not using bosh-bootloader, you will need to add your key manually and upload the certificate to your VPC, as follows:

```
$ aws iam upload-server-certificate --server-certificate-name <YOUR_CERT_NAME> \
    --certificate-body file://<YOUR_CERT.pem> \
        --private-key file://<YOUR_KEY.pem>
```

One final point: be sure to register your chosen domain name in Route53 by creating the appropriate record to point to your ELB.

Summary

Cloud Foundry is a complex distributed system that requires forethought prior to deploying. How you configure and deploy Cloud Foundry becomes even more important if you intend to use your environment for production applications. Appropriate effort and assessment at the outset can help mitigate challenges such as future resource contention or infrastructure and component failure. This chapter explored both the technical and non-technical topics that require upfront consideration prior to deploying Cloud Foundry.

Although upfront sizing and architectural assessment is vital, keep in mind that timely progression toward an end state is always better then stagnation due to indecision. The benefit of Cloud Foundry's rolling-upgrade capability is that it offers you the freedom to modify your environment at any point in the future.

Now that you are aware of the prerequisites, considerations, and decision points that are required prior to installing Cloud Foundry, Chapter 5 walks you through a Cloud Foundry installation.

Installing and Configuring Cloud Foundry

This chapter explores the steps required for bootstrapping BOSH and installing the Cloud Foundry BOSH release. The general topic of how to install Cloud Foundry is nuanced and varied, depending on the approach taken. Nonetheless, there are some fundamental patterns required to achieve a new deployment of Cloud Foundry, and the steps for deploying Cloud Foundry are broadly the same regardless of the IaaS platform or the specific tooling used.

This chapter walks you through setting up Cloud Foundry along with the following key concerns and decision points:

- Using bosh-bootloader
- Installing Cloud Foundry
- Growing the platform
- Validating platform integrity in production
- Logical environment structure (Orgs and Spaces)
- Deploying an application

This chapter assumes that you are familiar with the Cloud Foundry components discussed in Chapter 3. It also assumes that you are familar with the basics of Cloud Foundry's release-engineering tool chain, BOSH (a recursive acronym meaning BOSH outer shell). I will provide you with all of the required BOSH commands for provisioning Cloud Foundry; however, if you would like a deeper overview of BOSH, feel free to jump ahead to Chapter 10.

The Canonical Approach to Bootstrapping Cloud Foundry

Until recently, there was no canonical way of getting up and running with BOSH and Cloud Foundry. Many open source approaches exist, such as Stark and Wayne's genesis (*https://github.com/starkandwayne/genesis*). Commercial products also exist such as Pivotal Cloud Foundry, which make it easy to install and configure BOSH, Cloud Foundry, and additional backing services. The Cloud Foundry community has recently added additional tooling and BOSH functionality to help bootstrap a Cloud Foundry environment.

Installation Steps

In "Installation Steps" on page 43, I described the prerequisites for installing Cloud Foundry:

1. Create and configure the IaaS environment (including any networks, security groups, blobstores, and load balancers).[1]

2. Set up the required external dependencies; this includes additional enterprise services (such as LDAP, syslog endpoints, monitoring and metrics dashboards).

After the prerequisites are in place, here is the next set of steps to actually install Cloud Foundry and BOSH:

1. Deploy the BOSH Director.

2. Create an IaaS/infrastructure-specific BOSH configuration such as cloud configuration.

3. Create a deployment manifest to deploy Cloud Foundry.

4. Integrate Cloud Foundry with the required enterprise services (via the deployment manifest).

5. Deploy Cloud Foundry.[2]

The rest of this chapter explores the necessary considerations for each step.

---

1 The IaaS environment is created and configured by bosh-bootloader for standard configurations. If you desire a different configuration, you will need to manually create the IaaS environment.

2 Deployment and configuration steps are significantly easier to manage if you're using a CI pipeline such as Concourse.ci.

Installing Cloud Foundry

To install Cloud Foundry, you need an infrastructure (in our case, an AWS VPC) and a BOSH Director. bosh-bootloader (*https://github.com/cloudfoundry/bosh-bootloader*) was created to bootstrap both of these concerns.

A single BOSH environment consists of both the Director and the deployments that it orchestrates. Therefore, to create an empty BOSH environment, we first need a Director. The Director VM includes all necessary BOSH components that will be used to manage different IaaS resources.

Bootstrapping just the Director was solved by the BOSH CLI, through:

```
$ bosh create-env
```

create-env provides only the Director, there still remains the requirement to provision and configure the VPC, subnets, security groups, ELB, databases, and blobstores.

You can install both BOSH and the required IaaS environment using bosh-bootloader. Bosh-bootloader is a command-line utility for setting up Cloud Foundry (and Concourse) on an IaaS. Under the hood, bosh-bootloader uses the BOSH CLI to set up the BOSH Director.

Before using bosh-bootloader, be sure to do the following:

- Create and change into a clean directory by running the following commands:

  ```
  $ mkdir bosh-bootloader;cd bosh bootloader
  ```

- Download the latest stable release and add it to a directory on your PATH, as in this example (assuming */usr/local/bin* is on your PATH):

  ```
  $ wget https://github.com/cloudfoundry/bosh-bootloader/releases/
  download/v2.3.0/bbl-v2.3.0_osx
  $ chmod +x bbl-v2.3.0_osx
  $ mv bbl-v2.3.0_osx /usr/local/bin/bbl
  ```

- Add the correct inline policy to your AWS user (see the bosh-bootloader repository for details)

- Export any required environment variables (see repo for details), such as the following:

  ```
  $ export BBL_AWS_ACCESS_KEY_ID=<YOUR ACCESS KEY>
  $ export BBL_AWS_SECRET_ACCESS_KEY=<YOUR SECRET KEY>
  $ export BBL_AWS_REGION=<YOUR AWS DEPLOYMENT REGION>
  ```

Now you are going to focus on bosh-bootloader:

1. To set up the AWS VPC and deploy the BOSH Director, run the following:

   ```
   $ bbl up
   ```

You should now have a BOSH Director residing in a new VPC with the appropriate subnets, security groups, and NAT in place.

 The BOSH team recommends updating your BOSH environment frequently to be sure you're using the latest version of BOSH. The sequence of steps that follows assumes that you are using BOSH 2.0.

2. Pull out the Director IP, ca-cert, username, and password from the bbl CLI and then log in to your BOSH Director. BOSH requires a ca-cert because the BOSH v2 CLI connects over HTTPS to the Director.

A typical approach is to alias the BOSH environment (Director IP address) and log in as follows:

```
$ bosh alias-env my-bosh -e <YOUR-BOSH-IP>
  Using environment '<YOUR-BOSH-IP>' as user 'user-********'

$ bosh -e my-bosh --ca-cert <(bbl director-ca-cert) \
  login --user $(bbl director-username)
  --password $(bbl director-password)
```

Alternatively, you might find it advantageous to set the Director credentials as environment variables and log in as follows:

```
$ export BOSH_CLIENT=$(bbl director-username)
$ export BOSH_CLIENT_SECRET=$(bbl director-password)
$ export BOSH_ENVIRONMENT=$(bbl director-address)
$ export BOSH_CA_CERT=$(bbl director-ca-cert)

# check if the above environment is set up correctly
$ $ bosh env

# At this point you can login to your BOSH Director
$ bosh login
```

You need only provide the credentials the first time you log in to BOSH.

 For any of the aforementioned bbl query commands to work, you need to run them from the same directory as your bbl-state.json file. This file is created in the directory where you first ran bbl up.

3. Create the ELB using the key and certificate you created in "Setting Up Domains and Certificates" on page 62:

```
$ bbl create-lbs --type cf --cert <YOUR-cert.pem> --key <YOUR-KEY.pem>
```

This command updates your `bbl-state.json`. Save this file in a secure location such as Lastpass after this step.

Cloud Foundry approaches deploying the platform in an unique way. Open source software often resides in a single repository and can be distributed as either a single binary or a set of binaries.

The Cloud Foundry cf-deployment (*https://github.com/cloudfoundry/cf-deployment*) does not ship as a single binary or even a set of binaries that you first compile then deploy. Instead, cf-deployment is a set of software packages pulled from other Git repositories. These software packages are automatically compiled from source as part of the BOSH deployment process.

As part of the deployment process, BOSH sets up separate, temporary VMs to compile packages and automatically store the results for subsequent distribution. These VMs are known as *compilation VMs*.

Before beginning a new installation of Cloud Foundry, be sure to use the latest stable BOSH v2 CLI obtained from *http://bosh.io*.

4. BOSH provides a way to capture all OS dependencies as one image, known as a *stemcell* (discussed later in "Stemcells" on page 176). Upload the appropriate stemcell for your IaaS environment; for example:

```
$ bosh -e my-bosh upload-stemcell \
https://bosh.io/d/stemcells/bosh-aws-xen-hvm-ubuntu-trusty-go_agent
```

5. Deploy Cloud Foundry. You can obtain the canonical manifest for deploying Cloud Foundry from the cf-deployment Git repository. In time, this repo will also contain tooling for aiding deployment.

To deploy Cloud Foundry, run the following:

```
$ bosh -e my-env -d cf deploy cf-deployment/cf-deployment.yml \
--vars-store env-repo/deployment-vars.yml \
-v system_domain=<YOUR-CFDomain.com>
```

The *cf-deployment.yml* manifest requires two additional parameter types:

- Environment-specific data; as of this writing, this is just your `system domain`
- Sensitive configuration information such as credentials

  You should propagate all other configurations by using option fields. For additional information, see cf-deployment (*https://github.com/cloudfoundry/cf-deployment*).

  To import these datasets, the BOSH CLI currently uses the `--vars-store` flag. This flag reads in *.yml* files and extracts the values present in those files to fill out the template represented by cf-deployment. The BOSH v2 CLI generates this *.yml* file with all of the necessary variables to populate the cf-deployment manifest. In the command in the previous example, the `--vars-store env-`

repo/deployment-vars.yml -v system_domain=$SYSTEM_DOMAIN generates a *deployment-vars.yml* file based on custom variables such as your Cloud Foundry system domain. Note that for production deployments, you should use config-server instead of var-store.

cf-deployment contains all required BOSH releases for deploying Cloud Foundry; for example:

```
releases:
- name: capi
  url: https://bosh.io/d/github.com/cloudfoundry/
  capi-release?v=1.15.0
  version: 1.15.0
  sha1: 2008137d5bb71e701cedba96cb363e1bfbdebd45
```

The BOSH CLI will inspect the release URL and then retrieve and upload releases to the Director's blobstore. There is no requirement to explicitly upload a release to the Director. Instead of linking to a tarball on bosh.io, as in the example here, you can link to a Git repository that then links to a release blobstore. This detail is explained further in "Packaging a Release" on page 199.

6. Use the following command to view your deployed environment:

```
$ bosh instances --ps #view everything deployed
```

Figure 5-1 shows the output.

One important point: be sure to register your chosen wildcard domain names in a DNS such as Route53, and create the appropriate records to point to your load balancer.

```
$ bosh -e vbox -d cf instances
Using environment '192.168.50.6' as client 'admin'

Task 317. Done

Deployment 'cf'

Instance                                              Process State   AZ   IPs
api/a2b6d507-e99d-49f8-bc24-76beaf4d4841              running         z1   10.244.0.135
blobstore/6da27024-5971-4a94-83a1-480f371ba304        running         z1   10.244.0.134
cc_bridge/c1475011-8c27-4b7b-9d23-bec7982e3cd7        running         z1   10.244.0.137
cc_clock/d7f96fb8-cf1c-42e9-a34b-5fee2da9149f         running         z1   10.244.0.136
consul/b4e2329c-9a2d-49d6-8943-ea1fe743aa1a           running         z1   10.244.0.2
diego-bbs/aa4d7308-05fd-4e8d-9913-e0bed321abc4        running         z1   10.244.0.129
diego-brain/827227fe-bc9f-4903-a852-74f328c4ef9b      running         z1   10.244.0.131
diego-cell/807c821f-be87-4c83-9822-b5e468040478       running         z1   10.244.0.132
doppler/eec8857d-b607-4c4e-8a80-4a8d0bf2696e          running         z1   10.244.0.138
etcd/da95849d-fd79-4732-9243-f8af03d94b2a             running         z1   10.244.0.128
log_controller/207177fb-6fae-46c0-ad43-5ddb8bba813f   running         z1   10.244.0.139
mysql/c8c2187e-a75c-4240-ba83-a247a814972d            running         z1   10.244.0.10
nats/a8252a64-a6dd-49c9-913f-4ecea202dfd2             running         z1   10.244.0.6
route-emitter/2d7d3aa2-019c-4111-ac24-a22be9fb89ba    running         z1   10.244.0.133
router/392e0f8a-537a-4733-b0a3-6f5e5b609c89           running         z1   10.244.0.34
uaa/483d41e4-43bf-4a7a-8482-f358a5e342e5              running         z1   10.244.0.130

16 instances

Succeeded
$
```

Figure 5-1. Deployed instance groups that comprise Cloud Foundry

7. Target the cf api domain and then log in as follows:

   ```
   $ cf api api.<YOUR-CFDomain.com> --skip-ssl-validation
   ```

8. Log in via cf login. For the administrator username and password, use the following values from the *deployment-vars.yml* file:

   user:

Pull uaa_scim_users_admin_name out of deployment-vars. This currently defaults to admin: password:. Pull uaa_scim_users_admin_password out of deployment-vars.yml. The final deployment should look something like that shown in Figure 5-2.

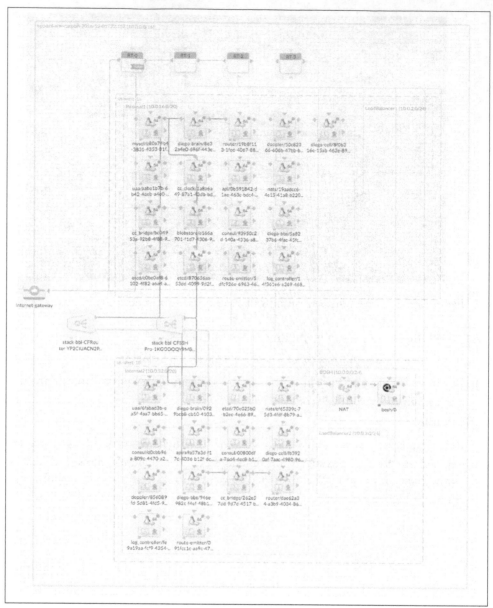

Figure 5-2. bbl and cf-deployment topology on AWS spanning two AZs (three AZs are preferable, but at the time of writing only two AZs are available in us-west)

Changing Stacks

As we discussed in "Stacks" on page 37, a stack is a prebuilt rootfs used along with droplets to provide the container filesystem used for running applications. The following Cloud Foundry command lists all the stacks available in a deployment:

```
$ cf stacks
```

To change a stack and restage an application, use this command:

```
$ cf push APPNAME -s STACKNAME
```

Growing the Platform

bosh-bootloader provides a reasonable, default configuration for getting started with Cloud Foundry. However, over time, your deployment and platform requirements are likely to grow in scope and external integration points. You will also need to upgrade the platform to take advantage of both security updates and new features.

As a distributed platform with many moving parts, Cloud Foundry supports rolling upgrades, which make it possible for you to make changes to platform configuration and underlying infrastructure. If you need additional or bigger Cells, you can resize them and/or increase their number and then simply redeploy Cloud Foundry using BOSH's ability to perform rolling upgrades. If you need additional IaaS capacity, you can grow your infrastructure to support your existing Cloud Foundry deployment. You can also deploy additional Cloud Foundry environments, as required.

The key is that you must make some important design decisions at the outset, but you are not locked into a static configuration and are free to grow and develop your Cloud Foundry environment, as needed.

Validating Platform Integrity in Production

This section discusses how to validate the health and integrity of your production environment. After you have successfully deployed Cloud Foundry, you should run the smoke tests and Cloud Foundry acceptance tests (CATS) to ensure that your environment is working properly. You should also maintain a dedicated sandbox to test any changes prior to altering any development or production environment.

Start with a Sandbox

If you run business-critical workloads on a production instance of Cloud Foundry, you should consider using a sandbox or staging environment prior to making any production platform changes. This approach allows you to test any production apps in an isolated environment before rolling out the platform changes (be it an infrastructure upgrade, stemcell change, Cloud Foundry release upgrade, buildpack change, or service upgrade) to production.

The sandbox environment should mirror the production environment as closely as possible. It should also contain a representation of the production apps and a mock up of the production services to ensure that you validate the health of the applications running on the platform. An example set of application tests could include the following:

- Use the `cf push` command to push the app
- Bind an application to a service(s)
- Start an app
- Target the app on a restful endpoint and validate the response
- Target the app on a restful endpoint to write to a given data service
- Target the app on a restful endpoint to read the written value
- Generate and log a unique string to validate application logging
- Stop an app
- Delete an app

This suite of tests should be designed to exercise the core user-facing functionality, including the applications interacting with any backing services.

Running these sorts of tests against each Cloud Foundry instance on a CI server with a metrics dashboard is the desired approach for ease of repeatability. Not only do you get volume testing for free (e.g., you can easily fill up a buildpack cache that way), you can publish the dashboard URL to your platform consumers and stakeholders alike. Tying these tests up to alerting/paging systems is also more efficient than paging people due to IaaS-level failures.

Production Verification Testing

Before making the production environment live, test the behavior of your platform by running the following:

- cf-smoke-tests (*https://github.com/cloudfoundry/cf-smoke-tests*)[3] to ensure core Cloud Foundry functionality is working

---

3 cf-smoke-tests are part of cf-deployment and will run as a one-off errand.

- cf-acceptance-tests (*https://github.com/cloudfoundry/cf-acceptance-tests*)[4] to test Cloud Foundry behavior and component integration in more detail

- Your own custom acceptance tests against the applications and services you have written, including any established or customized configuration (this ensures that the established application behavior does not break)

- External monitoring against your deployed apps

After you make the environment live, it is still important to identify any unintended behavior changes. Therefore, the ongoing periodic running of your own acceptance tests in production is absolutely recommended. For example, it is possible that you might uncover a problem with the underlying infrastructure that can be noticed only by repeatedly running acceptance tests in production.

Production Configuration Validation

cf-acceptance-tests (*https://github.com/cloudfoundry/cf-acceptance-tests*) (CATS) was never designed for live configuration validation. It is a developer workflow for engineers building Cloud Foundry to verify that changes have not adversely affected the platform. As a precheck, CATS is a valuable suite of tests to run. The Cloud Foundry engineering team is currently working on a production configuration validation test harness. If, in the meantime, you need ongoing production validation, you can run your own custom acceptance tests against the applications and services you have written, including any established or customized configuration. Due to the way CATS modifies global state across all running apps, running CATS against a live production environment is not recommended.

Logical Environment Structure

Earlier, in "IaaS and Infrastructure Design" on page 48, we described the need to both design and provision the infrastructure and IaaS layer to support a single Cloud Foundry foundation. After deploying Cloud Foundry, the next task is to divide the IaaS resources into logical environments for various teams, products, and users to utilize. These logical environments within Cloud Foundry are known as Orgs and Spaces.

As discussed in "Organizations and Spaces" on page 23, Orgs and Spaces provide a way to group users together for management purposes. All members of an Org share the same resource quota plan, services availability, and custom domain. Quota plans

---

4 cf-acceptance-tests are part of cf-deployment and will run as a one-off errand.

are associated with Orgs. A quota will apply to all the activities within a particular organization.[5]

Each Org will have at least one Space but can have multiple Spaces. Every application and service is scoped to a Space. Spaces provide a shared location for application development, deployment, and maintenance, and users will have specific Space-related roles. All members of a Space have access to any application environment variables configured in the Space. Therefore, the Space members must have a strict level of trust among one another.

Orgs and Spaces allow you to create a logical multitenant environment within your Cloud Foundry deployment. They give you a level of abstraction with which you can define who can do what in a particular environment. They also provide a way of allocating resources and governing chargeback.

You can define Orgs and Spaces any way that you like. Typically, Orgs are defined around constructs such as the lines of businesses or particular projects and initiatives. Spaces are generally defined in a couple of different ways:

- Typically, bigger organizations are broken down into "two-pizza teams," with each team owning its own Space. Usually, an individual team is responsible for developing an isolated component or components such as a specific microservice.

- When deploying through a pipeline, it is often useful to have a development space, test space, staging space, and a production space for the applications moving into production.

There is no right or wrong way to structure your Orgs and Spaces; an important point to keep in mind is that you are free to alter your logical Org and Space boundaries at any point.

To begin, you can use the default Org and simply create a Space, as demonstrated here:

```
$ cf create-space developer

Creating space developer in org default_org as admin...
OK
Assigning role SpaceManager to user admin in org default_org /
space developer as admin...
OK
Assigning role SpaceDeveloper to user admin in org default_org /
```

---

5 For a current view on what is governed by quota plans, check out the Cloud Foundry documentation on Creating and Modifying Quota Plans (*http://bit.ly/2qEFzf8*).

```
space developer as admin...
OK
```

You can then target the new `developer` space:

```
$ cf target -o "default_org" -s "developer"
```

Pushing Your First App

You can push many different apps to Cloud Foundry. If you do not have one on hand, you can download spring-music (*https://github.com/scottfrederick/spring-music*).

```
$ git clone https://github.com/scottfrederick/spring-music
$ cd spring-music
```

The Spring Music repository contains a sample app manifest. An app manifest provides an easy way to define and capture any required command-line arguments and application metadata. This is important because you can source-control the arguments you used when deploying your app. You do not need to deploy your app with an app manifest. If you prefer, you can simply provide any required arguments via the command line, as shown here:

```
---
applications:
- name: spring-music
  memory: 1G
  random-route: true
  path: build/libs/spring-music.jar
```

Therefore, to deploy the app, all you need to do is compile the code by using `./gradlew assemble` and then use `cf push`:

```
$ ./gradlew assemble
$ cf push
```

The `cf push` command should return a URL that you can then use to access your deployed app.

Summary

This chapter walked you through an end-to-end installation of Cloud Foundry using cf-deployment and bosh-bootloader. If you followed all the steps, you should have accomplished the following:

- Deployed the BOSH Director and created IaaS-specific components using bosh-bootloader
- Deployed a working instance of Cloud Foundry using BOSH and cf-deployment

- Successfully validated platform integrity through CATS smoke tests
- Set up an Org and Space
- Pushed an application

Now that you are up and running with Cloud Foundry, Chapter 6 introduces you to the underlying concepts and operational aspects of Diego.

Diego

Diego is the container runtime architecture for Cloud Foundry. It is responsible for managing the scheduling, orchestration, and running of containerized workloads. Essentially, it is the heart of Cloud Foundry, running your applications and one-off tasks in containers, hosted on Windows and Linux backends. Most Cloud Foundry users (e.g., developers) do not interact with Diego directly. Developers interact only with Cloud Foundry's API, known as CAPI. However, comprehending the Diego container runtime is essential for Platform Operators because, as an operator, you are required to interact with Diego for key considerations such as resilience requirements and application troubleshooting. Understanding Diego is essential for understanding how workloads are deployed, run, and managed. This understanding also provides you with an appreciation of the principles underpinning container orchestration.

This chapter explores Diego's concepts and components. It explains the purpose of each Diego service, including how the services interrelate as state changes throughout the system.

Implementation Changes

It is important to understand the fundamental concepts of the Diego system. The specific technical implementation is less consequential because it is subject to change over time. What Diego does is more important than how it does it.

Why Diego?

Residing at the core of Cloud Foundry, Diego handles the scheduling, running, and monitoring of tasks and long-running processes (applications) that reside inside managed containers. Diego extends the traditional notion of running applications to scheduling and running two types of processes:

Task

A process that is guaranteed to be run at most once, with a finite duration. A Task might be an app-based script or a Cloud Foundry "job"; for example, a *staging request* to build an application droplet.

Long-running process (LRP)

An LRP runs continuously and may have multiple instances. Cloud Foundry dictates to Diego the desired number of instances for each LRP, encapsulated as *DesiredLRPs*. All of these desired instances are run and represented as actual LRPs known as *ActualLRPs*. Diego attempts to keep the correct number of ActualLRPs running in the face of any network partitions, crashes, or other failures. ActualLRPs only terminate due to intervention, either by crashing or being stopped or killed. A typical example of an ActualLRP is an instance of an application running on Cloud Foundry.

Cloud Foundry is no longer solely about the *application as a unit of work*. The addition of running one-off tasks in isolation opens up the platform to a much broader set of workloads; for example, running Bash scripts or Cron-like jobs to process a one-off piece of data. Applications can also spawn and run tasks for isolated computation. Tasks can also be used for local environmental adjustments to ensure that applications adhere to service-level agreements (SLAs).

The required scope for what Cloud Foundry can run is ever increasing as more workloads migrate to the platform. Tasks and LRPs, along with the new TCPRouter (discussed in "The TCPRouter" on page 134), have opened up the platform to accommodate a much broader set of workloads. In addition to traditional web-based applications, you can now consider Cloud Foundry for the following:

- Internet of Things (IoT) applications such as aggregating and processing device data
- Batch applications
- Applications with application tasks
- Computational numerical modeling
- Reactive streaming applications
- TCP-based applications

By design, Diego is agnostic to preexisting Cloud Foundry components such as the Cloud Controller. This separation of concerns is compelling. Being agnostic to both client interaction and runtime implementation has allowed for diverse workloads with composable backends. For example, Diego has generalized the way container image formats are handled; Diego's container management API is Garden.

The Importance of Container Management

For a container image (such as a Docker image or other OCI–compatible image) to be instantiated and run as an isolated process, it requires a container-management layer that can create, run, and manage the container process. The Docker company provides its own Linux Container manager for running Docker images. Other container-management technologies also exist, such as rkt (*https://coreos.com/rkt/*) and runC (*https://runc.io/*). As a more generalized container management API, Cloud Foundry uses Garden to support a variety of container technologies. Garden is discussed further in "Why Garden?" on page 150.

Through Garden, Diego can now support any container image format that the Garden API supports. Diego still supports the original droplet plus a stack combination but can now accommodate other image formats; for example, OCI-compatible images such as Docker or Rocket. In addition, Diego has added support for running containers on any Garden-based container technology, including Linux and Windows-based container backends that implement the Garden API. Figure 6-1 illustrates Diego's ability to support multiple application artifacts and container image formats.

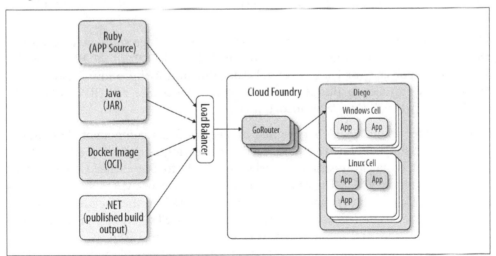

Figure 6-1. Developer interaction, cf pushing different application artifacts to Cloud Foundry

A Brief Overview of How Diego Works

Container scheduling and orchestration is a complex topic. Diego comprises several components, and each component comprises one or more microservices. Before getting into detail about these components and services, it is worth taking a moment to introduce the end-to-end flow of the Diego component interactions. At this point, I will begin to introduce specific component names for readability. The individual component responsibilities will be explained in detail in "Diego Components" on page 97.

At its core, Diego executes a scheduler. Scheduling is a method by which work, specified by some means, is assigned to resources that attempt to undertake and complete that work.

A Tip on Scheduling

Schedulers are responsible for using resources in such a way so as to allow multiple users to share system resources effectively while maintaining a targeted quality of service. Scheduling is an intrinsic part of the execution model of a distributed system. Scheduling makes it possible to have distributed multitasking spread over different nodes, with a centralized component responsible for processing. Within OSs, this processing unit is referred to as a CPU. Within Cloud Foundry, Diego acts as a centralized processing unit for all scheduling requirements.

Diego clients—in our case, the Cloud Controller (via a bridge component known as the CC-Bridge)—submit, update, and retrieve Tasks and LRPs to the BBS. The BBS service is responsible for Diego's central data store and API. Communication from the Cloud Controller to the BBS is via a remote procedure call (RPC)–style API implemented though Google protocol buffers.

The scheduler within Diego is governed by Diego's Brain component. The Brain's orchestration function, known as the Auctioneer service, retrieves information from the BBS and optimally distributes Tasks and LRPs to the cluster of Diego Cell machines (typically VMs). The Auctioneer distributes its work via an auction process that queries Cells for their capacity to handle the work and then sends work to the Cells. After the Auctioneer assigns work to a Cell, the Cell's Executor process creates a Garden container and executes the work encoded in the Task/LRP. This work is encoded as a generic, platform-independent recipe of composable actions (described in "Composable Actions" on page 85). Composable actions are the actual actions that run within a container; for example, a RunAction that runs a process in the container, or a DownloadAction that fetches and extracts an archive into the container. To assist in setting up the environment for the process running within the container,

Application Life-Cycle Binaries (e.g., Buildpacks) are downloaded from a file server that is responsible for providing static assets.

Application Life-Cycle Binaries

Staging is the process that takes an application and composes a executable binary known as a droplet. Staging is discussed further in "Staging" on page 159. The process of staging and running an application is complex and filled with OS and container implementation-specific requirements. These implementation-specific concerns have been encapsulated in a collection of binaries known collectively as the Application Life-Cycle. The Tasks and LRPs produced by the CC-Bridge download the Application Life-Cycle Binaries from a blobstore (in Cloud Foundry's case, the Cloud Controller blobstore). These Application Life-Cycle Binaries are helper binaries used to stage, start, and health-check Cloud Foundry applications. You can read more about Application Life-Cycle Binaries in "Application Life-Cycle Binaries" on page 112.

Diego ensures that the actual LRP (ActualLRP) state matches the desired LRP (DesiredLRP) state through interaction with its client (the CC-Bridge). Specific services on the CC-Bridge are responsible for keeping the Cloud Controller and Diego synchronized, ensuring domain freshness.[1]

The BBS also provides a real-time representation of the state of the Diego cluster (including all DesiredLRPs, running ActualLRP instances, and in-flight Tasks). The Brain's Converger periodically analyzes snapshots of this representation and corrects discrepancies, ensuring that Diego is eventually consistent. This is a clear example of Diego using a closed feedback loop to ensure that its view of the world is accurate. Self-healing is the first essential feature of resiliency; a closed feedback loop ensures that eventual consistency continues to match the ever-changing desired state.

Diego sends real-time streaming logs for Tasks/LRPs to the Loggregator system. Diego also registers its running LRP instances with the GoRouter via the Route-Emitter, ensuring external web traffic can be routed to the correct container.

Essential Diego Concepts

Before exploring Diego's architecture and component interaction, you need to be aware of two fundamental Diego concepts:

---

1 These services, along with the concept of domain freshness, are discussed further in "The CC-Bridge" on page 93.

- Action abstraction
- Composable actions

As work flows through the distributed system, Diego components describe their actions using different levels of abstraction. Diego can define different abstractions because the architecture is not bound by a single entity; for example, a single monolithic component with a static data schema. Rather, Diego consists of distributed components that each host one or more microservices. Although microservices architecture is no panacea, if designed correctly for appropriate use cases, microservices offer significant advantages by decoupling complex interactions. Diego's microservices have been composed with a defined boundary and are scoped to a specific component. Furthermore, Diego establishes well-defined communication flows between its component services. This is vital for a well designed system.

Components versus Services

Components like the Cell, Brain, and CC-Bridge are all names of VMs where Diego services are located. The location of those services is mutable, and depending on the deployment setup, some components can have more than one service residing on them. When describing the Diego workflow, consider the Diego components as though they were locations of specific services rather than the actual actors. For example, it makes sense to talk about distributing work to the Cells because a Cell is where the container running your workload will reside. However, the Cell does not actually create the container; it is currently the Rep service that is responsible for initiating container creation. Theoretically, the Rep could reside on some other component such as the BBS. Similarly, the Auctioneer is the service responsible for distributing work; the Brain is just the component VM on which the Auctioneer is running. In BOSH parlance, components are referred to as *instance groups* and services are referred to as *release jobs*.

Action Abstraction

Because each microservice is scoped to a specific Diego component, each service is free to express its work using its own abstraction. This design is incredibly powerful because bounded abstractions offer an unprecedented degree of flexibility. Abstraction levels move from course high-level abstractions to fine-grained implementations as work moves through the system. For example, work can begin its journey at the Cloud Controller as an app, but ultimately all work ends up as a scheduled process running within a created container. This low-level implementation of a *scheduled process* is too specific to be hardwired into every Diego component. If it were hardwired throughout, the distributed system would become incredibly complex for end users and brittle to ongoing change. The abstraction boundaries provides two key benefits:

- The freedom of a plug-and-play model
- A higher-level concern for Diego clients

Plug-and-play offers the freedom to replace key parts of the system when required, without refactoring the core services. A great example of this is a pluggable container implementation. Processes can be run via a Docker image, a droplet plus a stack, or in a Windows container. The required container implementation (both image format and container backend) can be plugged into Diego as required without refactoring the other components.

Moreover, clients of Diego have high-level concerns. Clients should not need to be concerned with underlying implementation details such as how containers (or, more specifically, process isolation) are created in order to run their applications. Clients operate at a much higher level of abstraction, imperatively requesting *"run my application."* They are not required to care about any of the underlying implementation details. This is one of the core benefits of utilizing a platform to drive application velocity. The more of the undifferentiated heavy lifting you allow the platform to undertake, the faster your business code will progress.

Composable Actions

At the highest level of abstraction, the work performed by a Task or LRP is expressed in terms of composable actions, exposed via Diego's public API. As described earlier, composable actions are the actual actions that run within a container; for example, a RunAction that runs a process in the container, or a DownloadAction that fetches and extracts an archive into the container.

Conceptually each composable action implements a specific instruction. A set of composable actions can then be used to describe an explicit imperative action, such as *"stage my application"* or *"run my application."*[2] Composable actions are, by and large, hidden from Cloud Foundry users. Cloud Foundry users generally interact only with the Cloud Controller. The Cloud Controller (via the CC-Bridge) then interacts with Diego through Diego's composable actions. However, even though as a Platform Operator you do not interact with composable actions directly, it is essential that you understand the available composable actions when it comes to debugging Cloud Foundry. For example, the UploadAction might fail due to misconfigured blobstore credentials, or a TimeoutAction might fail due to a network partition.

---

2 The available actions are documented in the Cloud Foundry BBS Release on GitHub (*https://github.com/cloud foundry/BBS/blob/master/doc/actions.md*).

Composable actions include the following:

1. RunAction runs a process in the container.

2. DownloadAction fetches an archive (*.tgz* or *.zip*) and extracts it into the container.

3. UploadAction uploads a single file, in the container, to a URL via POST.

4. ParallelAction runs multiple actions in parallel.

5. CodependentAction runs multiple actions in parallel and will terminate all codependent actions after any single action exits.

6. SerialAction runs multiple actions in order.

7. EmitProgressAction wraps another action and logs messages when the wrapped action begins and ends.

8. TimeoutAction fails if the wrapped action does not exit within a time interval.

9. TryAction runs the wrapped action but ignores errors generated by the wrapped action.

Because composable actions are a high-level Diego abstraction, they describe generic activity, not how the activity is actually achieved. For example, the UploadAction describes uploading a single file to a URL; it does not specify that the URL should be the Cloud Controller's blobstore. Diego, as a generic execution environment, does not care about the URL; Cloud Foundry, as a client of Diego, is the entity responsible for defining that concern. This concept ties back to the action abstraction discussed previously, allowing Diego to remain as an independently deployable subsystem, free from specific end-user concerns.

So, how do composable actions relate to the aforementioned Cloud Foundry Tasks and LRPs? Consider the steps involved when the Cloud Controller issues a *run command* for an already staged application. To bridge the two abstractions, there is a Cloud Foundry-to-Diego bridge component known as the Cloud Controller Bridge (CC-Bridge). This essential function is discussed at length in "The CC-Bridge" on page 93. For now, it is sufficient to know that the CC-Bridge knows how to take the various resources (e.g., a droplet, metadata ,and blobstore location) that the Cloud Controller provides, coupled with a desired application message. Then, using these composable actions, the CC-Bridge directs Diego to build a sequence of composable actions to run the droplet within the container, injecting the necessary information provided by the Cloud Controller. For example, the specific composable action sequence for a *run command* will be:

- DownLoadAction to download the droplet from the CC blobstore into a specified location inside the container.

- DownLoadAction to download the set of static plugin (AppLifeCycle) binaries from a file server into a specified location within the container.
- RunAction to run the start command in the container, with the correct parameters. RunAction ensures that the container runs the code from the droplet using the helper (AppLifeCycle) binaries that correctly instantiate the container environment.

Applications are broken into a set of *Tasks* such as *"stage an app"* and *"run an app."* All Diego Tasks will finally result in a tree of composable actions to be run within a container.

Layered Architecture

Diego is comprised of a number of microservices residing on several components. Diego is best explained by initially referring to the diagram in Figure 6-2.

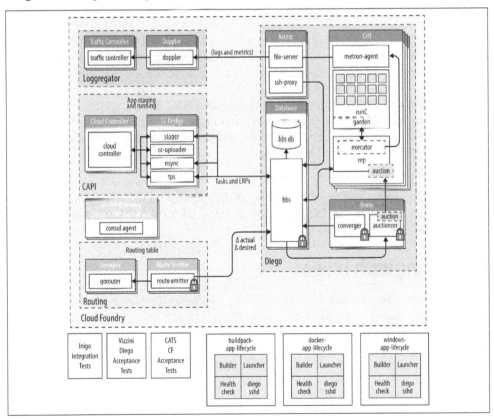

Figure 6-2. Diego components

We can group the components broadly, as follows:

- A Cloud Foundry layer of user-facing components (components with which you, as a platform user, will directly interact)
- The Diego Container Runtime layer (components with which the core Cloud Foundry components interact)

Each Diego component is a single deployable BOSH machine (known as an instance group) that can have any number of machine instances. Although there can be multiple instances of each instance group to allow for HA and horizontal scaling, some instance groups require a global lock to ensure that only one instance is allowed to make decisions.

Diego BOSH Releases

As with other Cloud Foundry components, you can deploy and run the Diego BOSH release as a standalone system. Having the property of being independently deployable is powerful. The engineering team responsible for the Diego subsystem has a smaller view of the distributed system allowing decoupling from other Cloud Foundry subsystems and faster iterative development. It also means that the release-engineering team can adopt more holistic granular testing in a heterogeneous environment of different subsystems. Because each Cloud Foundry subsystem can be deployed in isolation, more complex upgrade migration paths can now be verified because older versions of one subsystem, such as the Postgres release, can be deployed alongside the latest Diego release.[3]

We will begin exploring Diego by looking at the user-facing Cloud Foundry components that act as a client to Diego, and then move on to the specific Diego components and services.

Interacting with Diego

Cloud Foundry users do not interact with Diego directly; they interact with the Cloud Foundry user-facing components, which then interact with Diego on the user's behalf. Here are the Cloud Foundry user-facing components that work in conjunction with Diego:

---

3 You can find more information on Diego online, including the Diego BOSH release repository (*http://bit.ly/2q2TrTk*).

- CAPI components: the Cloud Foundry API (Cloud Controller and the CC-Bridge)
- The logging system defined by the Loggregator and Metron agents
- Routing (GoRouter, TCPRouter, and the Route-Emitter)

Collectively, these Cloud Foundry components are responsible for the following:

- Application policy
- Uploading application artifacts, droplets, and metadata to a blobstore
- Traffic routing and handling application traffic
- Logging
- User management including end-user interaction via the Cloud Foundry API commands[4]

Diego seamlessly hooks into these different Cloud Foundry components to run applications and tasks, route traffic to your applications, and allow the retrieval of required logs. With the exception of the CC-Bridge, these components were discussed at length in Chapter 3.

CAPI

Diego Tasks and LRPs are submitted to Diego via a Diego client. In Cloud Foundry's case, the Diego client is the CAPI, exposed by the Cloud Controller. Cloud Foundry users interact with the Cloud Controller through the CAPI. The Cloud Controller then interacts with Diego's BBS via the CC-Bridge, a Cloud Foundry-to-Diego translation layer. This interaction is depicted in Figure 6-3.

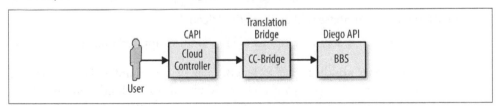

Figure 6-3. API interaction from the platform user through to Diego

The Cloud Controller provides REST API endpoints for Cloud Foundry users to interact with Cloud Foundry for commands including the following:

---

4 User management is primarily handled by the User Access and Authentication, which does not directly interact with Diego but still remains an essential piece of the Cloud Foundry ecosystem.

- Pushing, staging, running, and updating
- Pushing and running discrete one-off tasks
- Creating users, Orgs, Spaces, Routes, Domains and Services, and so on
- Retrieving application logs

The Cloud Controller (discussed in "The Cloud Controller" on page 33) is concerned with imperatively dictating policy to Diego, stating *"this is what the user desires; Diego, make it so!"*; for example, *"run two instances of this application."* Diego is responsible for orchestrating and executing the required workload. It deals with orchestration through a more autonomous subsystem at the backend. For example, Diego deals with the orchestration of the Cells used to fulfill a workload request through an auction process governed by the Auctioneer.

This design means that the Cloud Controller is not coupled to the execution machines (now known as Cells) that run your workload. The Cloud Controller does not talk to Diego directly; instead, it talks only to the translation component, the CC-Bridge, which translates the Cloud Controller's app-specific messages to the more generic Diego language of Tasks and LRPs. The CC-Bridge is discussed in-depth in "The CC-Bridge" on page 93. As just discussed, this abstraction allows the Cloud Foundry user to think in terms of apps and tasks, while allowing each Diego service to express its work in a meaningful abstraction that makes sense to that service.

Staging Workflow

To better understand the Cloud Controller interaction with Diego, we will explore what happens during a staging request. Exploring staging introduces you to two Diego components:

- The BBS: Diego's database that exposes the Diego API.
- Cells: the execution machines responsible for running applications in containers.

These two components are discussed at length later in this chapter. Understanding the staging process provides you with a clear picture of how Cloud Foundry interprets the $ cf push and translates it into a running ActualLRP instance. Figure 6-4 provides an overview of the process.

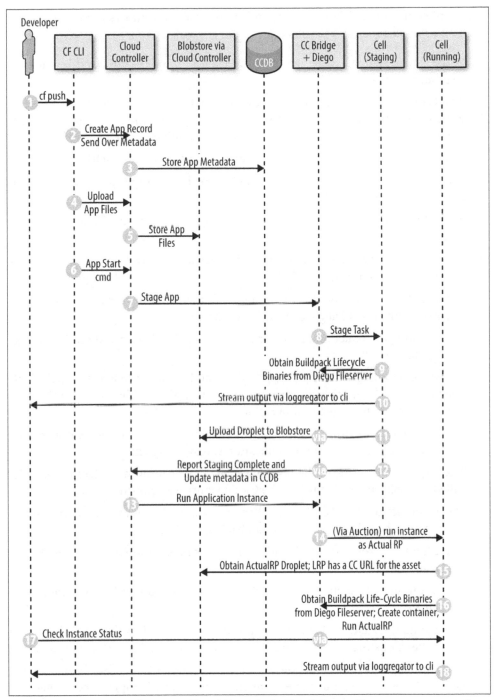

Figure 6-4. Interaction between Cloud Foundry's Cloud Controller components and Diego, while staging and running an application

The numbered list that follows corresponds to the callout numbers in Figure 6-4 and provides an explanation of each stage:

1. A developer/Platform Operator uses the Cloud Foundry command-line tool to issue a cf push command.

2. The Cloud Foundry command-line tool instructs the Cloud Controller to create a record for the application and sends over the application metadata (e.g., the app name, number of instances, and the required buildpack, if specified).

3. The Cloud Controller stores the application metadata in the CCDB.

4. The Cloud Foundry command-line tool uploads the application files (such as a *.jar* file) to the Cloud Controller.

5. The Cloud Controller stores the raw application files in the Cloud Controller blobstore.

6. The Cloud Foundry command-line tool issues an app start command (unless a no-start argument was specified).

7. Because the app has not already been staged, the Cloud Controller, through the CC-Bridge, instructs Diego to stage the application.

8. Diego, through an auction process, chooses a Cell for staging and sends the staging task to the Cell.

9. The staging Cell downloads the required life-cycle binaries that are hosted on the Diego file server, and then uses the instructions in the buildpack to run the staging task in order to stage the application.

10. The staging Cell streams the output of the staging process (to loggregator) so that the developer can troubleshoot application staging problems.

11. The staging Cell packages the resulting staged application into a tarball (*.tar* file) called a droplet and uploads it to the Cloud Controller blobstore.

12. Diego reports to the Cloud Controller that staging is complete. In addition, it returns metadata about the application back to the CCDB.

13. The Cloud Controller (via CC-Bridge) issues a run AI command to Diego to run the staged application.

14. Diego, through an auction process, chooses a Cell to run an LRP instance as an ActualLRP.

15. The running Cell downloads the application droplet directly from the Cloud Controller blobstore (the ActualLRP has a Cloud Controller URL for the asset).

16. The running Cell downloads the Application Life-Cycle Binaries hosted by the Diego file server and uses these binaries to create an appropriate container and then starts the ActualLRP instance.

17. Diego reports the status of the application to the Cloud Controller, which periodically receives the count of running instances and any crash events.

18. The Loggregator log/metric stream goes straight from the Cell to the Loggregator system (not via the CC-Bridge). The application logs can then be obtained from the Loggregator through the CF CLI.

Diego Staging

The preceding steps explore only staging and running an app from Cloud Foundry's perspective. The steps gloss over the interaction of the internal Diego services. After exploring the remaining Diego components and services, we will explore staging an LRP from Diego's perspective. Analyzing staging provides a concise way of detailing how each service interacts, and therefore it is important for you to understand.

The CC-Bridge

The CC-Bridge (Figure 6-5) is a special component comprised of four microservices. It is a translation layer designed to interact both with the Cloud Controller and Diego's API, which is exposed by Diego's BBS. The BBS is discussed shortly in "The BBS" on page 98.

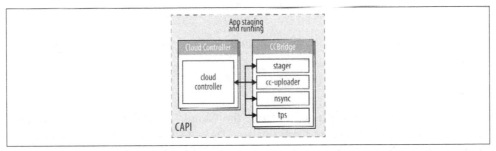

Figure 6-5. The CC-Bridge

The components on the CC-Bridge are essential for establishing *domain freshness*. Domain freshness means two things:

1. The actual state reflects the desired state.

2. The desired state is always understood.

Domain freshness is established through a combination of self-healing and closed feedback loops.

The Future of the CC-Bridge Component

For now, you can think of the CC-Bridge as a translation layer that converts the Cloud Controller's domain-specific requests into Diego's generic Tasks and LRPs. Eventually, Cloud Foundry's Cloud Controller might be modified to communicate directly with the BBS, making the CC-Bridge redundant. Either way, the function of the four services that currently reside on the CC-Bridge will still be required no matter where they reside.

CC-Bridge services translate the Cloud Controller's domain-specific requests of *stage* and *run* applications into Diego's generic language of LRP and Tasks. In other words, Diego does not explicitly know about applications or staging tasks; instead, it just knows about a Task or LRP that it has been requested to execute. The CC-Bridge services include the following:

Stager
   The Stager handles staging requests.

CC-Uploader
   A file server to serve static assets to the Cloud Controller's blobstore.

Nsync
   This service is responsible for handling domain freshness from the Cloud Controller to Diego.

TPS
   This service is responsible for handling domain freshness from Diego to the Cloud Controller.

Stager

The Stager handles staging requests from the Cloud Controller. It translates these requests into generic Tasks and submits the Tasks to Diego's BBS. The Stager also instructs the Cells (via BBS Task auctions) to inject the platform-specific Application Life-Cycle Binary into the Cell to perform the actual staging process. Application Life-Cycle Binaries provide the logic to build, run, and health-check the application. (You can read more about them in "Application Life-Cycle Binaries" on page 112.) After a task is completed (successfully or otherwise), the Stager sends a response to the Cloud Controller.

CC-Uploader

The CC-Uploader acts as a file server to serve static assets such as droplets and build artifacts to the Cloud Controller's blobstore. It mediates staging uploads from the Cell to the Cloud Controller, translating a simple generic HTTP POST request into the complex correctly formed multipart-form upload request that is required by the Cloud Controller. Droplet uploads to the CC-Uploader are asynchronous, with the CC-Uploader polling the Cloud Controller until the asynchronous UploadAction is completed.

Nsync and TPS

Nsync and TPS are the two components responsible for handling domain freshness, matching desired and actual state between Diego and the Cloud Controller. They are effectively two sides of the same coin:

- The Nsync primarily retrieves information from the Cloud Controller. It is the component responsible for constructing the DesiredLRP that corresponds with the application request originating from the Cloud Controller.
- The TPS primarily provides feedback information from Diego to the Cloud Controller.

Both components react to events via their listener process, and will periodically check state validity via their respective bulker/watcher processes.

Figure 6-6 shows the high-level component interaction between the Cloud Controller, Diego's Nsync, and Converger components right through to the Cell. The figure also illustrates the convergence from a DesiredLRP stored in the BBS to an ActualLRP running on a Cell.

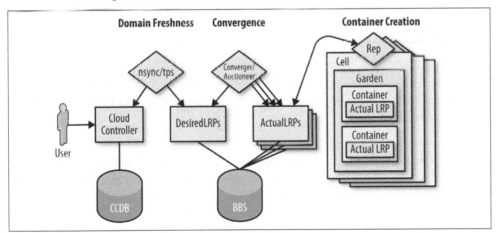

Figure 6-6. High-level process interaction involving domain freshness, convergence, and ActualLRP placement into a Cell's container

Domain Freshness

Diego's design has built-in resilience for its domain of responsibility—namely, running Tasks and LRPs. Diego's eventual-consistency model periodically compares the desired state (the set of DesiredLRPs) to the actual state (the set of ActualLRPs) and takes action to keep the actual and desired state synchronized. To achieve eventual consistency in a safe way, Diego must ensure that its view of the desired state is complete and up to date. Consider a rare scenario in which Diego's database has crashed and requires repopulating. In this context, Diego correctly knows about the ActualLRPs but has an invalid view of the DesiredLRPs, so it would be catastrophic for Diego to shut down all ActualLRPs in a bid to reconcile the actual and desired state.

To mitigate this effect, it is the Diego client's responsibility to repeatedly inform Diego of the desired state. Diego refers to this as the "freshness" of the desired state, or domain freshness. Diego consumers explicitly mark desired state as fresh on a domain-by-domain basis. Failing to do so will prevent Diego from taking actions to ensure eventual consistency (Diego will not stop extra instances if there is no corresponding desired state). To maintain freshness, the client typically supplies a *time-to-live* (TTL) and attempts to bump the freshness of the domain before the TTL expires (thus verifying that the contents of Diego's DesiredLRP are up to date). It is possible to opt out of this by updating the freshness with no TTL so that freshness will never expire, allowing Diego to always perform all of its eventual-consistency operations. Only destructive operations, performed during an eventual-consistency convergence cycle, will override freshness; Diego will continue to start and stop instances when explicitly instructed to do so.

The Nsync is responsible for keeping Diego *"in sync"* with the Cloud Controller. It splits its responsibilities between two independent processes: a bulker and a listener. Let's look at each of them:

Nsync-Listener

> The Nsync-Listener is a service that responds to DesiredLRP requests from the Cloud Controller. It actively listens for desired app requests and, upon receiving a request, either creates or updates the DesiredLRP via a record in the BBS database. This is the initial mechanism for dictating desired state from the Cloud Controller to Diego's BBS.

Nsync-Bulker

> The Nsync-Bulker is focused on maintaining the system's desired state, periodically polling the Cloud Controller and Diego's BBS for all DesiredLRPs to ensure that the DesiredLRP state known to Diego is up to date. This component pro-

vides a closed feedback loop, ensuring that any change of desired state from the Cloud Controller is reflected on to Diego.

The process status reporter (TPS) is responsible for reporting Diego's status; it is Diego's "hall monitor." It splits its responsibilities between two independent processes: listener and watcher submodules. Here's what each one does:

TPS-Listener
The TPS-Listener provides the Cloud Controller with information about currently running ActualLRP instances. It responds to the Cloud Foundry CLI requests for `cf apps` and `cf app <may-app-name>`.

TPS-Watcher
The TPS-Watcher monitors ActualLRP activity for crashes and reports them to the Cloud Controller.

Logging and Traffic Routing

To conclude our review of the Cloud Foundry layer of user-facing components, let look at logging.

Diego uses support for streaming logs from applications to Cloud Foundry's Loggregator system and provides support for routing traffic to applications via the routing subsystem. With the combined subsystems—Diego, Loggregator, and the routing subsystem—we have everything we need to do the following:

- Run any number of applications as a single user
- Route traffic to the LRPs
- Stream logs from the LRPs

The Loggregator aggregates and continually streams log and event data. Diego uses the Loggregator's Metron agent to provide real-time streaming of logs for all Tasks and LRPs in addition to the streaming of logs and metrics for all Diego components. The routing system routes incoming application traffic to ActualLRPs running within Garden containers on Diego Cells. (The Loggregator and routing subsystem were discussed in Chapter 3.)

Diego Components

At the time of writing, there are four core Diego component machines:

1. BBS (Database)
2. Cell
3. Brain

4. Access (an external component)

The functionality provided by these components is broken up into a number of microservices running on their respective component machines.

The BBS

The BBS manages Diego's database by maintaining an up-to-date cache of the state of the Diego cluster including a picture-in-time of all DesiredLRPs, running ActualLRP instances, and in-flight Tasks. Figure 6-7 provides an overview of the CC–Bridge-to-BBS interaction.

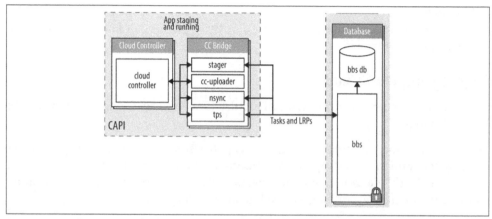

Figure 6-7. The BBS interaction with the Cloud Controller via the CC-Bridge

The BBS provides Diego's internal components and external clients with a consistent API to carry out the following:

1. Query and update the system's shared state (the state machine)

2. Trigger operations that execute the placement of Tasks and LRPs

3. View the datastore underpinning the state machine

For example, certain operations will cause effects. Consider creating a new LRP in the system. To achieve this, the CC-Bridge communicates to the BBS API endpoints. These endpoints will save any required state in the BBS database. If you specify a DesiredLRP with N instances, the BBS will automatically trigger the required actions for creating N ActualLRPs. This is the starting point of the state machine. Because understanding the state machine is important for debugging the platform, we cover it in more detail in "The Diego State Machine and Workload Life Cycles" on page 107.

Communication to the BBS is achieved through Google protocol buffers (protobufs).

Protocol Buffers

Protocol buffers (protobufs) provide an efficient way to marshal and unmarshal data. They are a language-neutral, platform-neutral, extensible mechanism for serializing structured data, similar in concept to eXtensible Markup Language (XML) but smaller, faster, and much less verbose.

The Diego API

The BBS provides an RPC-style API for core Diego components (Cell reps and Brain) and any external clients (SSH proxy, CC-Bridge, Route-Emitter). The BBS endpoint can be accessed only by Diego clients that reside on the same "private" network; it is not publicly routable. Diego uses dynamic service discovery between its internal components. Diego clients (the CC-Bridge) will look up the active IP address of the BBS using internal service discovery. Here are the main reasons why the Diego endpoint is not accessible via an external public route through the GoRouter:

- Clients are required to use TLS for communication with the BBS. The GoRouter is currently not capable of establishing or passing through a TLS connection to the backend.

- Clients are required to use mutual TLS authentication. To talk to the BBS, the client must present a certificate signed by a CA that both the client and BBS recognize.

The BBS encapsulates access to the backing database and manages data migrations, encoding, and encryption. The BBS imperatively directs Diego's Brain to state *"here is a task with a payload, find a Cell to run it."* Diego clients such as the CC-Bridge, the Brain, and the Cell all communicate with the BBS. The Brain and the Cell are both described in detail later in this chapter.

State versus Communication

The BBS is focused on data as opposed to communication. Putting state into an eventually consistent store (such as etcd, clustered MySQL, or Consul) is an effective way to build a distributed system because everything is globally visible. Eventual consistency is a data problem, not a communication problem. Tools like etcd and Consul, which operate as a quorum, handle consistency for you.

It is important that Diego does not store inappropriate data in a component designed for state. For instance, a "start auction" announcement is not a statement of truth; it is a transient piece of communication representing intent. Therefore, transient information should be communicated by messaging (i.e., NATS or HTTP—although direct communication over HTTPS is preferred). Communication via messaging is temporary and, as such, it can be lossy. For Diego auctions, loss is acceptable. Diego

---

can tolerate loss because of eventual consistency and the closed feedback loops described earlier.

For visibility into the BBS, you can use a tool called Veritas (*https://github.com/pivotal-cf-experimental/veritas*).

The Converger process

The Converger is a process responsible for keeping work eventually consistent.

Eventual Consistency

Eventual consistency is a consistency model used for maintaining the integrity of stateful data in a distributed system. To achieve high availability, a distributed system might have several "copies" of the data-backing store. Eventual consistency informally guarantees that, if no new updates are made to a given item of data, eventually all requests for that item will result in the most recently updated value being returned. To learn more about HA, see "High Availability Considerations" on page 263.

The Converger is a process that currently resides on the Brain instance group. It is important to discuss now, because it operates on the BBS periodically and takes actions to ensure that Diego attains eventual consistency. Should the Cell fail catastrophically, the Converger will automatically move the missing instances to other Cells. The Converger maintains a lock in the BBS to ensure that only one Converger performs convergence. This is primarily for performance considerations because convergence should be idempotent.

The Converger uses the converge methods in the runtime-schema/BBS to ensure eventual consistency and fault tolerance for Tasks and LRPs. When converging LRPs, the Converger identifies which actions need to take place to bring the DesiredLRP state and ActualLRP state into accord. Two actions are possible:

- If an instance is missing, a start auction is sent.
- If an extra instance is identified, a stop message is sent to the Cell hosting the additional instance.

In addition, the Converger watches for any potentially missed messages. For example, if a Task has been in the PENDING state for too long, it is possible that the request to hold an auction for the Task never made it to the Auctioneer. In this case, the Converger is responsible for resending the auction message. Periodically the Converger sends aggregate metrics about DesiredLRPs, ActualLRPs, and Tasks to the Loggregator.

Resilience with RAFT

Whatever the technology used to back the BBS (etcd, Consul, clustered MySQL), it is likely to be multinode to remove any single point of failure. If the backing technology is based on the Raft consensus algorithm, you should always ensure that you have an odd number of instances (three at a minimum) to maintain a quorum.

Diego Cell Components

Cells are where applications run. The term application is a high-level construct; Cells are concerned with running desired Tasks and LRPs. Cells are comprised of a number of subcomponents (Rep/Executor/Garden; see Figure 6-8) that deal with running and maintaining Tasks and LRPs. One Cell typically equates to a single VM, as governed by the CPI in use. You can scale-out Cells both for load and resilience concerns.

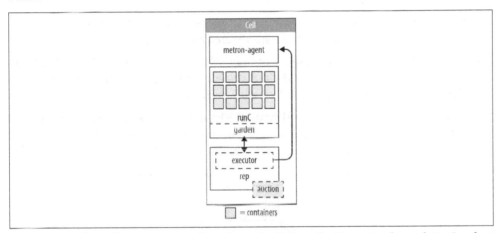

Figure 6-8. The Cell processes gradient from the Rep to the Executor through to Garden and its containers

There is a specificity gradient across the Rep, Executor, and Garden. The Rep is concerned with Tasks and LRPs, and knows the details about their life cycles. The Executor knows nothing about Tasks and LRPs but merely knows how to manage a collection of containers and run the composable actions in these containers. Garden, in turn, knows nothing about actions and simply provides a concrete implementation of a platform-specific containerization technology that can run arbitrary commands in containers.

Rep

The *Rep* is the Cell's API endpoint. It represents the Cell and mediates all communication between the BBS and Brain—the Rep is the only Cell component that communicates with the BBS. This single point of communication is important to understand; by using the Rep for all communication back to the Brain and BBS, the other Cell components can remain implementation independent. The Rep is also free to be reused across different types of Cells. The Rep is not concerned with specific container implementations; it knows only that the Brain wants something run. This means that specific container technology implementations can be updated or swapped out and replaced at will, without forcing additional changes within the wider distributed system. The power of this plug-and-play ability should not be underestimated. It is an essential capability for upgrading the system with zero-downtime deployments.

Specifically, the Rep does the following (see also Figure 6-9):

- Participates in the Brain's Auctioneer auctions to bid for Tasks and LRPs. It bids for work based on criteria such as its capacity to handle work, and then subsequently tries to accept what is assigned.

- Schedules Tasks and LRPs by asking its in-process Executor to create a container to run generic action recipes in the newly created container.

- Repeatedly maintains the presence of the Cell in the BBS. Should the Cell fail catastrophically, the BBS will invoke the Brain's Converger to automatically move the missing instances to another Cell with availability.

- Ensures that the set of Tasks and ActualLRPs stored in the BBS are synchronized with the active containers that are present and running on the Cell, thus completing the essential feedback loop between the Cell and the BBS.

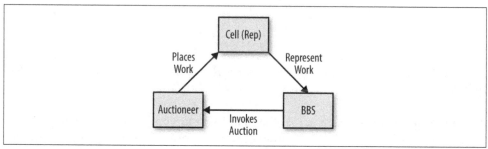

Figure 6-9. The BBS, auction, and Cell feedback loop

The Cell Rep is responsible for getting the status of a container periodically from Garden via its in-process Executor and reporting that status to the BBS database. There is only one Rep running on every Diego Cell.

Executor

The Executor is a logical process inside the Rep. Its remit is *"Let me run that for you."*[5] The Executor still resides in a separate repository, but it is not a separate job; it is part of the Rep.

The Executor does not know about the Task versus LRP distinction. It is primarily responsible for implementing the generic Executor "composable actions," as discussed in "Composable Actions" on page 85. Essentially, all of the translation between the Rep and Garden is encapsulated by the Executor: the Executor is a gateway adapter from the Rep to the Garden interface. The Rep deals with simplistic specifications (*execute this tree of composable actions*), and the Executor is in charge of actually interacting with Garden to, for example, make the ActualLRP via the life cycle objects. Additionally, the Executor streams Stdout and Stderr to the Metron-agent running on the Cell. These log streams are then forwarded to the Loggregator.

Garden

Cloud Foundry's container implementation, Garden, is separated into the API implementation and the actual container implementation. This separation between API and actual containers is similar to how Docker Engine has both an API and a container implementation based on runC.

Garden is a container API. It provides a platform-independent client server to manage Garden-compatible containers such as runC. It is backend agnostic, defining an interface to be implemented by container-runners (e.g., Garden-Linux, Garden-Windows, libcontainer, runC). The backend could be anything as long as it understands requests through the Garden API and is able to translate those requests into actions.

Container Users

By default, all applications run as the vcap user within the container. This user can be changed with a runAction, the composable action responsible for running a process in the container. This composable action allows you to specify, among other settings, the user. This means Diego's internal composable actions allow processes to run as any arbitrary user in the container. That said, the only users that really make sense are distinguished unprivileged users known as vcap and root. These two users are provided in the cflinuxfs2 rootfs. For Buildpack-based apps, Cloud Foundry always specifies the user to be vcap.

---

5 A conceptual adaption from the earlier container technology LMCTFY, which stands for *Let Me Contain That For You.*

Chapter 8 looks at Garden in greater detail.

The Diego Brain

We have already discussed the Brain's Converger process. The Brain (Figure 6-10) is also responsible for running the Auctioneer process. Auctioning is the key component of Diego's scheduling capability. There are two components in Diego that participate in auctions:

The Auctioneer
> Responsible for holding auctions whenever a Task or LRP needs to be scheduled

The Cell's Rep
> Represents a Cell in the auction by making bids for work and, if picked as the winner, running the Task or LRP

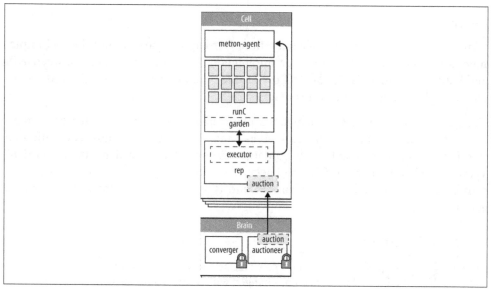

Figure 6-10. The Cell–Brain interaction

Horizontal Scaling for Controlling Instance Groups

Each core component (known in BOSH parlance as an instance group) is deployed on a dedicated machine or VM. There can be multiple instances of each instance group, allowing for HA and horizontal scaling.

Some instance groups, such as the Auctioneer, are essentially stateless. However, it is still important that only one instance is actively making decisions. Diego allows for lots of potential running instances in order to establish HA, but only one Auctioneer can be in charge at any one period in time. Within a specific instance group, the instance that is defined as "in charge" is specified by a global lock. Finding out which specific instance is in charge is accomplished through an internal service discovery mechanism.

When holding an auction, the Auctioneer communicates with the Cell Reps via HTTP. The auction process decides where Tasks and ActualLRP instances are run (remember that a client can dictate that one LRP requires several ActualLRP instances for availability). The Auctioneer maintains a lock in the BBS such that only one Auctioneer may handle auctions at any given time. The BBS determines which Auctioneer is active from a lock record (effectively the active Auctioneer holding the lock). When the BBS is at a point at which it wants to assign a payload to a Cell for execution, the BBS directs the Brain's Auctioneer by requesting, *"here is a task with a payload, find a Cell to run it."* The Auctioneer asks all of the Reps what they are currently running and what their current capacity is. Reps proactively bid for work and the Auctioneer uses the Reps' responses to make a placement decision.

Scheduling Algorithms

At the core of Diego is a distributed scheduling algorithm designed to orchestrate where work should reside. This distribution algorithm is based on several factors such as existing Cell content and app size. Other open source schedulers exist, such as Apache Mesos or Google's Kubernetes. Diego is optimized specifically for application and task workloads. The supply–demand relationship for Diego differs from the likes of Mesos. For Mesos, all worker Cells report, "*I am available to take N pieces of work*" and Mesos decides where the work goes. In Diego, an Auctioneer says, "*I have N pieces of work, who wants them?*" Diego's worker Cells then join an auction, and the winning Cell of each auctioned-off piece of work gets that piece of work. Mesos' approach is supply driven, or a "reverse-auction," and Diego's approach is demand driven.

A classic optimization problem in distributed systems is that there is a small lag between the time the system realizes it is required to make a decision (e.g., task placement) and the time when it takes action on that decision. During this lag the input criteria that the original decision was based upon might have changed. The system needs to take account of this to optimize its work-placement decisions.

Consequently, there are currently two auction actions for LRPs: LRPStartAuction and LRPStopAuction. Let's look at each:

LRPStartAuctions
> These occur when LRPs need to be assigned somewhere to run. Essentially, one of Diego's Auctioneers is saying, *"We need another instance of this app. Who wants it?"*

LRPStopAuctions
> These occur when there are too many LRPs instances running for a particular application. In this case, the Auctioneer is saying, *"We have too many instances of this app at index X. Who wants to remove one?"*

The Cell that wins the auction either starts or stops the requested LRP.

Simulations

Diego includes simulations for testing the auction orchestration. Diego values the tight feedback loops achieved with the auction algorithms. This feedback allows the engineers to know how Diego internals are working and performing. It is especially valuable for dealing with order dependency: *where "A" must run before "B."* Simulating this means it can be tested and reasoned over more quickly.

Simulations can be run either in-process or across multiple processes. Unit tests are great for isolation and integration tests exercise the traditional usage. Simulation testing provides an extra layer of performance testing.

The Access VM

The access VM contains the file server and the SSH proxy services.

File server

The file server serves static assets used by various Diego components. In particular, it provides the Application Life-Cycle Binaries to the Cells.

The SSH proxy

Diego supports SSH access to ActualLRP instances. This feature provides direct access to the application for tasks such as viewing application logs or inspecting the state of the container filesystem. The SSH proxy is a stateless routing tier. The primary purpose of the SSH proxy is to broker connections between SSH clients and

SSH servers running within containers. The SSH proxy is a lightweight SSH daemon that supports the following:

- Command execution
- Secure file copy via SCP
- Secure file transfer via SFTP
- Local port forwarding
- Interactive shells, providing a simple and scalable way to access containers associated with ActualLRPs

The SSH proxy hosts the user-accessible SSH endpoint so that Cloud Foundry users can gain SSH access to containers running ActualLRPs. The SSH proxy is responsible for the following:

- SSH authentication
- Policy enforcement
- Access controls

After a user successfully authenticates with the proxy, the proxy attempts to locate the target container, creating the SSH session with a daemon running within the container. It effectively creates a "man-in-the-middle" connection with the client, bridging two SSH sessions:

- A session from the client to the SSH proxy
- A session from the SSH proxy to the container

After both sessions have been established, the proxy will manage the communication between the user's SSH client and the container's SSH daemon.

The daemon is self-contained and has no dependencies on the container root filesystem. It is focused on delivering basic access to ActualLRPs running in containers and is intended to run as an unprivileged process; interactive shells and commands will run as the daemon user. The daemon supports only one authorized key and is not intended to support multiple users. The daemon is available on Diego's file server. As part of the application life cycle bundle, Cloud Foundry's LRPs will include a downloadAction to acquire the binary and then a runAction to start it.

The Diego State Machine and Workload Life Cycles

Diego's semantics provide clients with the ability to state, *"Here is my workload: I want Diego to keep it running forever. I don't care how."* Diego ensures this request becomes a reality. If for some reason an ActualLRP crashes, Diego will reconcile desired and actual state back to parity. These life cycle concerns are captured by Diego's state machine. It is important that you understand the state machine should you need to debug the system. For example, if you notice many of your ActualLRPs remain in UNCLAIMED state, it is highly likely that your Cells have reached capacity and require additional resources.

Stateful and Globally Aware Components

When it comes to state, Diego is comprised of three types of components: stateful components, stateless components, and stateless globally aware components. To describe the difference between the three components, consider the differences between the Cell, the BBS, and the Auctioneer.

A Cell has a global presence, but it is effectively stateless. Cells advertise themselves over HTTP to the BBS via a service discovery mechanism. They do not provide the entire picture of their current state; they simply maintain a presence in the BBS via recording a few static characteristics such as the AZ they reside in and their IP address. Maintaining a presence in the BBS allows the Auctioneer to contact the Cell at the recorded location in order to try to place work.

The BBS retains the global state associated with managing the persistence layer. The BBS also has the responsibility of managing migrations (between data migrations and schema migrations or API migrations reflected in the schema). For this reason, the BBS is an essential component to back up.

The Auctioneer is required to be globally aware; it has a global responsibility but is not directly responsible for system state. When a component has a global responsibility, there should only ever be one instance running at any one time.

An understanding of the state machine (see Figure 6-11) and how it relates to the app and task life cycles is essential for understanding where to begin with debugging a specific symptom.

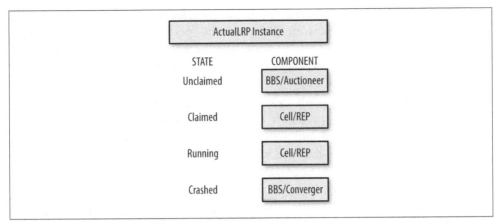

Figure 6-11. Diego's state machine

The responsibility for state belongs, collectively, to several components. The partition of ownership within the distributed system is dependent on the task or LRP (app) life cycle.

The Application Life Cycle

The application life cycle is as follows:

1. When a client expresses the desire to run an application, the request results in Diego's Nsync process creating an ActualLRP record.

2. An ActualLRP has a state field (a process globally unique identifier [GUID] with an index) recorded in the BBS. The ActualLRP begins its life in an UNCLAIMED state, resulting in the BBS passing it over to the Auctioneer process.

3. Work collectively is batched up and then distributed by the Auctioneer. When the Auctioneer has a batch of work that requires allocating, it looks up all the running Cells through service discovery and individually asks each Cell (Rep) for a current snapshot of its state, including how much capacity the Cell has to receive extra work. Auction activity is centrally controlled. It is like a team leader assigning tasks to team members based on their desire for the work and their capacity to perform it. The batch of work is broken up and distributed appropriately across the Cells.

4. An auction is performed and the ActualLRP is placed on a Cell. The Cell's Rep immediately transfers the ActualLRP state to CLAIMED. If placement is successful, the LRP is now RUNNING and the Rep now owns this record. If the ActualLRP cannot be placed (if a Cell is told to do work but cannot run that work for some reason), it reenters the auction process in an UNCLAIMED state. The Cell rejects the work and the Auctioneer can retry the work later.

5. The Cell's response on whether it has the capacity to do the work should not block actually starting the work. Therefore, the "perform" request from the Auctioneer instructs the Cell to try to undertake the work. The Cell then attempts to reserve capacity within the Executor's state management, identifying the extra resource required for the work.

6. The Cell quickly reports success or failure back to the Auctioneer. Upon success, the Cell then reserves this resource (as quickly as possible) so as not to advertise reserved resources during future auctions. The Executor is now aware that it has the responsibility for the reserved work and reports this back to the Rep, which knows the specifics of the Diego state machine for Tasks and LRPs.

7. Based on the current state that the Executor is reporting to the Rep, the Rep is then going to make decisions about how to progress workloads through their life cycles. In general, if anything is in reserved state, the Rep states to the Executor: "*start running that workload*." At that point, the Executor takes the container specification and creates a container in Garden.

8. The Auctioneer is responsible for the placement of workloads across the entire cluster of Cells. The Converger is responsible for making sure the desired and actual workloads are reconciled across the entire cluster of Cells. If the ActualLRP crashes, it is placed in a CRASHED state and the Rep moves the state ownership back to the BBS because the ActualLRP is no longer running. When the Rep undertakes its own local convergence cycle, trying to converge the actual running states in its Garden containers with its representation within the BBS, the Rep will discover the ActualLRP CRASHED state. The Rep then looks for the residual state that might still reside from its management of that ActualLRP. Even if the container itself is gone, the Executor might still have the container represented in a virtual state. The virtual state's "COMPLETED" state information might provide a clue as to why the ActualLRP died (e.g., it may have been placed in failure mode). The Rep then reports to the BBS that the ActualLRP has crashed. The BBS will attempt three consecutive restarts and then the restart policy will begin to back off exponentially, attempting subsequent restarts after a delayed period.

9. The Brain's Converger runs periodically looking for "CRASHED" ActualLRPs. Based on the number of times it has crashed (which is also retained in the BBS), the Converger will pass the LRP back to the Auctioneer to resume the ActualLRP. The Converger deals with the mass of unclaimed LRPs, moving them to ActualLRPs "CLAIMED" and "RUNNING". The Converger maps the state (held in the BBS) on to the desired LRPs. If the BBS desires five instances but the Rep only reports on four records, the Converger will make the fifth record in the BBS to kickstart the placement.

10. There is a spectrum of responsibilities that extends from the Converger to the BBS. Convergence requires a persistence-level convergence, including the

required cleanup process. There is also a business-model convergence in which we can strip away any persistence artifacts and deal with the concepts we are managing—and Diego ensures that the models of these concepts are in harmony. The persistence layer always happens in the BBS, but it is triggered by the Converger running a convergence loop.

Task Life Cycle

Tasks in Diego also undergo a life cycle. This life cycle is encoded in the Task's state as follows:

PENDING
When a task is first created, it enters the PENDING state.

CLAIMED
When successfully allocated to a Diego Cell, the Task enters the CLAIMED state and the Task's Cell_id is populated.

RUNNING
The Task enters the RUNNING state when the Cell begins to create the container and run the defined Task action.

COMPLETED
Upon Task completion, the Cell annotates the TaskResponse (failed, failure_reason, result), and the Task enters the COMPLETED state.

Upon Task completion, it is up to the consumer of Diego to acknowledge and resolve the completed Task, either via a completion callback or by deleting the Task. To discover if a Task is completed, the Diego consumer must either register a completion_callback_url or periodically poll the API to fetch the Task in question. When the Task is being resolved, it first enters the RESOLVING state and is ultimately removed from Diego. Diego will automatically reap Tasks that remain unresolved after two minutes.

Additional Components and Concepts

In addition to its core components, Diego also makes use of the following:

- The Route-Emitter
- Consul
- Application Life-Cycle Binaries

The Route-Emitter

The Route-Emitter is responsible for registering and unregistering the ActualLRPs routes with the GoRouter. It monitors DesiredLRP state and ActualLRP state via the information stored in the BBS. When a change is detected, the Route-Emitter emits route registration/unregistration messages to the router. It also periodically emits the entire routing table to the GoRouter. You can read more about routing in Chapter 7.

Consul

Consul (*https://www.consul.io*) is a highly available and distributed service discovery and key-value store. Diego uses it currently for two reasons:

- It provides dynamic service registration and load balancing via internal DNS resolution.

- It provides a consistent key-value store for maintenance of distributed locks and component presence. For example, the active Auctioneer holds a distributed lock to ensure that other Auctioneers do not compete for work. The Cells Rep maintains a global presence in Consul so that Consul can maintain a correct view of the world. The Converger also maintains a global lock in Consul.

To provide DNS, Consul uses a cluster of services. For services that require DNS resolution, a Consul agent is co-located with the hosting Diego component. The consul-agent job adds 127.0.0.1 as the first entry in the nameserver list. The consul-agent that is co-located on the Diego component VM serves DNS for consul-registered services on 127.0.0.1:53. When Consul tries to resolve an entry, the Consul domain checks 127.0.0.1 first. This reduces the number of component hops involved in DNS resolution. Consul allows for effective intercomponent communication.

Other services that expect external DNS resolution also need a reference to the external DNS server to be present in */etc/resolv.conf*.

Like all RAFT stores, if Consul loses quorum, it may require manual intervention. Therefore, a three-Consul-node cluster is required, preferably spanning three AZs. If you restart a node, when it comes back up, it will begin talking to its peers and replay the RAFT log to get up to date and synchronized with all the database history. It is imperative to ensure that a node is fully back up and has rejoined the cluster prior to taking a second node down; otherwise, when the second node goes offline, you might lose quorum. BOSH deploys Consul via a rolling upgrade to ensure that each node is fully available prior to bringing up the next.

Application Life-Cycle Binaries

Diego aims to be platform agnostic. All platform-specific concerns are delegated to two types of components:

- the Garden backend
- the Application Life-Cycle Binaries

The process of staging and running an application is complex. These concerns are encapsulated in a set of binaries known collectively as the *Application Life-Cycle Binaries*. There are different Application Life-Cycle Binaries depending on the container image (see also Figure 6-12):

- Buildpack-Application Life Cycle implements a traditional buildpack-based life cycle.
- Docker-Application Life Cycle implements a Docker-based OCI-compatible life cycle.
- Windows-Application Life Cycle implements a life cycle for .NET applications on Windows.

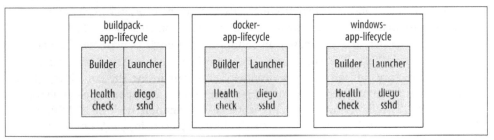

Figure 6-12. The Application Life-Cycle Binaries

Each of the aforementioned Application Life Cycles provides a set of binaries that manage a specific application type. For the Buildpack-Application Life Cycle, there are three binaries:

- The Builder stages a Cloud Foundry application. The CC-Bridge runs the Builder as a Task on every staging request. The Builder performs static analysis on the application code and performs any required preprocessing before the application is first run.
- The Launcher runs a Cloud Foundry application. The CC-Bridge sets the Launcher as the Action on the app's DesiredLRP. The Launcher executes the user's start command with the correct system context (working directory, environment variables, etc.).
- The Healthcheck performs a status check of the running ActualLRP from within the container. The CC-Bridge sets the Healthcheck as the Monitor action on the app's DesiredLRP.

The Stager Task produced by the CC-Bridge downloads the appropriate Application Life-Cycle Binaries and runs them to invoke life cycle scripts such as *stage*, *start*, and *health-check* in the ActualLRP.

This is a pluggable module for running OS-specific components. Because the life cycle is OS specific, the OS is an explicitly specified field required by the LRP. For example, the current Linux setting references the cflinuxfs2 rootfs. In addition to the rootfs, the only other OS-specific component that is explicitly specified is the back-end container type.

RunAction and the Launcher Binary

When Diego invokes `start-command` for an app (ActualLRP), it does so as a RunAction. A Task or LRP RunAction invokes a process that resides under the process identifier (PID) namespace of the container within which it is invoked. The RunAction process is not like a simple `bash -c "start-command"`. It is run through the launcher binary, which adds additional environmental setup for the process before the process calls `exec` to spawn `bash -c "start-command"`. The launcher is invoked after the container is created and is focused on setting up the environment for the `start-command` process (e.g., the launcher sets appropriate environmental variables, the working directory, and all other environment concerns inside the container). This environment setup is not very extensive; for example, for buildpack apps, it changes HOME and TMPDIR, puts some per-instance information in VCAP_APPLICATION, and then sources any scripts the buildpack placed in *.profile.d*. When the launcher runs, it uses the `exec` system call to invoke the start command (and so disappears). When you review the process tree within the Garden container, you can observe that after the launcher finishes running and setting up the environment, the top-level process is `init` (the first daemon process started when booting the system), and your applications will be a child of `initd`.

In addition to the Linux life cycle, Diego also supports a Windows life cycle and a Docker life cycle. The Docker life cycle (to understand how to stage a Docker image) is based on metadata from the Cloud Controller, based on what type of app we want to run. As part of the information for *"stage these app bits,"* there will be some indication of what branching the Stager is required to undertake. The binaries have tried to ensure that, as much as possible, these specifications are shared.

Putting It All Together

We discussed what happens when staging an application in "Staging Workflow" on page 90. Specifically, we discussed the following interactions:

- The CLI and the Cloud Controller

- The Cloud Controller and CC-Bridge
- The CC-Bridge and Diego, including Diego Cells

Up to this point, we have glossed over the interaction of the internal Diego components. This section discusses the interaction between the Diego components during staging LRPs. This section assumes you are staging an app using the buildpack Application Life-Cycle Binaries as opposed to pushing a prebuilt OCI-compatible image.

Staging takes application artifacts and buildpacks and produces a binary droplet artifact coupled with metadata. This metadata can be anything from hosts and route information to the detected buildpack and the default start command. Essentially, any information that comes out of the entire buildpack compilation and release process can be encapsulated via the buildpack's metadata.

 The internals of Diego know nothing about buildpacks. The Cloud Controller, via the Application Life-Cycle Binaries, provides all the required buildpacks to run in a container. The Cloud Controller can be conservative on what it downloads; if you specify a buildpack (e.g., the JBP), only that buildpack will be downloaded. If no buildpack is specified, the Cloud Controller will download all buildpacks. Additionally, individual Cells can cache buildpacks so that they do not need to be repeatedly downloaded from the Cloud Controller. Chapter 9 looks at buildpacks in greater detail.

The steps for staging are as follows:

1. The staging process begins with a cf push request from the Cloud Foundry CLI to the Cloud Controller (CAPI). Diego's role in the process occurs when the Cloud Controller instructs Diego (via the CC-Bridge) to stage the application. All Tasks and LRPs are submitted to the CC-Bridge via Cloud Foundry's Cloud Controller. The Cloud Controller begins the staging process by sending a *"stage app bits"* request as a task.

2. The CC-Bridge's Stager picks up and handles the *"stage app bits"* request. The Stager constructs a staging message and forwards it to the BBS. Thus, the Stager represents a transformation function.

3. The first step of the BBS is to store the task information. When the task request is stored in the BBS, the BBS is responsible for validating it. At this stage the task request is only stored; no execution of the task has taken place.

4. Diego is now at a point at which it wants to assign a payload (the Task) to a Cell that is best suited to run it. The BBS determines which of the Brain's Auctioneers is active by looking for the Auctioneer that currently holds the lock record. The BBS communicates to the Auctioneer, directing it to find a Cell to run the Task.

5. The Auctioneer optimally distributes Tasks and LRPs to the cluster of Diego Cells via an auction involving the Cell Reps. The Auctioneer asks all of the Reps what they are currently running. It uses the Reps' responses to make a placement decision. After it selects a Cell, it directs the chosen Cell to run the desired Task. You can configure it so that this auction is done every time you push an application; however, you can also batch auctions for performance to reduce the auction overhead.

   There is additional scope for sharding this auction process by AZ. It is inappropriate to cache the auction results because state is changing all the time; for example, a task might complete or an ActualLRP might crash. To look up which Cells are registered (via their Reps), the Auctioneer communicates with the BBS to get the shared system state. Reps report to BBS directly to inform BBS of their current state. When the Auctioneer is aware of the available Reps, it contacts all Reps directly.

6. The chosen Rep is assigned the Task. After a Task/LRP is assigned to a Cell, that Cell will try to allocate containers based on its internal accounting. Inside the Rep, there is a gateway to Garden (the Executor). (We introduced Garden in "Garden" on page 103 and it is discussed further in Chapter 8.) The Rep runs Tasks/ActualLRPs by asking its in-process Executor to create a container to run generic action recipes. The Executor creates a Garden container and executes the work encoded in the Task/ActualLRP. This work is encoded as a generic, platform-independent recipe of composable actions (we discussed these in "Composable Actions" on page 85). If the Cell cannot perform the Task, it responds to the Auctioneer, announcing that it was unable to run the requested work. Payloads that are distributed are a batch of Tasks rather than one Task per request. This approach reduces chatter and allows the Cell to attempt all requested tasks and report back any Task it was unable to accomplish.

7. The staging Cell uses the instructions in the buildpack and the staging task to stage the application. It obtains the buildpack through the buildpack Application Life-Cycle Binaries via the file server.

8. Assuming that the task completes successfully, the staging task will result in a droplet, and Garden reports that the container has completed all processes. This information bubbles up through the Rep and the Task is now marked as being in a completed state. When a Task is completed it can call back to the BBS using the callback in the Task request. The callback URL then calls back to the Stager so that the Stager knows that the task is complete (Stagers are stateless, so the callback will return to any Stager). The callback is the process responsible for uploading the metadata from Cell to Stager, and the Stager passes the metadata back to the Cloud Controller.

9. The Cloud Controller also provides information as to where to upload the droplet. The Cell that was responsible for staging the droplet can asynchronously

upload the droplet back to the Cloud Controller blobstore. The droplet goes back to the Cloud Controller blobstore via the Cell's Executor. The Executor uploads the droplet to the file server. The file server asynchronously uploads the blobstore to the Cloud Controller's blobstore, regularly polling to find out when the upload has been completed.

10. Additionally the staging Cell streams the output of the staging process so that the developer can troubleshoot application staging problems. After this staging process has completed successfully, the Cloud Controller subsequently issues a *"run application droplet command"* to Diego to run the staged application.

From a developer's perspective, you issue a command to Cloud Foundry and Cloud Foundry will run your app. However, as discussed at the beginning of this chapter, as work flows through the distributed system, Diego components describe their actions using different levels of abstraction. Internal interactions between the Cloud Controller and Diego's internal components are abstracted away from the developer. They are, however, important for an operator to understand in order to troubleshoot any issues.

Summary

Diego is a distributed system that allows you to run and scale N number of applications and tasks in containers across a number of Cells. Here are Diego's major characteristics and attributes:

- It is responsible for running and monitoring OCI-compatible images, standalone applications, and tasks deployed to Cloud Foundry.
- It is responsible for container scheduling and orchestration.
- It is agnostic to both client interaction and runtime implementation.
- It ensures applications remain running by reconciling desired state with actual state through establishing eventual consistency, self-healing, and closed feedback loops.
- It has a generic execution environment made up of composable actions, and a composable backend to allow the support of multiple different Windows- and Linux-based workloads.

When you step back and consider the inherent challenges with any distributed system, the solutions to the consistency and orchestration challenges provided by Diego are extremely elegant. Diego has been designed to make the container runtime subsystem of Cloud Foundry modular and generic. As with all distributed systems, Diego is complex. There are many moving parts and the communication flows between them are not trivial. Complexity is fine, however, if it is well defined within bounded contexts. The Cloud Foundry team has gone to great lengths to design explicit boundaries for the Diego services and their interaction flows. Each service is free to express its work using its own abstraction, and ultimately this allows for a modular composable plug-and-play system that is easy both to use and operate.

## CHAPTER 7

Routing Considerations

This chapter looks at Cloud Foundry's routing mechanisms in more detail. User-facing apps need to be accessed by a URL, often referred to in Cloud Foundry parlance as a *route*. End users target the URL for the app that they want to access. The app then hopefully returns the correct response. However, there is often a lot more going on behind that simple request–response behavior.

Operators can use routing mechanisms for reasons such as to provide additional security, ease deployment across a microservices architecture, and avoid downtime during upgrades through well-established techniques such as deploying canaries and establishing blue/green deployments. For these reasons, an understanding of Cloud Foundry's routing mechanisms along with an appreciation of the routing capabilities is an important operational concern. Additionally, understanding how different Cloud Foundry components dynamically handle routing is important for debugging platform- or app-routing issues.

Routing Primitives

The Cloud Foundry operator deals with the following:

- Routes
- Hostnames
- Domains
- Context paths
- Ports

The Cloud Foundry documentation (*http://bit.ly/2qoUBYM*) explores these concepts at length. This chapter explores the key considerations for establishing routing best practices. We begin with a brief introduction to the terms and then move on to the routing mechanisms and capabilities.

Routes

To enable traffic from external clients, apps require a specific URL, known as a route. For example, developers can create a route by mapping the route `myapp.shared-cf-domain.com` to the app `myapp`.

You can construct routes via a combination of the following:

- Domain
- Host
- Port
- Context path

Route construction is explained further in a later section.

Each Cloud Foundry instance can have a single default domain and further additional domains that can be shared across organizations (Orgs) in a single Cloud Foundry instance. Routes are then based on those domains. Routes belong to a Space, and only apps in the same Space as that route can be mapped to it. A developer of one Space cannot create or use a route if it already exists in another Space. For this reason, many developers place `app-name-${random-word}` in their route to ensure that their app route is unique during the dev/test phase.

One app, one route, multiple app instances

You can map an individual app to either a single route or, if desired, multiple routes. Because apps can have multiple app instances (ActualLRPs), all accessed by the single route, each route has an associated array of host:port entries stored in a routing table on the GoRouter. Figure 7-1 shows that the host is the Diego Cell machine running the LRP in a container and the port corresponds to a dedicated host port for that container. The router regularly recomputes new routing tables based on the Cell IP addresses and the host-side port numbers for the containers, as illustrated in Figure 7-1. In a cloud-based distributed environment, both desired and actual state can rapidly change; thus, it is important to dynamically update routes both periodically and immediately in response to state changes.

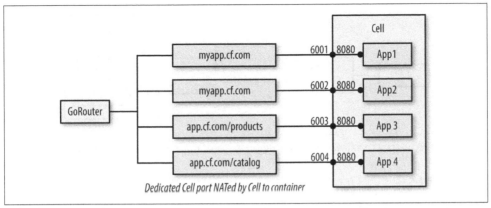

Figure 7-1. Cell-to-container port mapping

One app, multiple routes

You can also map an individual app to multiple routes, granting multiple URLs access to that app. This capability is illustrated in Figure 7-2.

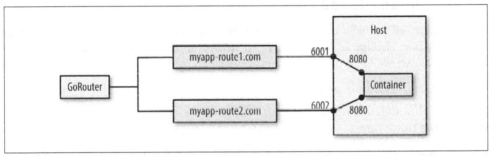

Figure 7-2. One app mapped to two different routes

Mapping more than one route to an app can be a valuable feature for establishing techniques such as blue/green deployments. You can read more about blue/green deployments in the Cloud Foundry Documentation (*http://bit.ly/2pCoB0g*).

Several apps, one route

In addition to being able to map all identical app instances to a single route, as depicted in Figure 7-3, you can also map independent apps to a single route. This results in the GoRouter load-balancing requests for the route across all instances of all mapped apps, as demonstrated in Figure 7-3. This feature is also important for enabling the use of blue/green and *canary* deployment strategies. It is also used when dealing with different apps that must work collectively with a single entry point; for example, microservices architecture (discussed shortly).

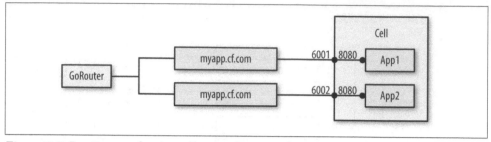

Figure 7-3. Routing mechanism allowing for several apps mapped to the same route

Hostnames

Cloud Foundry provides the option of creating a route with a *hostname*. A hostname is a name that can be explicitly used to specify an app, as shown in the following code:

```
$ cf create-route my-space shared-domain.com --hostname myapp
```

This creates the unique route `myapp.shared-domain.com` comprising the host that is prepended on to the shared domain.

At this stage, all we have done is reserved the route so that the route is not used in another Space. The app is only routable by this route after it is mapped to the route, as in the following:

```
$ cf mapp-route app-name domain hostname
```

Note that although this route is created for the Space `my-space`, the Space is not featured in the route name.

Routes created for shared domains must always use a hostname. Alternatively, you can create a route without a hostname. This approach creates a route for the domain itself and is permitted for private domains only. You can create private domains as follows:

```
$ cf create-route my-space private-domain.com
```

This example creates a route in the Space `my-space` from domain `private-domain.com`. After configuring your DNS, Cloud Foundry will route requests for `http(s)://private-domain.com` or any context path under that URL (e.g., `private-domain.com/app1`) to apps that are mapped to that route or context path. Any subdomain (e.g., `*foo*.private-domain.com`) will fail unless additional routes are specified for that subdomain and then mapped to a subsequent app.

You can use wildcard routes here as a catch-all (e.g., `*.private-domain.com`); for example, to serve a custom 404 page or a specific homepage.

Domains

Cloud Foundry's use of the terms *domain*, *shared domain*, and *private domain* differ from their common use:

- Domains provide a namespace from which to create routes.
- Shared domains are available to users in all Orgs, and every Cloud Foundry instance requires a single default shared domain.
- Private domains allow users to create routes for privately registered domain names.

As discussed in "Hostnames" on page 122, by default apps are assigned a route with a hostname my-app, and the app domain my-app.apps.cf-domain.com, resulting in the route my-app.apps.cf-domain.com.

The presence of a domain in Cloud Foundry indicates that requests for any route created from that domain will be routed to a specific Cloud Foundry instance. This provision requires a DNS to be configured to resolve the domain name to the IP address of a load balancer that fronts traffic entering Cloud Foundry.[1]

The recommended practice is to have a wildcard canonical name (CNAME) that you can use as a base domain for other subdomains. An example of a wildcard CNAME is *.cf-domain.com.

To use a subdomain of your registered domain name with apps on Cloud Foundry, configure the subdomain as a CNAME record with your DNS provider, pointing at any shared domain offered in Cloud Foundry.

When installing Cloud Foundry, it is good practice to have a subsequent system domain and one or more app domains; for example, system.cf-domain.com for your system domain, and apps.cf-domain.com for (one of) your app domain(s). Multiple app domains can be advantageous and are discussed further later.

The system domain allows Cloud Foundry to receive requests for and send communication between its internal components (like the UAA and Cloud Controller). Cloud Foundry itself can run some of its components as apps. For example, a service broker can deploy an app. The app domain guarantees that requests for routes based off that domain will go to a specific Cloud Foundry instance.

If we had only one combined system and app domain, there would be no separation of concerns. A developer could register an app domain name that infers it is a potential system component. This can cause confusion to the Cloud Foundry operator with

---

1 The enterprise load balancer you use is your choice. Cloud Foundry is not opinionated about the load-balancing strategy that fronts it.

respect to what are system apps and what are developer-deployed apps. Moreover, mapping an arbitrary app to a system component can cause fundamental system failures, as we will explore in "Scenario Five: Route Collision" on page 241. For these reasons, it is recommended that you always have at least one default system domain and default app domain per environment.

All system components should register routes that are extensions of the system domain; for example, `login.system.cf-domain.com`, `uaa.system.cf-domain.com`, `doppler.system.cf-domain.com`, and `api.system.cf-domain.com`.

Using Wildcard Domains

For an operator not to have to create a new certificate for every app, Cloud Foundry depends on wildcard domains. Wildcard SSL certificates (referred to as "certs") are extremely beneficial for rapid app development and deployment. You will need to generate wildcard certificates based on your chosen domains for use in Cloud Foundry. You can either generate these certificates using your own CA, or through any other tool for generating certificates, such as Cloud Foundry's "Generate Self-Signed Certificate" tool.

Certs are necessary for the platform to operate, but this does not mean that your external load balancer must use these wildcard domains and/or wildcard certificates. However, it is worth mentioning that if you do not use wildcard certs at your load balancer, every time you want to deploy a new app, you will need to set up a new DNS record and then generate a new certificate for that app and install that cert on your load balancer. This approach adds time and an additional burden that delays the velocity of pushing new apps to Cloud Foundry. To put it bluntly, not using wildcard domains in your TLS certificates violates the entire reason for using Cloud Foundry.

Multiple app domains

There are some advantages to using multiple app domains. For example, an operator might want to establish a dedicated app domain with a dedicated cert and VIP. If you issue a certificate for a critical app on a dedicated app domain, and for some reason that certificate becomes compromised, you have the flexibility of revoking just that certificate without affecting all of your other apps that are on a different app domain.

Context Path Routing

Context path routing allows for routing to be based not only on the route domain name (essentially the host header), but also the path specified in the route's URL. The GoRouter inspects the URL for additional context paths and, upon discovery, can then route requests to different apps based on that path. Here are a couple of examples:

- `myapp.mycf-domain.com/foo` can be mapped to the `foo` app.
- `myapp.mycf-domain.com/bar` can be mapped to the `bar` app.

This is important when dealing with a microservices architecture. With microservices, a single "big-A" apps can be comprised of a suite of smaller microservices apps, as shown in Figure 7-4. The smaller applications often require the same single top-level route `myapp.mycf-domain.com` to offer a single entry point for the user. Context path routing allows different microservices apps (e.g., `foo` and `bar`), all served by the same parent route, to provide support for different paths in the URL, based on their unique context path.

With context path-based routing, you can also independently scale up or down those portions of your big-A app that are being heavily utilized.

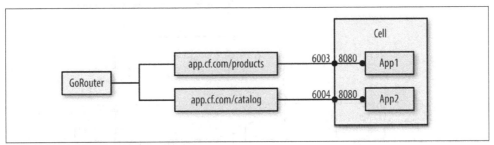

Figure 7-4. Routing using a single route and context paths to target a specific app

Routing Components Overview

There are several components involved in the flow of ingress Cloud Foundry traffic. We can broadly group these as follows:

- Routing tier (load balancer, GoRouter, TCPRouter)
- The control plain and user management (Cloud Controller and UAA)
- The app components (Cells and the SSH proxy)

Figure 7-5 provides a high-level view of the components.

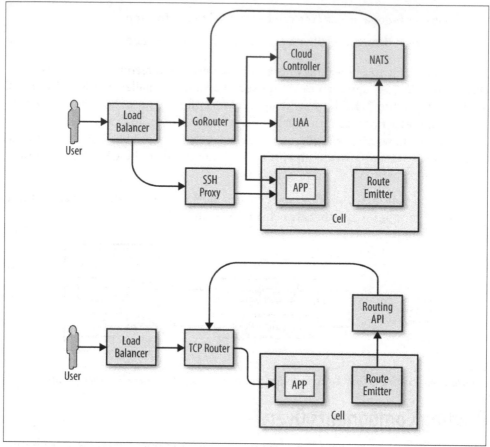

Figure 7-5. Routing components and communication flow

Let's take a closer look at each of these components:

Load balancer

All HTTP-based traffic first enters Cloud Foundry from an external load balancer fronting Cloud Foundry. The load balancer is primarily used for traffic routing to Cloud Foundry routers.

GoRouter

The GoRouter receives all incoming HTTP(s) traffic from the load balancer. The GoRouter also receives WebSocket requests and performs the HTTP-to-WebSocket upgrade to establish a consistent TCP connection to the backend.

TCPRouter

The TCPRouter receives all incoming (non-HTTP) TCP traffic from the load balancer.

Cloud Controller and the UAA

Operators address the Cloud Controller through Cloud Foundry's API. As part of this flow, identity management is provided by the UAA.

Cells and SSH_Proxy

App users target their desired apps via a dedicated hostname and/or domain combination. The GoRouter will route app traffic to the appropriate app instance (ActualLRP) running on a Diego Cell. If multiple app instances are running, the GoRouter will round-robin traffic across the app instances to distribute the workload. App users can use SSH to the app's container running on a host Cell via the SSH proxy service.

Routing Flow

All traffic enters Cloud Foundry from an external load balancer. The load balancer routes the traffic as follows:

- HTTP/HTTPS and WebSocket traffic to the GoRouter
- (Non-HTTP) TCP traffic to the TCPRouter

App traffic is routed from the routers to the required app. If you're running multiple app instances (ActualLRPs), the routers will load-balance the traffic across the running ActualLRPs. If an app requires the user to authenticate, you can redirect requests to the UAA's login server. Upon authentication, the user is passed back to the original app. The Cloud Controller provides an example of this behavior.

Platform users target the Cloud Controller. Requests come in from the load balancer through the GoRouter and hit the CAPI. If the user has yet to log in, requests are redirected to the UAA for authentication. Upon authentication, the user is redirected back to the Cloud Controller.

Route-Mapping Flow

When you create a route in the routing table (either directly via Cloud Foundry `map-route` command or indirectly via `cf push`), the Route-Emitter is listening to events in Diego's BBS and notices all newly created routes. It takes the route-mapping info (of Cell host:port) and then dynamically updates the route mapping in the routing table. Any additional changes—for example, a deleted or moved app—will also result in the emitter updating the routing table. We discuss route mapping and the Route-Emitter further in "Routing Table" on page 131.

Load Balancer Considerations

Although the choice of load balancer is yours to make, there are some specific considerations required:

- Setting the correct request header fields.
- Determining where to terminate SSL.
- Configuring the load balancer to handle HTTP upgrades to WebSockets (assuming these requests are then being passed on to the TCPRouter). Ideally, you should avoid this with the WebSocket upgrade; you should instead use the GoRouter.

Setting Request Header Fields

When a client connects to a web server through an HTTP proxy or load balancer, it is possible to identify the originating IP address and the send protocol by setting the X-Forwarded-For and X-Forwarded-Proto request header fields, respectively. These headers must be set on the load balancer that fronts the traffic coming into Cloud Foundry. HTTP traffic passed from the GoRouter to an app will include these headers. If an app wants to behave differently based on the transport protocol used, it can inspect the headers to determine whether traffic was received over HTTP or HTTPS.

X-Forwarded-For

X-Forwarded-For (XFF) provides the IP address of the originating client request. For example, an XFF request header for a client with an IP address of 203.0.56.67 would be as follows:

```
X-Forwarded-For: 203.0.56.67
```

If you did not use XFF, connections through the router would reveal only the originating IP address of the router itself, effectively turning the router into an anonymizing service and making the detection and prevention of abusive access significantly more difficult. The usefulness of XFF depends on the GoRouter truthfully reporting the original host IP address. If your load balancer terminates TLS upstream from the GoRouter, it must append these headers to the requests forwarded onto the GoRouter.

X-Forwarded-Proto

X-Forwarded-Proto (XFP) identifies the client protocol (HTTP or HTTPS) used from the client to connect to the load balancer. The scheme is HTTP if the client made an insecure request, or HTTPS if the client made a secure request. For example, an XFP for a request that originated from the client as an HTTPS request would be as follows:

```
X-Forwarded-Proto: https
```

As with most client-server architectures, the GoRouter access logs contain only the protocol used between the GoRouter and the load balancer; they do not contain the protocol information used between the client and the load balancer. XFP allows the router to determine this information. The load balancer stores the protocol used between the client and the load balancer in the XFP request header and passes the header along to the router.

XFP is important because you can configure apps to reject insecure requests by inspecting the header for the HTTP scheme. This header is as important, or even more so, for system components than for apps. The UAA, for example, will reject all login attempts if this header is not set.

WebSocket Upgrades

WebSockets is a protocol providing bidirectional communication over a single, long-lived TCP connection. It is commonly implemented by web clients and servers. Web-Sockets are initiated via HTTP as an upgrade request. The GoRouter supports WebSocket upgrades, holding the TCP connection open with the selected app instance.

Supporting WebSockets is important because the Firehose (the endpoint of all aggre-gated and streamed app logs) is a WebSockets endpoint that streams all event data originating from a Cloud Foundry deployment. To support WebSockets, operators must configure their load balancer to pass WebSockets requests through as opaque TCP connections. WebSockets are also vital for app log streaming, allowing develop-ers to view their app logs.

Some load balancers are unable to support listening for both HTTP and TCP traffic on the same port. Take, for example, ELB offered by AWS. ELB can listen on a port in either HTTP(s) mode or TCP mode. To pass through a WebSocket request, ELB must be in TCP mode. However, if ELB is terminating TLS requests on 443 and appending the XFF and XFP headers, it must be in HTTP mode. Therefore, ELB can-not handle WebSockets on the same port. In this scenario, you can do the following:

- Configure your load balancer to listen for WebSocket requests on a nonstandard port (e.g., 8443) and then forward WebSocket requests to this port in TCP mode to the GoRouter on port 80 or 443. App clients must make WebSockets upgrade requests to this port.

- Add a second load balancer listening in TCP mode on standard port 80. Configure DNS with a dedicated hostname for use with WebSockets that resolves to the new load balancer serving port 80 in TCP mode.

The PROXY Protocol

As just described, WebSockets require a TCP connection; however, when using TCP mode, load balancers will not add the XFF HTTP protocol headers, so you cannot identify your clients. Another solution for client identification is to use the Proxy protocol. This protocol allows your load balancer to add the Proxy protocol header so that your apps can still identify your clients even when you use TCP mode at the load balancer.

Another scenario is to terminate TLS with a component that does not support HTTP and operates only in TCP mode. Therefore, an HTTP connection is then passed on to the GoRouter.

A point to note is that some load balancers in TCP mode will not give you HTTP multiplexing and pipelining (*https://en.wikipedia.org/wiki/HTTP_pipelining*). This could cause a performance problem unless you have a content delivery network (CDN) in front.

TLS Termination and IPSec

Although Cloud Foundry is a distributed system, conceptually we can consider it as a software appliance. It is designed to sit in a dedicated network with defined egress and ingress firewall rules. For this reason, if the load balancer sits within or on the edge of the private network, it can handle TLS decryption and then route traffic unencrypted to the GoRouter.

However, if the load balancer is not dedicated to Cloud Foundry and it is located on a general-purpose corporate network, it is possible to pass the TLS connection on to the GoRouter for decryption. To implement this, you must configure your load balancer to re-sign the request between the load balancer and the GoRouter using your wildcard certificate. You will also need to configure the GoRouter with your Cloud Foundry certificates.

There might be situations in which you require encryption directly back to the app and data layer. For these scenarios, you can use the additional IPSec BOSH add-on that provides encrypted traffic between every component machine.

GoRouter Considerations

The GoRouter serves HTTP(S) traffic only. HTTP(S) connections to apps from the outside world are accepted only on ports 80 or 443. (Protocol upgrade requests for WebSockets are also acceptable.)

All router logic is contained in a single process. This approach removes unnecessary latency introduced through interprocess communication. Additionally, with full control over every client connection, the router can more easily allow for connection upgrades to WebSockets and other types of traffic (e.g., HTTP tunneling and proxying via HTTP CONNECT).

Routing Table

The router uses a routing table to keep track of available apps. This table contains an up-to-date list of all the routes to the Cells and containers that are currently running ActualLRPs. As described earlier, you can map multiple routes to an app and map multiple apps to a route. The routing table keeps track of this mapping. It provides the source of truth for all routing, dynamically checking for and pruning dead routes to avoid 404 errors.

Diego uses its Route Emitter component to consume event streams from the Diego Database—the BBS—and then pushes the route updates to the router. Additionally, the Route-Emitter performs a bulk lookup operation against its database every 20 seconds to fetch all the desired and actual routes.

The GoRouter then recomputes a new routing table based on the IP addresses of each Cell machine and the host-side port numbers for the Cell's containers. This ensures that the routing table information is up to date in the event that an app fails.

Router and Route High Availability

GoRouters should be clustered both for resiliency and for handling a large number of concurrent client connections.

When GoRouters come on line, they send `router.start` messages informing Route-Emitters that they are running. Route-Emitters are monitoring desired and actual LRP events in the BBS to establish and map routes to app instances. They compute the routing table and send this table to the GoRouter via NATS at regular intervals.

This ensures that new GoRouters update their routing table and synchronize with existing GoRouters. Routes will be pruned from the routing table if an app connection goes stale. To maintain an active route, the route must be updated by default at least every two minutes.

An important implementation consideration for the GoRouter is that because it uses NATS, it must be brought online after the NATS component in order to function properly.

Router Instrumentation and Logging

Like the other Cloud Foundry components, the GoRouter provides logging through its Metron agent. In addition, a /routes endpoint returns the entire routing table as JSON. Because of the nature of the data present in /routes, the endpoint requires HTTP basic authentication credentials served on port 8080. These credentials are obtained from the deployment manifest under the router job:

```
status:
  password: some_password
  port: 8080
  user: some_user
```

The credentials can also be obtained from the GoRouter VM at */var/vcap/jobs/gorouter/config/gorouter.yml*.

Each route contains an associated array of host:port entries, which is useful for debugging:

```
$ curl -vvv "http://some_user:some_password@127.0.0.1:8080/routes"
```

In addition to the routing table endpoint, the GoRouter offers a healthcheck endpoint on /health:

```
$ curl -v "http://10.0.32.15:8080/health"
```

This is particularly useful when performing healthchecks from a load balancer. This endpoint does not require credentials and should be accessed at port 8080. Because load balancers typically round-robin the GoRouters, by regularly checking the GoRouter health, they can avoid sending traffic to GoRouters that are temporarily not responding.

You can configure the GoRouter logging levels in the Cloud Foundry deployment manifest. The meanings of the router's log levels are as follows:

fatal
> An error has occurred that makes the current request unserviceable; for example, the router cannot bind to its TCP port, or a Cloud Foundry component has published invalid data to the GoRouter.

warn
> An unexpected state has occurred. For example, the GoRouter tried to publish data that could not be encoded as JSON.

info, debug

An expected event has occurred. For example, a new Cloud Foundry component was registered with the GoRouter, and the GoRouter has begun to prune routes for stale containers.

Sticky Sessions

For compatible apps, the GoRouter supports *sticky sessions* (aka session affinity) for incoming HTTP requests.

When multiple app instances are running, sticky sessions will cause requests from a particular client to always reach the same app instance. This makes it possible for apps to store session data specific to a user session. Generally, this approach is not good practice; however, for some select pieces of data such as discrete and lightweight user information, it can be a pragmatic approach.

Sticky Sessions

A single app can have several instances running concurrently. Functional use of the local filesystem is limited to local caching because filesystems provided to apps are ephemeral unless you use a filesystem service. By default, changes to the filesystem are not preserved between app restarts, nor are they synchronized or shared between multiple app instances.

This means Cloud Foundry does not natively maintain or replicate HTTP session data across app instances, and all cached session data will be discarded if the app instance hosting the sticky session is terminated. If you require session data to be saved, it must be offloaded to a backing service that offers data persistence.

To support sticky sessions, apps must return a JSESSIONID cookie in their responses.

If an app returns a JSESSIONID cookie to a client request, the GoRouter appends an additional VCAP_ID cookie to the response, which contains a unique identifier for the app instance. On subsequent client requests, the client provides both the JSESSIONID and VCAP_ID cookies, allowing the GoRouter to forward client requests back to the same app instance.

If the app instance identified by the VCAP_ID is no longer available, the GoRouter attempts to route the request to a different instance of the app. If the GoRouter finds a healthy instance of the app, it initiates a new sticky session.

The TCPRouter

Support for non-HTTP workloads on Cloud Foundry is provided by the TCPRouter. The TCPRouter allows operators to offer TCP routes to app developers based on reservable ports.

When pushing an app mapped to a TCP route:

```
$ cf p myapp -d tcp.mycf-domain.com --random-route
```

the response from the Cloud Controller includes a port associated with the TCP route. Client requests to these ports will be routed to apps running on Cloud Foundry through a layer 4 protocol-agnostic routing tier.

Both HTTP and TCP routes will be directed to the same app port, identified by environment variable $PORT.

The developer experience for TCP routing is similar to previous routing-related workflows. For example, the developer begins by discovering a domain that supports TCP routing through cf domains. cf domains will show whether a specific domain has been enabled for TCP routing by setting up DNS for that domain to point to the load balancers, and load balancers then pointing to the TCPRouters.

The discovered domain gives a developer an indication that requests for routes created from that domain will be forwarded to apps mapped to that route. It also provides a namespace allowing operators to control access for one domain or another.

After you choose your domain, you can then create a route from that domain via the usual create route and map route commands. However, the cf push experience is streamlined because the appropriate route will be configured for that app simply by selecting a TCP domain. For example, to create a TCP route for the app myapp using the domain tcp-example-domain.com you can run the following:

```
$ cf push myapp -d tcp-example-domain.com --random-route
```

TCP routes are different from HTTP routes because they do not use hostnames; instead, routing decisions are based on a port. For each TCP route, we reserve a port on the TCPRouter. This requires clients of apps that receive TCP app traffic to support these arbitrary ports.

TCP Routing Management Plane

The TCP routing management plane (see Figure 7-5) has similar functionality to the HTTP routing management plane. There is a Route-Emitter listening to events in Diego's BBS. For example, whenever a new app is created or an app is moved or scaled, the BBS is updated.

The emitter detects these events, constructs the routing table, and then sends this table on to the routing API. The routing API effectively replaces the need for NATS; it maintains the routing table and then makes the configuration available across a tier of TCPRouter instances. Therefore, TCPRouters receive their configuration from the routing API and not via NATS. Both the TCPRouter and the Route-Emitter receive their configuration from both periodic bulk fetches and real-time server sent events.

TCP routing introduces some complexity through additional NAT involving different ports at different tiers, as illustrated in Figure 7-6. There is a route port to which clients send requests. This port is reserved on the TCPRouter when you create a TCP route. Behind the scenes, the TCPRouter makes a translation between that route port and the app instances. Containers include app ports (that default to 8080). These ports are not directly accessible via the TCPRouter, because containers are running in a Cell providing an additional NAT for the container. Therefore, the ports made known to the TCPRouter are the Cell ports (the backend port).

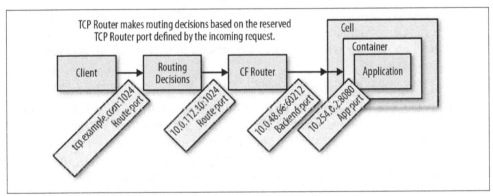

Figure 7-6. TCPRouter port mappings from the load balancer through to the app

TCPRouter Configuration Steps

Here are the deployment steps required for configuring TCP routing:

1. Choose a domain name from which developers will create their TCP routes.
2. Configure DNS to point to that domain name via the load balancer.
3. Choose how many TCP routes the platform should support based on the reserved ports on the TCPRouter.
4. Configure the load balancer to listen on the port range[2] and then forward requests for that port range and domain to the TCPRouters.

---

2 Make sure your port range accounts for sufficient capacity because every TCP connection will require a dedicated port from your reserved port range.

5. Configure the TCPRouter group within Cloud Foundry with the same port range.

6. Create a domain associated with that TCPRouter group.

7. Configure a quota to entitle Orgs to create TCP routes.

Route Services

Apps often have additional requirements over and above traditional middleware components, such as databases, caches, and message buses. The additional app requirements include tasks such as authentication, or might require a special firewall or rate limiting. Traditionally, these burdens have been placed on the developer and app operator to build additional (nonbusiness) capabilities into the app or directly use and configure some other external capability such as an edge caching appliance.

The route services capability makes it possible for developers to select a specific route service from the marketplace (in a similar fashion to middleware services) and insert that service into the app request path. They offer a new point of integration and a new class of service.

As seen in Figure 7-7, route services give you the ability to dynamically insert a component (in the case of Figure 7-7, Apigee) into the network path as traffic flows to apps. Traditionally, developers had to file a ticket to get a new load balancer configuration for additional firewall settings, or IT had to manually insert additional network components for things like rate limiting. Route services now offer these additional capabilities dynamically via integration with the router.

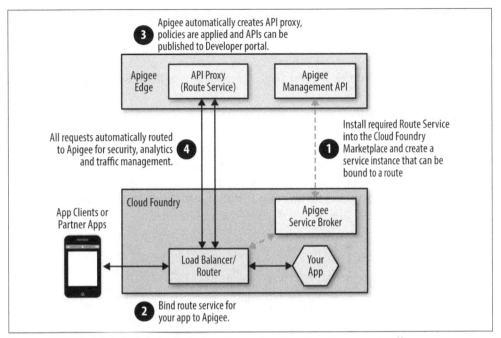

Figure 7-7. The Route Service showing the path of application user traffic to an app, accessing an API Proxy Service (in this case provided by Apigee)

Unlike middleware marketplace services that are bound to an app, route services are bound to a route for a specific app. New requests to that app can then be modified via a route service. Just like the middleware services in the marketplace, the route service might not necessarily be Cloud Foundry, or BOSH-deployed and managed. For example, a route service could be the following:

- An app running on Cloud Foundry
- A BOSH-, Puppet-, or Chef-deployed component
- Some other external enterprise service provided by a third party such as Apigee

Route Service Workflow

All requests arrive (1) via the external load balancer, which passes traffic on to the GoRouter (2). The GoRouter checks for a bound route service for a route, and if no service exists, it will simply pass traffic on to the appropriate LRP (3). If a route service does exist for the route, the router will then pass that traffic on to the service that is bound to the route.

Before passing the request on to the service, the router generates an encrypted short-lived message to include both the requested route and the route service GUID. The router then appends this message to the request header and forwards the request to the bound route service. After the specific route service has undertaken its work (e.g., header modification or rate limiting) the service can do one of two things:

- Respond directly to the request (e.g., serve an access-denied message if acting as an app firewall)
- Pass the traffic to the app

The route service passes traffic to the app (4) by resolving via DNS back to the load balancer (5), then to the router (6), and then to the app. The response traffic then follows that same flow backward to return a response to the client (7/8/9/10/11/12). This allows the service to do further modification on the returned response body if required. Figure 7-8 provides an overview of the architecture.

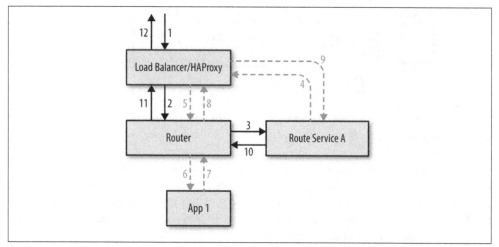

Figure 7-8. Route service workflow showing the redirection of app traffic to the route service before being directed back to the app via the load balancer (note that the return flow retraces the same path in reverse)

Route Service Use Cases

You can consider any use cases that can be on the request path as eligible for a route service. Here are some examples:

- Gateway use cases such as rate limiting, metering, and caching
- Security use cases such as authentication, authorization, auditing, fraud detection, and network sniffing
- Analytics use cases such as monetization, chargeback, and utilization
- Mobile backend as a service (MBaaS) such as push notifications and data services

In line with the rest of Cloud Foundry, the key goal of routing services is to increase app velocity. Without the developer self-service that route services provide, most organizations are left with the pain of ticketing systems and extra configuration to achieve these use-case capabilities.

Summary

The core premise of Cloud Foundry is to allow apps to be deployed with velocity and operated with ease. The routing abstractions and mechanisms within Cloud Foundry have been designed and implemented to support that premise:

- Routing is an integral part of deploying and operating apps.
- Cloud Foundry provides a rich set of abstractions and mechanisms for supporting fast deployment, rolling upgrades, and other complicated routing requirements.
- Establishing the most appropriate routing architecture is essential for app security, resiliency, and updatability.
- With the introduction of the TCPRouter and additional route services, the platform can take on more diverse workloads with broader, more granular routing requirements.

## CHAPTER 8

Containers, Containers, Containers

Containers, as a concept, is not new technology. However, in recent years, there has been rapid adoption of new container-based technologies such as Docker, Garden, and Rocket. Many organizations regard containers as a key enabler for adopting technologies such as microservices-based architectures or continuous delivery pipelines. Therefore, containers have become a critical part of the digital transformation strategy of most companies.

Some companies I work with establish a mandate to adopt containers but cannot articulate a specific use case or problem that would be solved by adopting containers. Others believe containers will help them deploy apps quicker but cannot explain why, or they believe containers will provide better utilization but have not profiled their existing infrastructure utilization. The use of container technology absolutely can provide significant benefits. It is essential to understand how those benefits are achieved in such a way as to derive the most from container technology.

The Meaning of "Container"

Like the term "platform," the term *container* is also overloaded. This chapter is not about traditional app server containers such as Tomcat; it is about OS–level containers such as runC.

What Is a Container?

Despite their huge popularity, there still are a lot of misconceptions about containers. Principally, in the Linux world at least, containers are not a literal entity, they are a logical construct. Strictly speaking, a container is nothing more than a controlled user process. Container technology typically takes advantage of OS kernel features to constrain and control various resources, and isolate and secure the relevant containerized processes. In addition, the term "container" conflates various concepts, which adds to the confusion.

Containers have two key elements:

Container Images

These package a repeatable runtime environment (encapsulating your app and all of its dependencies, including the filesystem) in a format that is self-describing and portable, allowing for images to be moved between container hosts. The self-describing nature of container images specifies instructions on how they should be run, but they are not explicitly self-executable, meaning that they cannot run without a container management solution and container runtime. However, regardless of the container contents, any compliant container runtime should be able to run the container image without requiring extra dependencies.

Container management

Often referred to as container engine, the management layer typically uses OS kernel features (e.g., Linux kernel primitives such as control groups and namespaces) to run a container image in isolation, often within a shared kernel space. Container-management engines typically expose a management API for user interaction and utilize a backend container runtime such as runC or runV that is responsible for building and running an isolated containerized process.

Container Terminology

The challenge in discussing containers is that implementation terminology can mean different things to different people, and it can be implementation-specific. I have tried to be as generic as possible in my description, but it is important to note that different terms like *engine* or *backend* can have meanings relating to a specific technology implementation.

Container images can be created through a concept of containerization: the notion of packaging up a filesystem, runtime dependencies, and any other required technology artifacts to produce a single encapsulated binary image. You can then port these images around and run them in different container backends via the container API/ management layer. The container backend implementation is host-specific; for example, the term *Linux container* is a reference to the Linux technology (originally based on LXC) for running containerized images. Currently, Linux containers are by far the most widely adopted container technology. For this reason, the rest of this chapter focuses on Linux containers to explain the fundamental container concepts.

Container Fervor

Why have containers become so popular so quickly? Containers offer three distinct advantages over traditional VMs:

- Speed and efficiency because they are lightning fast to create
- Greater resource consolidation, especially if you overcommit resources
- App stack portability

Because containers use a slice of a prebuilt machine or VM,[1] they are generally regarded to be significantly faster to create than a new VM. Effectively, to create a new container, you simply fork and isolate a process.

Containers also allow for a greater degree of resource consolidation because you can run several container instances in isolation on a single host machine by a single OS kernel.

In addition, containers have enabled a new era of app-stack portability because apps and dependencies developed to run in a container backend can easily be packaged into a single container *image* (usually containing a tarball with some additional metadata). You can then deploy and run container images in several different environments. Container images make it easy to efficiently ship deltas, and therefore moving whole images between different host machines becomes practical. App-stack portability is one of the key reasons why containers have become so popular. Container images have become a key enabler for trends such as DevOps and CD by enabling both the app artifacts and all of the related runtime dependencies to migrate unchanged, as a layered binary image, through a CI pipeline into production. This has provided a unified approach to delivering software into production as opposed to the old and defunct *"it worked on my machine"* approach. Chapter 9 discusses this unified approach and its various merits in further detail.

Increased deployment efficiency becomes paramount when deploying apps using a microservices architecture because there are more moving parts and more overall churn. Container-based infrastructure has therefore become a natural choice for teams using a microservices architecture.

Containers, as with all technology, are a means to an end. It is not technology itself that is important; it is how you take advantage of it that is key. For example, we discussed using container images to propagate apps through a pipeline and into production. However, the pipeline itself can also effectively use containers. For example, the Concourse CI (*http://concourse.ci*) controls pipeline inputs so that results are always

---

1 The terms "VM" and "machine" are used interchangeably because containers can run in both environments.

repeatable. Rather than sharing state, every task runs in its own container, thus controlling its own dependencies. Containers are created and then destroyed every time a task is run, ensuring repeatability by avoiding build "pollution." Concourse's use of containers is a perfect example of how we can use container technology to provide a clear tangible benefit over more traditional approaches that experience polluted build-up due to a pattern of VM reuse.

Linux Containers

Linux containers provide a way of efficiently running an isolated user process. As just discussed, strictly speaking, Linux containers do not exist in a purely literal sense: there are no specific Linux kernel container features. Existing kernel features are combined together to produce the behavior associated with containers, but Linux containers themselves remain a high-level abstract concept.

The essence of container abstraction is to run processes in an isolated environment. Linux container technologies use lower Linux primitives and kernel features to produce container attributes such as the required process isolation. Other Unix OSs implement containers at the OS kernel level; for example, BSDJails or Solaris Zones.

How do containers differ from VMs? There are two key elements:

- Where processes are run
- What is actually run

Although the container backend (the runtime) can, technically, be backed by a VM, traditionally speaking, containers are fundamentally different in concept. A VM virtualizes the entire machine and then runs the kernel and device drivers that are then isolated to that VM. This approach provides superb isolation; however, historically, at least, VMs have been considered relatively slow and expensive to create. Containers, on the other hand, all share the same kernel within a host machine, with isolation achieved by using various kernel features to secure processes from one another. Creating a container amounts to forking a process within an existing host machine. This is orders of magnitude faster than instantiating a traditional VM.

Containers versus VMs

The container versus VM debate is blurring in many ways. Specialized, minimal, single-address-space machine images known as *unikernels* allow for fast VM instantiation. You can replace container backends like runC with VM equivalents such as runV. At the end of the day, the important concern is not what runs your containerized process, but that your process is being run with the appropriate isolation guarantees and resource constraints.

The core Linux primitives and kernel features that produce container attributes include the following:

- Namespaces to enforce isolation between containers
- Control groups to enforce resource sharing between containers

We look at both of these kernel features in more detail a little later in the chapter. It is worth keeping in mind that the typical Cloud Foundry developer or operator does not require a deep understanding of containers, because the Cloud Foundry platform handles the container creation and orchestration concerns. However, gaining a deeper understanding is valuable for both the curious and the security-minded operator.

Namespaces

Namespaces provide isolation. They offer a way of splitting kernel resources by wrapping global system resources in an abstraction. The process within a namespace sees only a subset (its own set) of those kernel resources. This produces the appearance of the namespaced process having its own isolated instance of the global resource. Changes to a resource governed by a namespace are visible only to other processes that are members of that namespace; they cannot be seen by processes outside of the namespace.

A process can be placed into the following namespaces:

PID
> These processes view other processes running inside the same (or a child) namespace.

network
> These processes have their own isolated view of the network stack.

cgroup
> These processes have a virtualized view of their CGroups root directories.

mount
> These processes have their own view of the mount table; mounts and unmounts do not affect processes in other namespaces.

uts/username
> These processes have their own hostname and domain name.

ipc
> These processes can communicate only with other processes within the same namespace via system-level IPCs (interprocess communication).

`user`
> These processes have their own user and group IDs. Host users and groups are remapped to local users and groups within the user namespace.

Take, for example, the `PID` namespace. Processes are always structured as a tree with a single root *parent* process. A Linux host uses `PID` `1` for the root process. All the other processes are eventually parented (or grandparented) by `PID` `1`.

A container's first process—which might have a `PID` `123` in the host—will appear as `PID` `1` within the container. All other processes in the container are similarly mapped. Processes that are not in the container's `PID` namespace do not appear to exist to the namespaced process. Effectively, both the namespaced process and the host have different views of the same `PID`. It is the kernel that provides this mapping.

Upon container creation, a clone of the container process is created within the newly created namespace. This cloned process becomes `PID` `1` in the newly created namespace. If that process then makes a kernel call asking *"what is my Process ID,"* the kernel does the mapping for the process transparently. The process is unaware it is running within a `PID` namespace.

As another example, take `user` namespaces. The host views a `user` namespaced process with, for example, `UID` `4000`. With `user` namespaces, the process can ask *"what is my User ID"?* If the process is running as root user, the namespaced response from the kernel will be `UID` `0` (root). However, the kernel has explicitly mapped the namespaced process such that the process thinks it is root. The host still knows the process as, for example, `UID` `4000`. If the process attempts to open a file owned by the host root, the kernel maps the process to `UID` `4000`, checks the UID against the host filesystem, which is actually mapped to 0, and will then correctly deny the process access to that host file because of invalid permissions.

> The preceding is just an illustration. With the abstraction of containers in Cloud Foundry, host files are not even visible to try to open them. For other container scenarios outside of Cloud Foundry, there can be, however, some value in joining only a subset of namespaces. For example, you might join the same network namespace to another process but not the mount namespace. This would allow you to achieve an independent container image that shares just the network of another container. This approach is known as a *sidecar container*.

Security through namespaces

When running processes in a dedicated VM, the responsibility for sharing physical resources is pushed down to the hypervisor. Containers that run on a single host are at the mercy of the kernel for security concerns, not an isolated hypervisor. Even though container isolation is achieved through namespaces, the namespaces still share the underlying resource.

Cloud Foundry provides multilayered security for containers. Principally, Garden—Cloud Foundry's container creation and management API—does not allow processes to run as root (the host's root). Garden can run two types of containers:

- Privileged containers that have some root privileges (useful for testing Garden itself)
- Unprivileged containers secured as much as possible; for example, processes running as pseudo root not host root

For tighter security, Cloud Foundry recommends that everything be run in unprivileged containers. A buildpack-built app will never run as root; it will always run as the Cloud Foundry created user vcap. In addition, for buildpack-built apps, Cloud Foundry uses a trusted secure rootfs provided by the platform. The Cloud Foundry engineering team has hardened the rootfs to remove exploits that could enable a user to become root. Building containers from the same known and trusted rootfs becomes a powerful tool for release engineering, as discussed in "Why BOSH?" on page 170.

Isolating the use of the root user is not unique to containers; this is generally how multiuser systems are secured. The next layer of security is containerization itself. The act of containerization uses Linux namespaces to ensure each container has its own view of system resources. For example, when it comes to protecting app data, each container has its own view of its filesystem with no visibility of other containers' files.

For Linux, conceptually, the kernel is unaware that a process is running in a container. (Remember, there is no actual container, only an isolated process.) Without the use of namespaces, any non-namespaced kernel call that provides access to a host resource could allow one process to directly affect another. Namespaces therefore provide additional security for processes running in a shared kernel.

A point to be aware of is that Docker containers can run as root and, therefore, if not mitigated, could potentially compromise the underlying host. To address this vulnerability, Cloud Foundry uses a namespaced root for Docker images, so a Docker container still cannot read random memory. Assuming that you have PID and user namespaces, you should never have the ability to read a random process's RAM.

Data Locality

Data is generally regarded to be the principal attack surface as opposed to simply another app process. Therefore, it is critical to maintain data isolation between processes. Container technology uses namespaces to isolate system resources such as filesystem access. Arguably, containers are still less secure than a dedicated VM because VMs are not sharing memory at the OS level. The only way to access another process's isolated memory would be to break out of the VM on to the host hypervisor. With containers, if a file descriptor is left open, because container processes reside in the same OS, that file descriptor becomes more exposed. For the Cloud Foundry model, this should not be a major issue, because, generally speaking, data is not stored on the local filesystem but rather in a backing service.

CGroups

Namespaces provide containers with an isolated view of the host; however, they are not responsible for enforcing resource allocation between containers. A Linux kernel feature known as control groups (CGroups) is used for resource control, accounting, and isolation (CPU, memory, disk I/O, network, etc.). CGroups enforce fair sharing of system resources such as CPU and RAM between processes. You can apply CGroups to a collection of processes; in our case, a namespaced set of container processes.

Disk Quotas

Resource limits (R limits) define things such as how many files can be opened or how many processes can be run. However, the Linux kernel does not provide any way to limit disk usage; therefore, disk quotas have been established. Disk quotas were originally dependent on quotas based on user IDs. However, because in Docker a process can be root, that process could create a new user to get around disk quotas, given that all new users will be provisioned with a new disk. This loophole allows disk usage to keep growing. As a result, today disk quotas tend to use a layered—copy-on-write—filesystem for Linux. This allows Linux to scale for the storage that will be available, with the ability to administer and manage the filesystem with a clean interface and a clear view of what is being used.

Filesystems

The filesystem image format comes from either a preexisting container image (e.g., if you use Docker) or it will be Cloud Foundry–created based on available stemcells. Cloud Foundry–created containers are known as *trusted containers* because of their use of a hardened rootfs. Trusted containers use a single-layer filesystem known as a *stack.* The stack works in combination with a buildpack to support apps running in containers.

 A stack is a prebuilt root filesystem (rootfs). Stacks support a specific OS; for example, Linux-based filesystems require /usr and /bin directories at their root. Cloud Foundry app machines (Diego Cells) can support multiple stacks.

Upon creation, every trusted container uses the same base image (or one of a small set of base images). The container manager in Cloud Foundry, Garden, can create multiple containers from its base images. Cloud Foundry uses a layered filesystem. If every newly created container required a new filesystem, around 700 MB would have to be copied from the base image. This would take multiple seconds or even minutes, even on a fast solid-state drive (SSD), and would result in wasted unnecessary storage. The layered approach amounts to immediately instantiating a filesystem because it provides a read-only view of the filesystem.

Here's how it works:

1. On every Cell, there resides a tarball containing the container's rootfs.

2. When a Cell starts, it untars the rootfs (for argument's sake, to /var/rootfs).

3. When Garden creates a new container, it takes in a parameter called rootfs (passing in /var/rootfs) and imports the contents of that directory into a layered filesystem graph.

4. For this new container and only this container, Garden then makes a layer on top of this rootfs; this layer is the resulting filesystem for this container.

5. When a second container is used, it recognizes that the base layer is already in place, and will create a sibling (a second layer) on the base rootfs for the new container.

6. The host has a tree structure consisting of a single base rootfs for all containers, with each container having a layer on top of that base. All containers are therefore siblings of one another.

7. On a write, the container copies that write to a layer above the base image.

8. When the container does a read, it first checks the top level and then goes down for the read-only content.

Untrusted containers (containers such as Docker that can run as a pseudo root) also often use a layered filesystem. A Docker container image is slightly more complex than just a single filesystem. Docker images are constructed from a Dockerfile, a script containing a set of instructions for building a Docker image very similar to a vagrant script used for building VMs. Every line in the script becomes a layer stored upon the previous layer. The Docker image can then build up multiple filesystem layers on top of one another. In addition to the layered filesystem, Docker images usually also contain metadata such as environment variables and entry points. Cloud Foundry must apply a quota to the rootfs to stop users from pushing containers with, for example, 100 GB of MapReduce data.

Container Implementation in Cloud Foundry

There is currently a degree of confusion and misinformation in the marketplace with respect to containers. This is largely because, as described earlier in "What Is a Container?" on page 141, the term "container" conflates various concepts. Moreover, the terminology used to describe container concepts tends to differ based on specific implementations. For example, when people refer to *running containers*, what they are really describing is the running of containers plus a number of other things such as package management, distribution, networking, and container orchestration. Containers are of limited value if considered in isolation because there are additional concerns surrounding them that must be addressed in order to run production workloads at scale; for example, container orchestration, clustering, resiliency, and security.

Cloud Foundry's container manager, Garden, runs container processes using the runC backend runtime, which is a CLI tool for spawning and running containers.

When Cloud Foundry uses the Garden API to make a container (running a process within runC), a couple of additional things happen:

File/volume system management
Containers require a filesystem. Whether that comes from Cloud Foundry's rootfs or a Docker image on Docker Hub or some other Docker registry, broadly speaking, the container engine sets up a volume on disk that a container can use as its root filesystem. This mechanism provides filesystem isolation. The filesystem is a path on a disk and Garden imperatively tells the container, *"make this filesystem path the root filesystem of the container."*

Networking
runC has no opinions about the network. The runC API allows Garden to specify a container that should be run within a network namespace. Therefore, Cloud Foundry provides additional code that will set up interfaces and assign IPs for each container so that it can provide each container with its own IP in order for it to be addressable.

Why Garden?

Garden offers some key advantages when used with Cloud Foundry. First, because Garden uses runC for the container runtime, it allows both Docker images and buildpack-staged containers to be run in Cloud Foundry. Therefore, the use of Garden does not preclude the use of Docker images.

The primary reason why Garden is the right choice for Cloud Foundry is that good architecture (especially, complex distributed architecture) must support change. Garden provides a platform-neutral, lightweight container abstraction so that it can be backed by multiple backends. Currently, Cloud Foundry Garden supports both a Linux backend and a Windows backend. This allows Cloud Foundry to support a wider array of apps. For example, Windows-based .NET apps can run on Cloud Foundry along with other apps running in Linux containers such as .NET Core, Java, Go, and Ruby.

The Garden API contains a set of interfaces that each platform-specific backend must implement. These interfaces contain methods to perform the following actions:

- Create/delete containers
- Apply resource limits to containers
- Open and attach network ports to containers
- Copy files to and from containers
- Run processes within containers, streaming back stdout and stderr data
- Annotate containers with arbitrary metadata
- Snapshot containers for zero-downtime redeploys

In Diego, the Garden API is currently implemented by the following:

- Garden-runC (Garden backed by runC), which provides a Linux-specific implementation of a Garden interface.
- Garden-Windows, which provides a Windows-specific implementation of a Garden interface.

OCI and runC

As discussed earlier in "Linux Containers" on page 144, Linux achieves container-like behavior through isolation, resource sharing, and resource limits. The first well-known Linux container implementation was LXC. Both Docker and Cloud Foundry's first container manager, Warden, originally used LXC and then built container management capability on top. Both Docker and Cloud Foundry have since moved to employing runC as the technology that spawns and runs the container process.

runC is a reference implementation according to the Open Container Project (OCP), governed by the OCI. OCI is an open-governance structure for creating open industry standards around container formats and runtime.

OCI has standardized backend formats and provided the runC reference implementation, which many higher-level systems have now adopted (e.g., Garden and Docker). runC was established primarily through Docker pulling out the non-Docker-specific container creation library (libcontainer) for reuse.

Container implementation should not be a concern to the developer, because it is just an implementation detail. Developers are more productive by focusing on their app, and Cloud Foundry makes it possible for them to keep their focus on the higher level of abstraction of apps and tasks. So, with this in mind, why focus on runC, which is a specific implementation? Why is runC important?

The answer is unification for the good of all! Container fervor is exploding. Various technologies (such as VMs and containers) are, in some cases, blending together, and in other cases (such as container orchestration), pulling in opposite directions. In this complex, emerging, and fast-moving space, standards serve to unite the common effort around a single goal while leaving enough room for differentiation, depending on the use case. This promise of containers as a source of lightweight app portability requires the establishment of certain standards around both format and runtime. These standards must do the following:

- Not be bound to a specific product, project, or commercial vendor
- Be portable across a wide variety of technologies and IaaS (including OSs, hardware, CPU architectures, etc.)

The OCI specification defines a *bundle*. A bundle is JSON that describes the container, stating the following:

- It should have *this* path as the rootfs.
- It should have *this* process and be in *these* namespaces.

It is the bundle that should become truly portable. Users should be able to push this OCI bundle to any number of OCI-compatible container environments and expect the container to always run as designed. The debate on the use of a specific container technology such as Garden versus Docker Engine is less important because both of these technologies support the same image format and use runC. These technologies are just an implementation detail that a platform user never sees nor need ever be concerned about. Most container orchestration tools are increasingly agnostic about what actually runs the container backend. For example, if you want to swap out runC for runV—a hypervisor-based runtime for OCI—this should not affect the running of your OCI container bundle.

Container Scale

Cloud Foundry is well suited for apps that can scale-out horizontally via process-based scaling. Cloud Foundry can also accommodate apps that need to scale vertically to some extent (such as increased memory or disk size); however, this limit is bound by the size of your containers and ultimately the size of your container host.

One app should not consume all of the available RAM or disk space on a host machine. Generally speaking, apps that scale memory vertically do so because they hold some state data in memory. Apps that scale disk space vertically do so because they write data to a local disk. As a best practice, you should avoid holding excessive state in memory or writing user data to local disk, or you should look to minimize these and offload them to a dedicated backing service such as a cache or database wherever possible.

Container Technologies (and the Orchestration Challenge)

All mainstream container technologies allow you deploy container images (at the moment, generally in Docker image format, although other standards exist) in a fairly similar way. Therefore, as mentioned earlier, the key concern is not the standardized backend implementation, but the user experience of the container technology.

You should not run containers in isolation. Low-level container technology alone is insufficient for dealing with scale and production environment concerns. Here are a few examples:

- If your container dies (along with your production app), who will notice, and how will it be restarted?

- How can you ensure that your multiple container instances will be equally distributed across your VMs and AZs?

- How will you set up and isolate your networks on demand to limit access to specific services?

For these reasons, container orchestration, container clustering, and various other container technologies have been established. As a side effect of the explosive growth in the container ecosystem over recent years, there is a growing list of container orchestration tools including Kubernetes, Docker Swarm, Amazon EC2 Container Service, and Apache Mesos. In addition, some companies still invest in in-house solutions for container orchestration.

Container orchestration is a vital requirement for running containers at scale. Orchestration tools handle the spawning and management of the various container processes within a distributed system. Container orchestration manages the container life cycle and allows for additional functions such scheduling or container restarts. Container services provide a degree of control for the end user to determine how containers interact with other containers and backing services. Additionally, orchestration makes it possible for you to group containers into clusters to enable them to scale to accommodate increased processing loads.

As discussed in Chapter 1 and "Do More" on page 9, Cloud Foundry provides the additional capabilities required for running containers in production at scale. At its heart, Cloud Foundry uses Diego as its container orchestration mechanism. (Chapter 6 reviewed Diego in detail.)

Summary

Containers have become immensely popular in recent years because they offer app deployment speed and resource efficiency through greater resource consolidation. They also allow app-stack portability across different environments. All of these benefits are appealing to DevOps cultures who desire to deliver software with velocity and avoid the *"it worked on my machine"* challenge. Containers become even more critical when working with microservices and CI pipelines for which rapid, repeatable, lightweight deployment is essential.

The challenge with containers is that because they have only recently become mainstream, there has been some confusion in the marketplace as to what container solution to adopt and how best to operationalize and orchestrate them in production. The key to obtaining benefits from containers is to move away from concerns surrounding image format or the backend runtime and ensure that you approach containers at the right level—namely, the tooling and orchestration that allow you to use running containers in production at scale.

Here's how Cloud Foundry supports this approach:

- Garden, a pluggable model for running different container images. Garden enables Cloud Foundry to support buildpack apps and Docker apps on Linux (via the runC backend) and Windows apps (via the Windows backend).
- Diego, which handles the container life cycle and orchestration including scheduling, clustering, networking, and resiliency.

When all is said and done, as impressive as container technology is, containers are just an implementation detail and not a developer concern. The key consideration in taking advantage of containers is not the container itself but the user experience of container orchestration. Removing developer concern from container construction and refocusing attention back on apps is vital for app velocity. This is where Cloud Foundry along with its Diego runtime really excels. Chapter 9 looks at Cloud Foundry's use of containers through buildpacks and Docker images.

Buildpacks and Docker

As we explored in Chapter 8, apps[1] that have been deployed to Cloud Foundry run as containerized processes. Cloud Foundry supports running OCI–compatible container images such as Docker as first-class citizens. It also supports running a standalone app artifact (e.g., *.jar* file or Ruby app) deployed "*as is,*" containerizing apps on the user's behalf.

Users can deploy a containerized image by using the cf push command. This command, along with additional arguments, is used for deploying both standalone apps and OCI-compatible container images.

When deploying just a standalone app artifact, Cloud Foundry stages your pushed app by composing a binary artifact known as a *droplet*. A droplet is an encapsulated version of your app along with all of the required runtime components and app dependencies. Cloud Foundry composes this droplet via its buildpack mechanism. The resulting droplet, combined with a stack (filesystem), is equivalent to a container image. Cloud Foundry runs this droplet in the same way as any other OCI-compatible container image: as an isolated containerized process.

When you push an app, Cloud Foundry automatically detects how to run that app and then invokes the use of Application Life-Cycle Binaries (ALB). The correct set of ALBs will be installed on the Cell (the Diego machine) where the app needs to run. For example, if a Docker image is pushed, the Docker ALBs will be used. If your app requires further compilation via a buildpack, using the buildpack ALBs, Cloud Foundry will additionally detect which buildpack is required to stage and run the app.

---

1 Apps in this context refers both to Long-Running Processes and tasks. Conceptually, a task is simply a short-lived application with finite characteristics and is guaranteed to run at most once.

The ability to deploy both individual apps and Docker images allows for flexibility. Companies already extensively using Docker images can deploy their existing Docker images to Cloud Foundry. Companies that want to keep their focus on just their apps can use Cloud Foundry to containerize their app artifacts for them. Although Cloud Foundry supports both approaches, there are trade-offs and benefits to each one. This chapter explores those trade-offs and benefits. It then further explains the nature of buildpacks, including a review of their composition, how they work, and how you can modify them.

Why Buildpacks?

There is an explicit ethos to the buildpack approach. The buildpack model promotes a clean separation of roles between the Platform Operator, who provides the buildpack, and the developer, who produces an app, which then consumes the buildpack in order to run. For example, the Platform Operator defines the language support and the dependency resolution (e.g., which versions of Tomcat or OpenJDK are supported). The developer is then responsible only for providing the app artifacts. This separation of concerns is advantageous to both the developer and the app operator.

Generally speaking, developers should not need to be concerned with building containers or tweaking middleware internals; their focus should be on the business logic of their app. By adopting the use of buildpacks, the developers' focus shifts from building containers and tinkering with middleware to just providing their app artifact. This shift aims to remove the undifferentiated heavy lifting of container construction in order to promote velocity of the app's business code.

Containerizing apps on the developer's behalf also offers additional productivity, security, and operational benefits because you can always build the resulting container image from the same known, vetted, and trusted components. Explicitly, as you move your app artifact between different Cloud Foundry environments (e.g., the app is pushed to different spaces as it progresses through different stages of a CI pipeline), the resulting compiled droplet can and should be staged with the same app, dependencies, and stack. The buildpack configuration facilitates this repeatability. This leaves only the app source code to require additional vulnerability and security scanning on every commit.

An additional feature of buildpacks is increased velocity when patching common vulnerabilities and exposures (CVEs) that affect the app. You can update buildpacks to Cloud Foundry when runtime CVEs emerge. Rather than updating and then redeploying each container image in turn, the Platform Operator simply updates the buildpack or runtime dependency once. Cloud Foundry can then restage and redeploy each app with the latest updates and patches.

Finally, there is a clear benefit to separating the build and run stages. A droplet is built during the compile phase of the buildpack. Building (staging) the droplet is done on a new container that is then destroyed after the droplet is created and uploaded to a blobstore. To run the app, the compiled droplet is then downloaded into a freshly created container. This separation between staging and running an app means that build tools do not end up alongside the executed droplet, further reducing the attack surface of the running app.

Why Docker?

The Docker image format (along with the standard OCI image format) has gained a huge amount of traction in many companies. There are benefits to encapsulating your app and all of its dependencies into a single executable image that can be moved between different environments. An often-cited benefit is that what you run in development is guaranteed to be the same in your production environment because you are not repeatedly rebuilding the container image per environment. With Cloud Foundry, every cf push results in a new droplet because you are restaging the application with a buildpack. This means that if your CI pipeline does a cf push to a staging environment and then a cf push to a production environment, you will have created two different droplets albeit with exactly the same components. A single image removes any doubt that development and production apps could have subtle differences. For example, with the buildpack approach, if your buildpack dependency configuration is too broad, there is a small risk that you can update a dependency during the execution of your pipeline resulting in a subtly different droplet. It is easy to mitigate this by locking down the buildpack dependency scope through configuration. Nonetheless, this is an important consideration to be aware of at this point. In the future, Cloud Foundry will allow droplets to be portable across different environments through download/upload mechanisms.

Another benefit of using Docker is that Docker images work well on desktop computers, allowing for a fast "getting started" experience. For comparison, a full Cloud Foundry installation on a local box (bosh-lite) requires BOSH skills and therefore some upfront investment. However, you can obtain a lightweight, easy-to-use, single-tenant version of Cloud Foundry by using PCFDev (*https://pivotal.io/pcf-dev*).

The trade-off of using Docker images is that more responsibility remains with the developer who constructs the image. Additionally, there are more components requiring a package scan on every new code commit. For example, the opaque nature of Docker images makes detecting and patching CVEs significantly more difficult than containers constructed and managed by the platform.

Whatever approach you decide on, by design, Cloud Foundry natively supports it. This leaves the choice down to what best suits your operational requirements.

App and Dependency Security Scanning

Many companies have already invested heavily in app security scanning. This includes the app and all of its external build and runtime dependencies. Therefore, there are some compelling benefits of using buildpacks to create a droplet for you. From a security and operational standpoint, it is likely to be more secure to keep just the app as the unit of deployment and allow the vetted components of the platform to handle all remaining dependencies.

Buildpacks Explained

Buildpacks are an essential component when deploying app artifacts to Cloud Foundry. Essentially, a buildpack is a directory filesystem that provides the following:

- Detection of an app framework and runtime support
- App compilation (known as staging), including all the required app dependencies
- Application execution

You can locate buildpacks remotely; for example, on GitHub, accessed via any Git URL, as in the case of the Java Buildpack (*https://github.com/cloudfoundry/java-buildpack*). Buildpacks can also reside natively on Cloud Foundry through a process of being packaged and uploaded for offline use.

You can specify additional buildpack metadata, such as the app name, RAM, service-binding information, and environment variables, on the command line or in an app manifest file.

Using an app manifest provides an easy way to handle change control because you can check manifests into source control. You can see a simple example of an app manifest in the spring-music (*https://github.com/cloudfoundry-samples/spring-music*) repository:

```
applications:
- name: spring-music
  memory: 512M
  instances: 1
  random-route: true
  path: build/libs/spring-music.war
```

Buildpacks typically examine the user-provided artifacts (applications along with their manifest and any CF CLI arguments) to determine the following:

- Which dependencies should be downloaded

- How apps and runtime dependencies should be configured

Unlike pushing a Docker image, buildpack-built containerized processes undergo a process known as *staging*.

Staging

Buildpacks only make one requirement on the filesystem: it must contain a *bin* directory containing three scripts:

1. Detect
2. Compile
3. Release

Detect, compile, and release are the three life-cycle stages of the buildpack. The three stages are completely independent and it is not possible to pass variables between these scripts.

Collectively, the detect, compile, and release stages are known in Cloud Foundry parlance as staging. Staging happens on a new clean container. The output of staging is a droplet that is uploaded to the Cloud Controller blobstore for later use.

You can write buildpacks in any language. For Ruby-based buildpacks, the buildpack scripts invoke the following piece of Ruby to ensure that Ruby is passed to the environment to run the scripts:

```
#!/usr/bin/env ruby
```

This basically instructs Bash to use the Ruby interpreter when it is executing the script. Alternatively, if you had a buildpack written in Node.js, the script would provide the path to Node.js. For buildpacks written in Bash, you simply invoke the detect, compile, and release scripts in the buildpack's bin directory, as shown here:

```
$ bin/detect <build-dir>
```

The Java Buildpack

Technically, you can make no assumptions about the environment in which the three buildpack scripts will run, and so historically buildpacks were written using Bash. Cloud Foundry ensures that Ruby will be present, thus the Java buildpack (JBP) has deviated from the standard buildpacks to be written in Ruby. There is a difference in philosophy between the JBP and other buildpacks. With other buildpacks such as the Ruby buildpack, the ability to handle things like enterprise proxy servers is handled by setting up a lot of the environment by hand. The JBP is different. It attempts to handle as much of this environment configuration for you via the buildpack components directly.

For the rest of this chapter, we will use the JBP as a great example of how buildpacks work.

Detect

Detect is called only if Cloud Foundry does not know which buildpack to run. Assuming that the user did not specify which buildpack to use at the outset, detect will be the first script to be run. It is invoked when you push an app to Cloud Foundry. Cloud Foundry will iterate through all known buildpacks, based on buildpack ordering, until it finds the first available buildpack that can run the app.

The detect script will not be run if a particular buildpack was specified by the user; for example:

```
$ cf push <my_app> -b my-buildpack
```

Detect is required to return very little. Strictly speaking, detect only needs to return an exit code (either 0 or some other nonzero integer). The JBP, however, returns a list of key–value pairs that describe what it is going to do; for example, use Java Version = Open Jdk JRE 1.8.0_111 and Tomcat = 8.0.38, etc.

System Buildpack Ordering

There are some important considerations when using the detect script. Because the detect script uses the first available buildpack that can run the app, it is important to define the correct ordering of system buildpacks. For example, both the JBP and a TomEE buildpack could run a WAR file. When you use the cf push command without explicitly defining the buildpack, the first buildpack in the buildpack list is used.

For this reason, it is best practice to always explicitly define your desired buildpack and to do so using a manifest that you can check into a source-control repository. With that said, because some users might still rely on the detect script, both the Cloud Foundry operator and user should always pay strict attention to buildpack ordering.

Compile

Compile is responsible for all modification tasks that are required prior to execution. Compile takes the pushed app and turns it to a state in which it is ready to run. The /bin/compile script can move files around, change file contents, delete artifacts, or do anything else required to get the app into a runnable state. For example, in the case of Java, it downloads Java (Open JDK), Tomcat, JDBC drivers, and so on, and places all of these dependencies in their required location. If compile needs to reconfigure anything, it can reach into your app and, in the example of the JBP, rewrite the Spring configuration to ensure that everything is properly set up. The compile phase is when you would make any other modifications such as additional app-specific load balancer configurations.

The JBP Compile Phase

The workflow for the JBP is subtly different from other buildpacks. Most other buildpacks will accept app source code. The JBP requires a precompiled app at the code level; for example, a JAR or WAR file.

As discussed in "A Marketplace of On-Demand Services" on page 37, an app can have various services bound to it; for example, database or app monitoring. The compile script downloads any service agents and puts them in the correct directory. Compile also reconfigures the app to ensure that the correct database is configured. If cf push specifies that a specific service should be used, but the service is not available, the deployment will fail and the app will not be staged.

The JBP has some additional capabilities; for example, the Tomcat configuration contains some Cloud Foundry–specific values to enable sending logging output to the Loggregator's Doppler component.

Release

The release stage provides the execution command to run the droplet. The release script is part of the droplet and will run as part of staging.

Some buildpacks (such as Java) need to determine how much memory to allocate. The JBP achieves this by using a program that calculates all required settings, such as how big the heap should be. You can run the script at the start of the application as opposed to only during the staging process. This flexibility allows for scaling because the script will be invoked every time a new instance is instantiated. cf scale can scale the number of instances and the amount of memory. If you change the amount of RAM, there is no restaging, but the app will be stopped and restarted with the required amount of memory specified, based on the specific memory weightings used.

The rest of the release script sets up variables and the runtime environment. For example, with Java, environment variables such as JAVA_HOME and JAVA_OPTS (see Java Options Framework (*http://bit.ly/2qstMQW*)) are set, and then finally, the release script will invoke any app server scripts such as *Catalina.sh* to start Tomcat.

Buildpack Structure

The three aforementioned life-cycle stages (detect, compile, release) are echoed by the code. The code sits in the *<buildpack>/lib* directory, all the tests sit in *<buildpack>/spec*, and, in the case of Ruby-based buildpacks, rake is the task executor.

The *<buildpack>/config* directory contains all the configurations. *Components.yml* is the entry point containing a list of all the configurable components.

For example, when looking at the JREs section, we see the following:

```
jres:
  - "JavaBuildpack::Jre::OpenJdkJRE"
# - "JavaBuildpack::Jre::OracleJRE"
# - "JavaBuildpack::Jre::ZuluJRE"
```

 The Oracle JRE is disabled because you need a license from Oracle to use it.

Here's the OpenJDK configuration YAML (*http://bit.ly/2qsmCfi*):

```
jre:
  version: 1.8.0_+
  repository_root: "{default.repository.root}/openjdk/{platform}/{architecture}"
memory_calculator:
  version: 1.+
  repository_root: "{default.repository.root}/memory-calculator/{platform}/↵
{architecture}"
  memory_sizes:
    metaspace: 64m..
    permgen: 64m..
  memory_heuristics:
    heap: 75
    metaspace: 10
    permgen: 10
    stack: 5
    native: 10
```

This specifies the use of Java 8 or above ("above" being denoted via the "+") and the repository root where the JRE is located. In addition, it contains the required configuration for the memory calculator app, including the memory weightings.[2]

Modifying Buildpacks

Cloud Foundry ships with a set of default built-in system buildpacks. To view the current list of built-in system buildpacks, run the $ cf buildpacks command via the Cloud Foundry CLI.

If some of the buildpacks require adjustment, in some cases you can override specific configuration settings.

If your app uses a language or framework that the Cloud Foundry system buildpacks do not support, you can write your own buildpack or further customize an existing buildpack. This is a valuable extension point. Operators can, however, choose to disable custom buildpacks in an entire Cloud Foundry deployment if there is a desire for uniformity of supported languages and runtime configuration.

After you have created or customized your new buildpack, you can consume the new buildpack by doing either of the following:

- Specifying the URL of the new repository when pushing Cloud Foundry apps
- Packaging and uploading the new buildpack to Cloud Foundry, making it available alongside the existing system buildpacks

For more information on adding a buildpack to Cloud Foundry, go to the Cloud Foundry documentation page (*http://bit.ly/2qsrvVO*).

---

2 The use of memory weightings for the memory calculator is in the process of being simplified.

Overriding Buildpacks

If you only need to change configuration values such as, in the case of Java, the default version of Java or the Java memory weightings, you can override the buildpack configuration by using environment variables. The name of the overriding environment variable must match the configuration file that you want to override (with the *.yml* extension) and it must be prefixed with `JBP_CONFIG`. The value of the environment variable should be valid inline YAML.

As an example, to change the default version of Java to 7 and adjust the memory heuristics, you can apply the following environment variable to the app:

```
$ cf set-env my-application JBP_CONFIG_OPEN_JDK_JRE '[jre: {version: 1.7.0_+},
+ memory_calculator: {memory_heuristics: {heap: 85, stack: 10}}]'
```

If the key or value contains a special character such as ":", you will need to escape them by using double quotes. Here is an example showing how to change the default repository path for the buildpack:

```
$ cf set-env my-application JBP_CONFIG_REPOSITORY
+ '[ default_repository_root: "http://repo.example.io" ]'
```

You cannot apply a new configuration using this process: you can only override an existing configuration. All new configurations require buildpack modifications, as discussed in "Modifying Buildpacks" on page 163.

The ability to override any configuration in a *config.yml* file has made simple configuration changes to the JBP very straightforward. You can specify environment variables both on the command line or in an app manifest file. You can find more detailed advice on extending the JBP at *https://github.com/cloudfoundry/java-buildpack/blob/master/docs/extending.md*.

Using Custom or Community Buildpacks

It is worth noting that the Cloud Foundry community provides additional external community buildpacks for use with Cloud Foundry.

> You can find a complete list of community buildpacks at *https://github.com/cloudfoundry-community/cf-docs-contrib/wiki/Build packs*.

Forking Buildpacks

You might have a requirement to extend or modify the buildpack; for example, maybe you need to add an additional custom monitoring agent. The buildpack feature supports modification and extension through the use of the Git repository forking functionality to create a copy of the buildpack repository. This involves making any required changes in your copy of the repository. When forking a buildpack, it is recommended you synchronize subsequent commits from upstream.

Best practice is that if the modifications are generally applicable to the Cloud Foundry community, you should submit the changes back to Cloud Foundry via a pull request.

Restaging

After the first `cf push`, both app files and compiled droplets are retained in the Cloud Controller's blobstore. When you use `cf scale` to scale your app, Cloud Foundry uses the existing droplet.

From time to time, you might want to restage your app in order to recompile your droplet; for example, you might want to pick up a new environment variable or a new app dependency.

The droplet that results from a restage will be completely new. Restage reruns the buildpack against the existing app files (source, JAR, WAR, etc.) stored in the Cloud Controller blobstore. The restage process picks up all new buildpack updates and any new runtime dependencies that the buildpack can accept. For example, if you, the Platform Operator, have specified the use of Java 8 or above (jre version: 1.8.0_+), the latest available version of Java 8 will be selected. If a specific version of Java was specified (such as jre version: 1.8.0_111), only that version will be selected.

As with `cf push`, `cf restage` runs whatever buildpack is associated with the app. By default, you do not need to specify a buildpack; the platform will run the buildpack *detect* script in the order specified by the command `system buildpacks`. Alternatively, you can explicitly specify a buildpack name or URL. Diego Cells support both *.git* and *.zip* buildpack URLs.

Packaging and Dependencies

There are different approaches that you can take when accessing a buildpack and its dependencies. The approach you choose is determined by two concerns:

- How you access the buildpack
- How you access the buildpack dependencies

You can access the buildpack either remotely, via a Git URL, or by packaging and uploading to Cloud Foundry. You can access buildpack dependencies either by the buildpack remotely (often referred to as online or remote dependencies) or packaged along with a packaged buildpack (referred to as offline dependencies).

Given these considerations, there are three standard approaches to consuming build-packs:

Online
> You access this via a Git URL with both buildpack and dependencies being pulled from a remote repository.

Minimal-package
> This is a packaged version of the buildpack that is as minimal as possible. The buildpack is uploaded to Cloud Foundry's blobstore, but it is configured to connect to the network for all dependencies. This package is about 50 KB in size.

Offline-package
> This version of the buildpack is designed to run without network access. It packages the latest version of each dependency (as configured in the *config* directory) and disables remote_downloads. This package is about 180 MB in size.

Cloud Foundry deployments residing within an enterprise often have limited access to dependencies due to corporate regulations. Therefore, the second or third options are generally established within an enterprise setting.

With all three approaches, it is recommended that you maintain a local mirror of the buildpack dependencies (*https://java-buildpack.cloudfoundry.org*) hosted by Cloud Foundry on Amazon S3. To clone this repository, follow the instructions at the Cloud Foundry GitHub repo (*http://bit.ly/2pHawSl*). With technologies such as Artifactory, you can set up a pull-through model that watches the source blobstore and pulls down any updates onto your local mirror for internal use only. This approach allows the security team to package-scan all dependencies and provides the Platform Operators with a level of governance over what dependencies can be consumed. It also makes it possible for you to run Cloud Foundry without requiring internet access.

Thus, the decision criterion for these options is one of flexibility versus governance.

The offline-package approach allows for complete control over the buildpack and dependencies. Packing provides an explicit guarantee of known, vetted, and trusted dependencies used to deploy the app. The downside is that you will need an additional CI pipeline (see the section that follows) to build and upload any buildpack and dependency changes.

The advantage of the online approach is that it provides the flexibility to make changes to both the buildpack and the consumption of dependencies without the need to run the changes through a pipeline. You can mitigate concerns surrounding control by strict governance of the mirrored dependency repository. For example, if you want to disable the use of Java 7, you can simply remove it from the repository and update the buildpack accordingly. If a developer then reconfigures his custom buildpack to use Java 7, his deployment will fail. Online buildpacks provide the most flexibility, but without the proper governance, this approach can lead to buildpack sprawl. This governance is managed in a production environment through the use of a pipeline to deploy apps. Buildpack sprawl during development is not a bad thing, provided developers keep in mind the available buildpack options and availability of app dependencies in the production environment.

Buildpack and Dependency Pipelines

When using the JBP, the approach of using a local mirror for dependencies involves forking the buildpack and updating the dependency repository. Keeping this mirror and forked buildpack up-to-date and synchronized with the online buildpack and latest dependencies is vital to ensure that you are guarding against the latest CVEs. To this point, it is prudent to set up a pipeline to maintain buildpack concurrency.

You can set up the dependency pipeline flow as follows:

- Trigger weekly updates from an RSS feed of CVEs that pertain to java_buildpack dependencies (or invoked as soon as a patch is added to the Amazon S3 repository via a pull-down mechanism)
- Use scripts to pull down pertinent items from Cloud Foundry's Amazon S3 buckets (see the Cloud Foundry GitHub repo (*http://bit.ly/2pHawSl*))
- Push all new dependencies to the local mirror repository, removing any outdated or compromised dependencies

You can set up the buildpack pipeline flow for packaging the java_buildpack as follows:

- Git clone and pull down the latest version of the java_buildpack repository
- Override the dependency repository to point to your local buildpack repository (e.g., an Artifactory repository)
- Push the online buildpack to Cloud Foundry
- Build offline buildpack and push offline buildpack to Cloud Foundry
- Restage all affected apps

Note that even if you are using the online-buildpack approach, it is still valuable to have the offline buildpack available in case there is any downtime of your local repository.

Summary

Cloud Foundry supports pushing Docker images and standalone apps and tasks. Upon pushing an app or task, Cloud Foundry uses a buildpack to containerize and run your app artifact. Buildpacks are a vital component in the deployment chain because they are responsible for transforming deployed code into a droplet, which can then be combined with a stack and executed on a Diego Cell in a container.

Buildpacks enable Cloud Foundry to be truly polyglot and provide an essential extension point to Cloud Foundry users. They also facilitate a separation of concerns between operators who provide the language support and runtime dependencies, and developers who are then free to keep their focus on just their app code.

Whatever approach you choose, be it deploying a standalone app or a Docker image, Cloud Foundry supports both as first-class citizens.

## CHAPTER 10

BOSH Concepts

BOSH is a release-engineering tool chain that provides an easy mechanism to version, package, and deploy software. It makes it possible for you to create software deployments that are both reproducible and scalable. This chapter covers BOSH concepts and primitives.

BOSH is an open source project originally developed to deploy Cloud Foundry. It is often overlooked as just another component of Cloud Foundry, but the truth is that BOSH is the bedrock of Cloud Foundry and an amazing piece of the ecosystem.

BOSH is a recursive acronym that stands for *BOSH outer shell*. The outer shell refers to BOSH being a release tool chain that unifies release-engineering, deployment, and life-cycle management of cloud-based software. To put it simply, the BOSH outer shell runs Cloud Foundry so that Cloud Foundry can run your apps.

 For readability I talk about BOSH deploying to VMs as simply machines; as is typically the case, however, BOSH can actually deploy VMs, containers, and in some cases, you can use it to configure physical servers.

BOSH can provision and deploy software packages either onto a single machine or at scale over hundreds of machines, with minimal configuration changes. It also performs monitoring, failure recovery, and software updates with zero-to-minimal downtime.

Release Engineering

IT operations are tasked with achieving operational stability. Historically, operational stability was achieved by reducing risk through limiting change. Limiting change is in direct conflict with frequently shipping features. To manage risks involved in frequent software releases, we use release-engineering tool chains. Release engineering involves members of the operations team, who are typically concerned with turning source code into finished software components or products through the following steps:

- Compilation
- Versioning
- Assembly/packaging
- Deploying

Automating release-engineering concerns through a tool chain reduces deployment risk, allowing for faster deployments with little to no human interaction.

Release engineering is typically concerned with the compilation, assembly, and delivery of source code into finished software components or products. Periodically, these software components require updating and repackaging in order to fix defects and provide additional features. After they are updated, the components might require redeployment over a distributed cluster of servers or repackaging for deployment to third-party servers.

Release-engineering tool chains are essential because they provide consistent repeatability. Source code, third-party components, data, and deployment environments of a software system are integrated and deployed in a repeatable and consistent fashion. Release-engineering tool chains also provide a historical view to track all changes made to the deployed system. This provides the ability to audit and identify all components that comprise a particular release. Security teams can easily track the contents of a particular release and re-create it at will if the need arises. In summary, *consistent repeatability de-risks software releases.*

Why BOSH?

Teams operating within a DevOps culture typically deploy their updated software to their own production environment after all of their tests have passed. The CI pipeline will often involve a number of different staging and integration environments that are similarly configured to their production environments. This ensures that updates run as expected when reaching production. These staging environments are often complex and time consuming to construct and administer. There is an ongoing challenge between trying manage configuration drift and maintaining consistency between environments.

Tools such as Chef, Puppet, and Salt Stack have become valuable assets to DevOps for provisioning new environments. Containerization technologies have further enabled developers to port their entire stack as a single reusable image as it moves through the different CI environments. Other tools have also come into the mix. The goal of versioning, packaging, and deploying software in a reproducible fashion often results in a bespoke integration of a variety of tools and techniques that provide solutions to individual parts of the stated goal.

BOSH has been designed to be a single tool covering the entire end-to-end set of requirements of release engineering. It has been purposefully constructed to address the four principles of modern release engineering (*https://en.wikipedia.org/wiki/ Release_engineering*) in the following ways:

Identifiability
This is the ability to identify all of the source, tools, environment, and other components that make up a particular release. BOSH achieves identifiability through the concept of *software release*. A software release packages up all related artifacts including source code, binary assets, scripts, and configuration. This enables users to easily track contents of a particular release. In addition to software releases, BOSH provides a way to capture all dependencies as one image, known as a *stemcell*.

Reproducibility
This is the ability to integrate source, third-party components, data, and deployment externals of a software system in order to guarantee operational stability. The BOSH tool chain achieves reproducibility through a centralized server, known as the BOSH Director. The BOSH Director manages software releases, OS images, persistent data, and system configuration. It provides a clean and reproducible way of interacting with deployed systems.

Consistency
This encompasses the mission to provide a stable framework for development, deployment, audit, and accountability for software components. BOSH achieves consistency through defined workflows that are used throughout both the development and deployment of the software system. The BOSH Director gives users the ability to view and track all changes made to the deployed system.

Agility
This entails ongoing research into the repercussions of modern software engineering practices on productivity in the software cycle; in other words, CI. The BOSH tool chain achieves agility by providing the ability to easily create automated releases of complex systems. Furthermore, it allows for subsequent updates through simple commands. BOSH integrates well with established current trends of software engineering such as CD and CI technologies.

The Cloud Provider Interface

BOSH supports deploying to multiple IaaS providers including VMware's vSphere, AWS, GCP, and OpenStack. BOSH achieves its infrastructure-agnostic capabilities by implementing a *cloud provider interface* (CPI) for each supported IaaS. The CPI contains implementations of the necessary verbs that drive the underlying IaaS layer. These include instructions such as `create VM` and `create disk`. You can extend BOSH support to additional infrastructure providers such as RackHD and Apache CloudStack by implementing a CPI for the required infrastructure, as demonstrated in Figure 10-1.

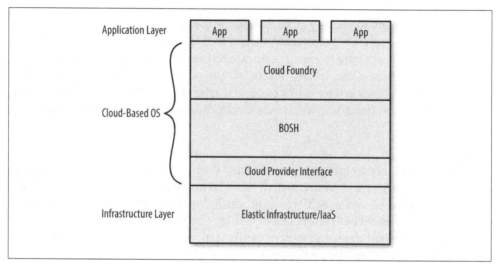

Figure 10-1. The Cloud Foundry infrastructure stack

Infrastructure as Code

BOSH focuses on defining your infrastructure as a piece of code. The traditional approach with other infrastructure-as-code provisioning tools involve having a pre-established set of servers or VMs that are then used for deploying and updating software. More recently, the traditional infrastructure-as-code tools have been extended with capabilities to preprovision VMs prior to laying down the OS and software components.

The difference between these approaches and BOSH is that BOSH, by design, tries to abstract away the differences between all of the infrastructure platforms (IaaS or physical servers) into a generalized cross-platform description of your deployment. Differences between infrastructures are, where possible, handled by the CPI layer. The BOSH user works with a manifest, and that manifest will, by and large, be the same across the different infrastructures to which the BOSH release will be deployed.

Other powerful provisioning tools such as Terraform or AWS Cloud Formation, which also provide configuration to instantiate infrastructure, have not abstracted away infrastructure-specific configuration to the same degree, allowing infrastructure concerns to bubble up for the end user to handle.

With tools like Terraform, you can set up an entire data center from scratch, if, for example you are working on AWS, because Terraform knows you will be using AWS components such as Route53 and ELB. BOSH comes in at a place where all infrastructure platforms provide certain levels of abstraction for compute, disk storage, and some networking. Given those bare-minimum configurations, BOSH will have a common ground for actually creating VMs, attaching disks, and putting them in the correct networks. The BOSH user does not need to worry about concerns such as, *"If I am on AWS which AMI should I choose?"*

BOSH does not solve every conceivable use case. For example, BOSH does not try to handle IaaS networking configuration, because this is unique to each IaaS layer. There is no easy way to abstract away these concerns to a point where you are not losing required configuration benefits. Abstraction focuses on the common ground across infrastructure platforms, potentially cutting out features that are unique to a specific platform. Therefore, picking the right level of abstraction—to be feature-rich while portable across infrastructure—is the challenge that BOSH aims to address.

BOSH on the Server

Even though BOSH is primarily designed for deployment to IaaS, there are efforts to allow a hardware provisioning experience through projects such as Open Crowbar (*https://github.com/open crowbar/core*) and RackHD (*https://rackhd.readthedocs.org/en/ latest/*).

The other key feature of BOSH is its built-in resiliency. Traditional infrastructure-as-code provisioning tools do not check whether services are up and running. BOSH has strong opinions on how to create your release, forcing you to create a monitor script for every process. If a process dies, the monitor script (Monit for Linux) will restart the process. In addition, the BOSH Resurrector has the ability to re-create failed or unresponsive VMs. Upon re-creation, BOSH can deal with remounting persistent data.

The final key difference is that most other infrastructure-as-code provisioning tools run a series of package-management commands to build and release their software. Usually those commands download packages from the internet. This approach might lead to a nonreproducible environment (the packages have changed in the upstream repository or are no longer available). BOSH again takes an opinionated view to always ensure that every provisioned release is identical. A BOSH release has all dependencies packaged into the release. Therefore, you can deploy an old release again and again, and BOSH should produce the same results every time.

The value of BOSH goes beyond configuration management. It is focused on a seamless experience of delivering software and then ensuring that it remains highly available and resilient. Simply put, BOSH translates intent into action and then maintains that state.

Creating a BOSH Environment

A single BOSH environment consists of the Director VM and any deployments it orchestrates. Before deploying software releases, or, more specifically, BOSH releases, we first need to deploy the Director. The Director VM includes all necessary BOSH components that will be used to manage the different IaaS resources such as networks, compute, and disks. You can bootstrap a BOSH Director via `bosh-init`. You can find steps for bootstrapping a BOSH environment via `$bosh creat-env` on bosh.io (*https://bosh.io/*).

 BOSH Versions

It is recommended that you update your BOSH environment frequently to stay on the latest version. I have seen spurious deployment issues fixed simply by upgrading to a newer version of BOSH, the latest stemcell, and the latest BOSH CLI.

Both BOSH and Cloud Foundry make extensive use of manifests. This includes manifests for creating a BOSH environment, release manifests, deployment manifests, and app manifests for app deployment. Manifests are discussed further in "Understanding YAML Syntax" on page 202. It is important to note that the manifest used to create the BOSH Director currently currently has some differences from manifests used for BOSH deployments. You should refer to the bosh.io (*https://bosh.io/*) for a description of those differences.

Single-Node versus Distributed BOSH

Single-node BOSH is a complete BOSH environment that runs on a single machine. Although you can deploy BOSH in a distributed fashion, in reality, most deployments (including Cloud Foundry) work fine using a single-node BOSH machine. Even though being on a single machine can be considered a single point of failure, a single-node BOSH removes network segmentation faults, and it can be protected and mitigated by the IaaS layer. BOSH downtime does not cause downtime of Cloud Foundry or the apps running on it. The only real advantage of a multinode (distributed) BOSH is that it is easier to update because a single-node BOSH can then be used to upgrade the distributed BOSH.

BOSH Lite

Not everyone requires a full-blown deployment for their BOSH release. For example, if you just want to play around with Cloud Foundry, you might not want to incur the costs of running anywhere between 10 to 30 VMs on AWS. The solution to running an easy-to-configure, lightweight version of Cloud Foundry, or any other release, is BOSH Lite.

BOSH Lite is a prebuilt Vagrant box that includes the BOSH Director. However, instead of using a traditional IaaS CPI such as AWS, BOSH Lite utilizes a CPI for Garden. This means that instead of the CPI creating new VMs, the Garden CPI uses containers to emulate VMs. This makes BOSH Lite an excellent choice for scenarios such as these:

- General BOSH exploration without investing time and resources to configure an IaaS
- Getting started with BOSH and Cloud Foundry without incurring significant IaaS costs
- Development of BOSH releases
- Testing releases locally or as part of a CI/CD pipeline

BOSH Lite (*https://github.com/cloudfoundry/bosh-lite*) is a great environment for trying out Cloud Foundry, but be mindful that because everything is running on a single VM, it is suitable only for experimentation and not production workloads.

BOSH Top-Level Primitives

This section covers the BOSH primitives, including the BOSH concepts and components, and how they interact. Before bootstrapping a new BOSH environment, it is important to be aware of the top-level BOSH primitives that underpin a provisioned Cloud Foundry environment.

Primitives

Computing languages use primitives to describe the simplest elements available in a programming language.

Following are the top-level BOSH primitives:

1. Stemcells
2. Releases

---

3. Deployments

Figure 10-2 presents an overview of the top-level BOSH primitives.

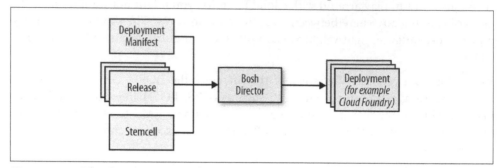

Figure 10-2. The three BOSH artifacts (deployment manifest, stemcell, and release) that the BOSH Director uses to create a new deployment (for example, a new Cloud Foundry instance)

Stemcells

In biology, a *stemcell* is an undifferentiated (or basic) cell that can differentiate into several types of specialized cells throughout the body. A BOSH stemcell follows this same principle; it is a hardened and versioned base OS image wrapped with minimal IaaS-specific packaging. A common example of stemcell hardening is that SSHD, the OpenSSH daemon program for SSH, has been reconfigured to support only appropriate cyphers, only allow specific users to log in, and enforce time-out of client connections. Another example is that all compilers have been removed from the stemcell to reduce the attack surface. A typical stemcell contains the following:

- A bare-minimum OS skeleton with essential preinstalled common utilities
- Configuration files to securely configure the OS
- A BOSH agent for communication back to the Director
- IaaS-specific packaging and versioning

IaaS Specifics

Certain infrastructures have different packaging schemes (e.g., raw, qcow, AMI), requiring stemcells to be packaged in a specific way. For this reason stemcells become infrastructure-specific. The base OS image is common across all infrastructure types. All installed packages and libraries should be identical across all stemcells of the same version.

All machines created by BOSH are created from stemcells, including the Director machine itself and any machine subsequently created by the Director.

Stemcells provide clear separation between the base OS and any later-installed software used to specialize the machine. Stemcells are agnostic to what will be installed on them. They do not contain specific or sensitive information relating to the downstream software used to specialized them, so they can be shared at will with other BOSH users. Stemcells ultimately become transformed into specialized VMs in the cluster through BOSH instantiating and installing additional software on them during a BOSH deployment. This specialized downstream software is referred to as a *BOSH release*.

This separation of the base OS (stemcells) and specialized downstream software (BOSH release) is a powerful concept. Stemcells capture a specific base OS image; for example, Ubuntu Trusty. They are exactly the same and you can use them across different software deployments and different VM types. Because the same base OS is reused, it becomes extremely easy to apply versioning changes to the OS; for example, OS security fixes. This property of generic stemcells makes it possible for BOSH users to effortlessly switch among different infrastructures without being concerned about potential differences between OS images. It is similar to Java's JVM aim of "write once, run anywhere" for compiled Java code. Because the same base OS is reused everywhere, it becomes easy to apply versioning changes systematically, to every deployed OS image. This benefit should not be underestimated; the ability to rapidly and confidently patch all machines within a distributed system is an extremely powerful capability.[1]

Stemcells are distributed as tarballs, and the Cloud Foundry BOSH team is responsible for producing and maintaining an official set of stemcells. You can view and download the most recent and currently supported stemcells at bosh.io (*https://bosh.io/$*).

Releases

BOSH deploys software that has been packaged into a self-contained BOSH release. A BOSH release is your software, including all configuration and dependencies required to build and run your software in a reproducible way. A single BOSH release contains one or more pieces of software that are designed to work in unison. Therefore, BOSH becomes an excellent choice for deploying both an individual component and an entire distributed system.

---

1 The word "patch" is used indicatively in this context; in reality, machines are not patched—they are recreated from a new patched stemcell. This approach further strengthens BOSH's intentional security posture.

A release is the software layer placed on top of a stemcell to transform it into a specialized component. Conceptually, a release is the packaging of your software (code) that you want to deploy. Releases are IaaS-agnostic, which allows for increased portability of your software across different IaaS environments. The key point here is that your BOSH releases and the subsequent deployment of those releases are not locked into any IaaS layer. This is because IaaS differences are abstracted away by the CPI layer and the Director's Cloud Configuration (discussed further in "Cloud Configuration" on page 180). This decoupling is powerful for your infrastructure strategy. With the rise of viable alternatives to vSphere and AWS, there is a genuine desire for portability across different IaaS offerings. For example, using only a small team, Pivotal moved its hosted version of Cloud Foundry, known as Pivotal Web Services (*https://run.pivotal.io*), from AWS to GCP in a matter of weeks with zero app downtime. This move was possible only because the Cloud Foundry software release is not tied into the underlying IaaS layer.

Releases are made up of one or more release jobs, and you can co-locate different releases during deployment. What you choose to actually deploy is not dictated by releases; you have the freedom to select which release jobs you would like to deploy and on which machines those jobs should reside. The anatomy of a release is discussed in "Anatomy of a BOSH Release" on page 192. For now, it is important to know that the release jobs you deploy to a VM form a specific component known as an *instance group*. Examples of instance group components are a Diego Cell and Cloud Foundry's Cloud Controller. As implied by the name, an instance group can run several instances of the same component; for example, you typically run several Cells within a Cloud Foundry deployment.

As discussed in Chapter 5, Cloud Foundry is encapsulated by the cf-deployment BOSH release, located at cf-deployment (*https://github.com/cloudfoundry/cf-deployment*).

Cloud Foundry Release Structure

The Cloud Foundry BOSH release is structured by the parent cf-deployment release, which links to a combination of smaller, independent releases (e.g., `etcd-release`, `UAA-release`, and `diego-release`). The `cf-deployment` release captures the exact versions of the specific releases necessary to deploy a full Cloud Foundry environment.

BOSH is designed for deploying distributed systems such as Cloud Foundry, but you can use it equally to deploy smaller individual components such as etcd (*https://github.com/coreos/etcd*) or redis (*http://redis.io/*). Because it can deploy almost any other software that is able to be run on the supported infrastructure, it has been used extensively within the Cloud Foundry ecosystem to deploy a wide variety of services such as databases, message brokers, and caching technologies. It is worth noting that many popular services such as RabbitMQ, MySQL, PostgreSQL, and Redis already have existing BOSH releases. Community service brokers are located in the Cloudfoundry-community GitHub repo (*https://github.com/cloudfoundry-community*).

This book does not delve into the detail of creating a new BOSH release; however, it is valuable to become familiar with release primitives and how releases are composed in order to understand how cf-deployment is structured and deployed. Understanding BOSH releases will also come in handy if you want to create additional BOSH releases for services that back your apps running on Cloud Foundry. Chapter 11 covers BOSH releases in detail.

Deployments

BOSH deploys software to the IaaS layer using a deployment manifest, one or more stemcells, and one or more releases. This is known in BOSH terminology as a *BOSH deployment*, which consists of a collection of one or more machines (VMs), as depicted in Figure 10-3. Machines are built from stemcells and then layered and configured with specified components from one or more BOSH releases. A BOSH deployment requires the following:

- The appropriate stemcell(s) for the IaaS of choice
- The releases (software) to deploy
- An IaaS environment (or infrastructure) to which to deploy the release
- A deployment manifest describing the deployment

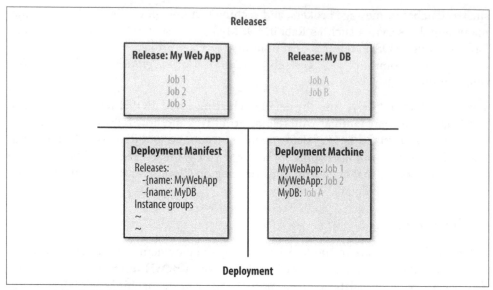

Figure 10-3. A BOSH deployment

BOSH creates the deployment using ephemeral resources and persistent disks. The deployment is stable because BOSH can keep your software running by re-creating machines that fail, or restarting failed processes. State stored on the persistent disk (e.g., database data files) can survive when BOSH re-creates a VM because persistent disks can be reattached. As just discussed, deployments are portable across different kinds of cloud infrastructure with minimal changes to the deployment manifest.

The anatomy of a deployment is discussed in Chapter 12.

BOSH 2.0

There are some great features of BOSH 2.0 that significantly reduce the complexity of deployment manifests. You can use the additional set of BOSH 2.0 features in conjunction with the original BOSH constructs.

Cloud Configuration

Previously, deployment manifests included all of the IaaS-specific resource configurations required for that deployment. To keep BOSH deployments IaaS-agnostic, you now can configure IaaS resource configuration (networks, resource pools, disk pools, compilation) in one location at the Director level. Each BOSH deployment can then reference the predefined IaaS resources by name. You can define the IaaS configuration in an additional manifest such as *iaas.yml*, as follows:

```
compilation:
  workers: 6
  network: my-network
  az: z1
  reuse_compilation_vms: true
  vm_type: m3.medium
  vm_extensions:
  - 100GB_ephemeral_disk

azs:
- name: z1
  cloud_properties:
    availability_zone: us-west-1a

networks:
- name: my-network
  type: manual
  subnets:
  - az: z1
    gateway: 10.0.16.1
    range: 10.0.16.0/20
    reserved:
    - 10.0.16.2-10.0.16.3
    - 10.0.31.255
    static:
    - 10.0.31.190-10.0.31.254
    cloud_properties:
      subnet: subnet-XXXXXXXX
      security_groups:
      - sg-XXXXXXXX

vm_types:
- name: m3.medium
  cloud_properties:
    instance_type: m3.medium
    ephemeral_disk:
      size: 1024
      type: gp2

vm_extensions:
- name: 100GB_ephemeral_disk
  cloud_properties:
    ephemeral_disk:
      size: 102400
      type: gp2
- name: router-lb
  cloud_properties:
    elbs:
    - stack-bbl-CFRouter-XXXXXXXX
    security_groups:
    - sg-XXXXXXXA
    - sg-XXXXXXXB
```

```
- name: ssh-proxy-lb
  cloud_properties:
    elbs:
    - stack-bbl-CFSSHPro-XXXXXXXX
    security_groups:
    - sg-XXXXXXXA
    - sg-XXXXXXXB

disk_types:
- name: 5GB
  disk_size: 5120
  cloud_properties:
    type: gp2
    encrypted: true
```

The cloud configuration construct provides the flexibility to stipulate IaaS-specific information once; for example, a small, medium, and large `vm-type`, which can then be used by the various different BOSH deployments. The preceding manifest example specifies information about the following:

- Compilation VM
- AZs
- Networks
- `vm_types`
- `vm_extensions`
- `disk_types`

The manifest specifies that the compilation VM resides on an AZ named `z1` and a network named `my-network`. The properties of `z1` and `my-network` are specified in the respective AZs and networks hashes. The compilation `vm_type` is specified as `m3.medium` with an `100GB_ephemeral_disk` `vm_extension`. Again, the details of `m3.medium` and `100GB_ephemeral_disk` are specified in the respective vm_types and vm_extensions hashes. The vm_extensions hash contains additional hashes that describe the required load balancers, named `router-lb` and `ssh-proxy-lb`. Finally, you can specify any other IaaS component in this manifest such as `disk_types`. If that description feels complex, don't worry, we will walk through the specifics of each component in a moment.

Because the entire IaaS configuration is now encapsulated in a separate cloud configuration manifest, the deployment manifest is not only simpler, it's significantly smaller. In the subsections that follow, we examine each section of the cloud configuration.

Networks

A BOSH network is an IaaS-agnostic representation of the networking layer. BOSH expresses networks as a logical view; a BOSH network is the aggregation of all assigned IaaS subnets. In the manifest, `networks` provides an array of networks (IaaS networks and subnets) to be used by deployed jobs.

BOSH Networking and IaaS Networking

The BOSH cloud configuration manifest has only a construct of networks. The IaaS networking can deal with both networks and subnets. Therefore, if you run out of IPs, you can simply add additional IaaS subnets to the BOSH networks' array. Second, as discussed in "AZs" on page 187, BOSH abstracts the AZ separation. Some IaaS offerings, such as AWS, do not allow subnets to span AZs. BOSH deals with this by allowing the operator to specify a single BOSH network and then add multiple IaaS subnets from different AZs to that single BOSH network.

Within the cloud configuration manifest, all networking is specified in one global networking section and then shared by multiple deployments. This provides the advantage that created VMs are assigned the same IPs. This also makes it easier to structure subnets, ensuring that they do not overlap. Specifying network information on a per-deployment manifest basis is significantly more difficult and error prone because you were required to be mindful of other deployments that might have been deployed to the same underlying IaaS network. Now, BOSH guarantees that subnets will not overlap because it keeps unique IPs all in one table. Therefore, you can even give multiple BOSH networks the same underlying IaaS subnet, and, still, BOSH will ensure each new deployment will use only unique IPs.

It is the Director's responsibility (with the help of the BOSH agent and the IaaS) to configure each of the instance group's network. Networking configuration is usually assigned when the machine is started. You can also apply it when the network configuration changes due to a manifest change for already-running instance groups. Here is an example of configuring the network:

```
networks:
- name: my-network
  type: manual
  subnets:
  - az: z1
    gateway: 10.0.16.1
    range: 10.0.16.0/20
    reserved:
    - 10.0.16.2-10.0.16.3
    - 10.0.31.255
    static:
```

```
      - 10.0.31.190-10.0.31.254
    cloud_properties:
      subnet: subnet-XXXXXXXX
      security_groups:
      - sg-XXXXXXXX
```

The reserved range is used for IPs that will be explicitly used by the network (such as the gateway VM or DNS). As such, BOSH will not use any IP in a reserved range for provisioning VMs.

BOSH networking supports automatic and static IP reservation types for manual networks:

Static
> The IP is explicitly requested by the Platform Operator in the deployment manifest.

Automatic
> The IP is selected automatically based on the network type.

You can use the static IP range for VMs that require a static IP. Components or VMs that you need to know about upfront, such as the HA_Proxy or the GoRouter, require a static IP so that you can point your DNS server to the load balancer and then point the load balancer at the GoRouter cluster.

If using BOSH links (discussed in "BOSH Links" on page 188), static IPs are not required for internal-facing BOSH-deployed components. BOSH links will maintain the IPs for you, and they do not need to be placed in the manifest. External-facing components such as a load balancer will still require a static IP.

There are three different BOSH network types:

- Dynamic
- Manual
- VIP

BOSH abstracts the networking away from the Platform Operator. If you are using a VIP network, you can assign elastic or floating IPs. Manual and dynamic networks allow you to assign private IPs. For a more detailed explanation about how to configure these network types, refer to bosh.io (*https://bosh.io*) for the latest guidance, as implementation details can change over time.

VM types

VM types is a collection of VM sizes with specific properties. They are created from the stemcell defined in the deployment manifest. Every VM created from the same VM type and stemcell will have the same configuration. The Platform Operator can define an array of VM types each with different VM settings; for example, varying CPU and RAM to offer small, medium, and large VMs to your deployment. Individual deployments no longer need to be concerned with what a small VM means because it is defined once per Director.

Each `instance_group` instance defined in the deployment manifest will run on a dedicated VM, and so the `instance_group` must reference the required stemcell and `vm-type`. This means that each instance group belongs to exactly one `vm-type` and stemcell combination.

In addition, there is a `cloud_properties` definition with which the Platform Operator can specify other VM characteristics and IaaS-specific settings that might be required when creating VMs; for example, `vm_extension` and `disk_type`.

A manifest for `bosh-init` might use the precursor to `vm_types` known as `resource_pools`. Resource pools contain IaaS-specific information about the VMs.

Configuring the disk type

Disks are used for machine storage. Disk types make it possible for you to specify persistent disks for use with the instance group VMs and compilation VMs (see "Compilation VMs" on page 187). It is possible to define two different types of storage solutions: ephemeral and persistent disks. This provides you with the flexibility to use a more cost-effective storage solution for the ephemeral storage and high-grade storage for persistent data.

Consider three different Cloud Foundry instance groups:

- API
- UAA
- etcd

Each instance group has a VM with two mounted ephemeral disk filesystems:

```
/dev/sda1 with / mounted
/dev/sdb2 with /var/vcap/data mounted
```

Instance groups that specify a persistent disk (such as `persistent_disk: 1024`) will have a third filesystem:

```
/dev/sdc1        1011416    8136    934688   1% /var/vcap/store
```

Looking at UAA, which has no persistent disk, you will observe two ephemeral disks with no `var/vcap/store`:

```
df -k
Filesystem      1K-blocks    Used Available Use% Mounted on
/dev/sda1       2886304 1293408   1426564  48% /
```

```
none                4        0        4  0% /sys/fs/cgroup
udev           498216        4   498212  1% /dev
tmpfs          101760      648   101112  1% /run
none             5120        0     5120  0% /run/lock
none           508784        0   508784  0% /run/shm
none           102400        0   102400  0% /run/user
/dev/sdb2     9182512   478144  8214872  6% /var/vcap/data
tmpfs            1024       16     1008  2% /var/vcap/data/sys/run
/dev/loop0     122835     1583   117321  2% /tmp
```

Looking at etcd, which does have a persistent disk, we see the addition of /var/vcap/store:

```
df -k
Filesystem      1K-blocks     Used Available Use% Mounted on
/dev/sda1       2886304  1293640   1426332  48% /
none                  4        0         4   0% /sys/fs/cgroup
udev             498216        4    498212   1% /dev
tmpfs            101760      656    101104   1% /run
none               5120        0      5120   0% /run/lock
none             508784        0    508784   0% /run/shm
none             102400        0    102400   0% /run/user
/dev/sdb2       9182512    57524   8635492   1% /var/vcap/data
tmpfs              1024       12      1012   2% /var/vcap/data/sys/run
/dev/loop0       122835     1550    117354   2% /tmp
/dev/sdc1       1011416     8136    934688   1% /var/vcap/store
```

In addition, one of the CF instance groups might use a blobstore such as a debian_nfs_server in vSphere or an Amazon S3 bucket in AWS.

The API instance group has mounted the filesystem /var/vcap/nfs. Data written to this location actually resides on an NFS blobstore under /var/vcap/store:

```
bosh_3x78y23hg@25e1aec0-36aa-424b-a70e-eff65b7b5490:~$ df -k
Filesystem                     1K-blocks      Used Available Use% Mounted on
/dev/sda1                        2886304   1296128   1423844  48% /
none                                   4         0         4   0% /sys/fs/cgroup
udev                              498216         4    498212   1% /dev
tmpfs                             101760       648    101112   1% /run
none                                5120         0      5120   0% /run/lock
none                              508784         0    508784   0% /run/shm
none                              102400         0    102400   0% /run/user
/dev/sdb2                        3057452    360844   2521584  13% /var/vcap/data
tmpfs                               1024        12      1012   2% /var/vcap/data/sys
                                                                   /run
/dev/loop0                        122835      1550    117354   2% /tmp
10.129.48.12:/var/vcap/store   103079936   2251776  95568896   3% /var/vcap/nfs
```

cf-deployment's manifest-generation capability will automatically configure the storage for your instance groups. You can reconfigure these after you generate the deployment manifest.

Compilation VMs

Compilation defines the machine settings for the VMs used to compile any individual packages from the release jobs into self-executable binaries, as follows:

```
compilation:
  workers: 6
  network: my-network
  az: z1
  reuse_compilation_vms: true
  vm_type: m3.medium
  vm_extensions:
  - 100GB_ephemeral_disk
```

It is generally considered fine to reuse compilation VMs as opposed to using a clean VM for every new compilation. Fewer workers can potentially result in longer deployments because less work might be done in parallel. However, it is worth noting that in the case of AWS, the IaaS might be slow to set up VMs compared to the time it takes to compile packages; thus it might be most performant to have fewer reusable workers.

AZs

AZs provide resiliency. By striping instances from a single instance group across multiple AZs, you ensure availability in the event of a total failure of a single AZ.

To simplify configuration of AZs, they have been pulled out of the deployment manifest into their own section. Previously, to stripe a single instance group across multiple AZs, the Platform Operator had to create multiple resource pools with slightly different cloud properties and multiple instance groups with slightly different names (e.g., web_az1, web_az2). This approach introduced extra complexity and repetition in the deployment manifest.

Since BOSH 2.0, each defined AZ specifies a name and the cloud properties to include any IaaS-specific properties required for placement information. For example, on AWS, AZs are encapsulated by an AWS availability_zone and on vSphere AZs might be a vSphere cluster and resource-pool combination.

The subnets of each network must define which AZ they belong to. Each instance group can be on one or more networks. Because each instance group can span multiple AZs, there must be a way to determine how to describe a network that spans multiple AZs. Most IaaS platforms require a separate subnet per AZ, so BOSH can abstract that away by defining a network based on multiple subnets from different AZs.

For deployments that still use resource pools, their cloud properties should only include VM sizing information such as instance types, RAM, CPUs, etc. When replacing resource_pools for the newer vm_types, each instance group must specify the Cloud Foundry AZ in which to reside.

BOSH Links

BOSH links give the Platform Operator a means to configure a deployment involving multiple VMs, where at least one instance group knows about another; for example, a web server that depends on a database. Traditionally, operators had to assign static IPs or DNS names to one job and pass it via properties to the other. This configuration was error-prone and unnecessary. It was also difficult to automate for the case of on-demand deployments.

Links provide a solution to this problem and abstract away manual versus dynamic (DNS-based) networking from the instance groups. Additionally, you can use links to share other non-networking configurations (job properties) between instance groups.

From the operator's perspective, introduction of links removes tedious cross-referencing of IPs and other properties between different BOSH releases and deployments.

To take advantage of links in releases, extra metadata needs to be specified by using the consumes and provides directives. Each release job that needs information about another release job must specify consumes with the name of the link type it consumes. Each release job that can satisfy link type must specify provides. BOSH also has a concept of explicit linking of release jobs. If a link type is provided by only one job within a deployment, all release jobs in that deployment that consume links of that type will be implicitly connected to that provider. You can find more information about BOSH links at *https://bosh.io/docs/links*.

Orphaned Disks

Orphaned disks provide an additional safety feature because losing persistent data is never good. If you require a larger disk size, you can modify this in the cloud configuration manifest (or select a larger instance from the disks listed in the cloud configuration); BOSH will detach the old disk and reattach the new disk, migrating data across to the new disk in the process. The challenge here is that if you rename your instance group (from nameA to nameB), BOSH sees this as a new instance group, as opposed to an upgraded instance group, and will delete the old instance group (and old persistent disks) without moving the data on the old disk. To address this valid but often unintended behavior, when deleting a disk, BOSH keeps old disks around for five days and will garbage-collect them retroactively. Therefore, if you accidentally delete a deployment, you can recover your persistent disk after the fact.

Addons

Addons provide the ability for you to add additional releases to BOSH deployments. This feature is extremely valuable for adding new capabilities to an existing or future deployment. Addons are especially powerful because they provide the ability for the operator to define Director-wide policies. For example, additional releases that you might want to "add on" could include a corporate security module or an IPSec BOSH release to encrypt communication between all deployed VMs. As a positive side effect, addons also remove some of the clutter from deployment manifests.

Your BOSH environment might consist of multiple release jobs (e.g., Cloud Foundry and additional service brokers). There might be requirements to add an additional release job to all deployed VMs. Instead of modifying the deployment manifest to add additional release templates and then redeploying, BOSH employs the concept of runtime-config in the form of BOSH addons. Addons are a new release job that can be co-located with existing instance groups. When a new bosh deploy is invoked, BOSH deploys the addons to the defined deployment.

Summary

This chapter covered the concepts of BOSH, the outer shell responsible for provisioning and running Cloud Foundry.

BOSH is a release-engineering tool chain that provides consistent, reproducible, and identifiable deployments. *Consistent repeatability de-risks software releases.*

BOSH is an essential component of the Cloud Foundry ecosystem, and it is important that you understand the role BOSH plays for both deploying and verifying the health of your Cloud Foundry environment and related services. Specifically, understanding the BOSH top-level primitives of stemcells, releases, and deployment helps you to understand how Cloud Foundry is deployed.

BOSH is complex, and there is a lot to it. For operators who want to gain a deeper understanding of BOSH, the next three chapters examine the anatomy of a BOSH release and deployments, and then we dive deeper into the individual BOSH components and basic BOSH commands.

## CHAPTER 11

BOSH Releases

Chapter 10 introduced BOSH concepts on a high level. For operators who want a deeper understanding of BOSH releases, this chapter presents an overview of how releases are structured and packaged.

A BOSH release is your software, including all configuration and dependencies required to build and run your software in a reproducible way. Gaining an understanding of releases will help you to comprehend how individual components work. For example, understanding how a release is composed and deployed can help you to pinpoint where each release job runs. This ability to determine exactly which processes run and where they run is invaluable for debugging.

Release Overview

Releases are self-contained and provide very specific software solely relating to the purpose of that release. Here's a simple example provided by bosh.io:

> [A] Redis release might include startup and shutdown scripts for Redis-server, a tarball with Redis source code obtained from the Redis official website, and a few configuration properties allowing cluster operators to configure that Redis-server.

A release consists of versioned release jobs and packages. A release job describes a single component that can be run in isolation to do its work. A release package contains the required dependencies for a specific job. A release exists as a versioned collection of the following artifacts:

- Configuration properties
- Configuration templates
- Scripts (including startup scripts and shutdown scripts) for the release jobs
- Source code

- Binary artifacts
- Anything else required to build and deploy software in a reproducible way

By allowing the separation and layering of releases on top of stemcells, BOSH is able to version and roll out updated software to the entire cluster on a machine-by-machine basis. Releases ensure that the same compiled software version is used repeatedly for every deployment, as opposed to running a package installer such as apt-get, which can potentially install a different binary every time, depending on from where you pull binaries. All the required configuration options and scripts for software deployment are captured and all software dependencies are explicitly recorded with all changes tracked. Packing enables versioning, tracking, and self-containment of IaaS—agnostic software releases. This means that you can deploy a release version without internet access.

Cloud Foundry BOSH Release

Installing Cloud Foundry does not require you to create a new release; you can simply deploy a current Cloud Foundry release version. The current canonical Cloud Foundry deployment is cf-deployment (*https://github.com/cloudfoundry/cf-deployment*). cf-deployment comprises several individual, self-contained component releases. This means that each Cloud Foundry component, such as the UAA, or Diego, or the GoRouter, resides in its own BOSH release. cf-deployment then draws these releases together via a canonical manifest for deploying Cloud Foundry. Chapter 12 discusses deployments, including how Cloud Foundry is deployed.

BOSH Director BOSH Release

The BOSH Director itself is a dedicated BOSH release. To install the BOSH Director, the $ BOSH create-env command will grab the BOSH Director BOSH release located on GitHub (*https://github.com/cloudfoundry/bosh*). This BOSH Director BOSH release has some subtle differences from typical BOSH releases. This chapter focuses on typical BOSH releases, such as Cloud Foundry.

Anatomy of a BOSH Release

A BOSH release has five release primitives, the most significant being *jobs*, *packages*, *src*, and *blobs*. These terms are discussed at length below. A typical release directory contains:

- A *jobs* directory that contains job metadata
- A *package* directory that contains package metadata
- A *config*, *blobs*, and *src* directory

- .dev_builds and .final_builds directories
- Any Git subdirectories

To create a typical release directory with one job and one package, navigate to the workspace where you want the release to reside. Then, using the BOSH v2 CLI, run the following:

```
$ bosh init-release <release_name>
$ cd <release-name>
$ bosh generate-job <job-name>
$ bosh generate-package <package-name>
```

You can now view the skeleton release directory tree:

```
$ tree .
.
├── blobs
├── config
│   └── blobs.yml
├── jobs
│   └── job_name
│       ├── monit
│       ├── spec
│       └── templates
├── packages
│   └── package-name
│       └── packaging
└── src
```

Release Naming

By convention, BOSH uses a lowercase naming convention with dashes in the release name; for example, cf-deployment. For all other filenames in the release, BOSH uses underscores; for example, job_name.

Jobs

A *release job* (or simply job) conceptually describes a single component. You can run a release job in isolation and it will do its work. The release job can be comprised of several individual processes (e.g., a master process coupled with a separate worker process for tasks such as log rotation). A release job might depend on other jobs, and there may be several steps to instantiate a release job, but the end state should be a single component that you can start and stop by a single Monit script.

Release Jobs and Instance Groups

Release jobs are individual software components that can run in isolation. An instance group is the deployment unit. A single instance group represents one or more release jobs to be deployed to a single VM. An instance group can have several running instances (VMs) such as several Diego Cells or several GoRouters.

The BOSH releases for each core Cloud Foundry component (such as the Cloud Controller or GoRouter) are broken into one or more release jobs. Usually, we do not append "release" to the release name. Appending release is useful only for descriptive purposes such as a GitHub repository or when the release is distributed as a *.tar* file. You can view a list of the current jobs associated with the deployed instance groups by running the following command:

```
$ bosh -e <bosh_env> -d <deployment> instances --ps
```

Each job has its own directory containing a Monit file, a specification file, and a *templates* directory. A job needs to be able to start and stop its processes. BOSH currently achieves this by using a control script and Monit.

Control scripts

We use control scripts to configure and control job processes, including commands such as `start` and `stop`. The job's control script is an embedded Ruby (ERB) template typically named *<job_name>*ctl.erb (arguably, it should just be called ctl.erb because it belongs to a specific job and so is already namespaced). It is stored in the job's templates directory. By BOSH convention, control scripts should configure the job to store logs in */var/vcap/sys/log/<job_name>*. If a release needs templates other than the control script, those templates should also reside in the templates directory.

ERB

ERB is a Ruby feature that provides a way to generate text from templates. The templates combine plain text with Ruby code for variable substitution and flow control.

When a release is deployed, BOSH transforms the control scripts into files, substituting the required variable values (properties), and then replicates these files onto the subsequent instance group VMs under */var/vcap/jobs/<job_name>*.

The */var/vcap* Directory Structure

By convention, the */var/vcap* directory is used as the parent directory to the */sys* and */jobs* subdirectories.

Monit

In addition to the `ctl.erb` template script, a release also requires a controlling and monitoring process that can start (or restart), monitor, and stop the job processes. In Linux you do this by using a Monit file (with an equivalent for Windows[1]) for each release job. The Monit file has two key responsibilities:

- Specifies the job's process ID (PID) file
- References all commands (e.g., start and stop) provided by the release job templates

The Monit file for a job typically contains the following:

```
check process <job_name>
  with pidfile /var/vcap/sys/run/<job_name>/pid
  start program "/var/vcap/jobs/<job_name>/bin/ctl start"
  stop program "/var/vcap/jobs/<job_name>/bin/ctl stop"
  group vcap
```

Note that the path to the `ctl` script is the path that will exist on the deployed instance group machine.

Specification Templates

Each job has a specification file that defines job metadata (including any additional templates) and any required job properties like db_password. Here is what the specification file lists:

`name`
    The job name

`packages`
    Includes both package dependencies and the packages created by this job

`templates`
    An array of ERB template names and paths

`properties`
    A list of properties required by the job

---

1 The concept is the same for Windows support; however, Windows uses a custom job supervisor with Windows services instead of Monit, and JSON in place of a `ctl` script.

Job Descriptions

Often, specification files will contain a description used to describe the job. This is not part of BOSH. You can write whatever you want in the specification file; however, BOSH will consider only names, packages, templates, and properties.

The job specification file's `templates` block contains a list of hashes. The template name is the key, and the path on the instance group machine's filesystem is the hash value.

File paths are always relative to the */var/vcap/jobs/<job_name>* directory on the instance group machine. By convention, these control scripts go in the *bin* directory. Therefore, on the instance group machine, *bin/ctl* becomes */var/vcap/jobs/<job_name>/bin/ctl*.

Templates can be required for things like scripts that set up environment variables. Any such script is generated via a template, with properties injected in by the Director, which accesses properties set in the deployment manifest. Properties are discussed further in "Properties" on page 207.

Packages

The *packages* directory contains the dependencies of a specific job. These dependencies are pulled in from the *blobs* and *src* directories. Packages provide BOSH with all of the information required to prepare the job binaries and job dependencies during the release-compile phase. A release can contain several jobs, each dependent on their specified packages.

1. Packages provide source code and dependencies to jobs
2. Src provides packages with the nonbinary files they need
3. Blobs provide packages with the binaries they need (other than binaries that are checked in to a source code repository)

Figure 11-1 shows the dependency graph for a release job.

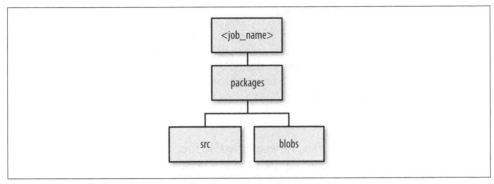

Figure 11-1. Job dependency graph

The *packages* directory also contains the packaging instructions so that BOSH can build each of the release job dependencies during the `create-release` compilation phase. A BOSH release has two kinds of dependencies: runtime dependencies and compile-time dependencies.

Runtime dependencies exist when a job depends on a package to run; for example, a Spring boot app depends on Java, or a Ruby app depends on Ruby. Compile-time dependencies occur when a package depends on another package at compile time; for example, Ruby depends on the YAML library to compile.

It is important to note that jobs are self-contained in that jobs can depend only on packages, not other jobs; however, packages can depend on other packages.

Src, Blobs, and Blobstores

As we just discussed in "Packages" on page 196, *src* and *blobs* directories contain the dependencies pulled in by the packages. The *src* contains source code that is explicitly part of the release. Job source code is either copied into the *src* directory or linked to it, using a mechanism such as a Git submodule or a Mercurial repository.

Most releases are highly dependent on a source code repository. However, releases often use blobs, such as *.tar* files or precompiled third-party libraries. Blob tarballs can contain both binaries or source code, and they usually contain all external dependencies. If the tarballs contain source code, the packaging script must define how to compile that code.

Typically, for components that are not your actual software (e.g., Ruby), you provide them via blobs. Components that you are responsible for releasing should be provided in the most generic form possible, namely source code.

Using Source over Binaries

You can compile dependencies from source as opposed to using prebuilt binaries. Binaries are usually tied to a specific OS architecture, so something that works on Ubuntu might not work on Centos. When you compile from source, you are creating binaries for the specific stemcell architecture defined in the deployment manifest.

A lot of source code repositories, for example GitHub, are not suitable for checking in large blobs. BOSH avoids the requirement to check blobs into a repository in two ways:

- For a dev release, BOSH uses local copies of blobs.
- For a final release, BOSH uploads blobs to a release blobstore.

For the latter, to deploy a release, the BOSH CLI needs to obtain the required blobs and then upload those blobs to the Director. Keep in mind that there are two unrelated blobstores in play here: a Director blobstore that the Director uses, and a release blobstore that is used only for managing a specific release.

The Director blobstore can reside anywhere the Director can reach it. A release blobstore is release-specific; for example, final UAA release saves the final artifacts in a UAA-specific blobstore.

The CLI has a number of ways to upload the release into the Director blobstore. The CLI can read the release blobstore location from a GitHub repo and then send the blobs over to the Director. This method means that the CLI must have access to both the Director blobstore as well as the release blobstore.

However, the BOSH Director does not require access to a release blobstore, which means that the Director does not require internet access. An operator can simply bring a release tarball that has been previously composed from the required blobs from the release blobstore and then upload that tarball to the Director. This method means that the tarball has no reference to the original release blobstore, and, as such, the Director and CLI do not require any access to the release blobstore.

Theoretically, a release can also be constructed from scratch if you can obtain all dependent blobs, or the release author places blobs in the blobs directory, but it is a better experience for your release consumers if you package a release for consumption, as discussed further in "Packaging a Release" on page 199.

All of the information about the release blobstore is recorded via the *config* directory. Two files reside in this directory:

final.yml
> This file names the blobstore and specifies its type. Type is either local to the BOSH Director VM or one of several other types that specify blobstore providers, such as a local NFS, or public blobstores such as Amazon S3.

private.yml
> This file specifies the blobstore path and secret key for accessing the blobstore. As such, for security reasons, it should not be checked into a repository.

The *config* directory also contains an automatically generated *blobs.yml* file.

Although a local blobstore is convenient for getting started, the resulting releases are held only locally and cannot be shared beyond the immediate BOSH deployment.

Packaging a Release

BOSH provides two main ways by which you can distribute a release version:

- Package the release in its entirety as a tarball and then store it somewhere.
- Use a Git repo and the *releases/<release-name>/release.yml* file that points to the release blobstore.

To upload a release, run the following:

```
$ bosh -e <env> upload-release <your-release>
```

This upload-release command accepts different URL schemes. Typically you can provide an HTTPS URL for the entire tarball, or you can clone the release's Git repo into a local directory and then provide, for example, the *releases/cf/cf-x.yml*. This *<release>.yml* file tells the CLI with the information on what the publisher published for that release version. Specifically, it contains pointers to blobstore objects (packages and jobs) that are required for a given release version. These blobs usually reside either locally (for a development release) or in the release blobstore (for a final release). From that YAML file, the BOSH CLI is able to create a release tarball that can be uploaded from the release blobstore to the Director blobstore.[2]

These blobs are resolved within the *.final_builds* file, which references the release blobstore for final jobs and packages (each referenced by one or more releases). For storing final releases, the config provides the URLs and access credentials to the release blobstore. Any Git subdirectories provide local Git hooks to pull those subdirectories in.

---

[2] The new BOSH v2.0 CLI has a Git syntax that can clone a Git repository in the background for you by using the command $ git clone, and then use the specified version of the YAML file to upload the release tarball.

You might want to create a BOSH release for additional custom Cloud Foundry services. It is important to note that you do not need to create a new release version for installing Cloud Foundry, because you can use the existing release version. For example, you can simply clone and use a Git URL by invoking $ `bosh -c <env> upload-release releases/cf-x.yml`. This has the same behavior as accessing a release directly from bosh.io. Using bosh.io is completely optional.

Compilation VMs

Some releases might still require further compilation (from source code to binary, based on the appropriate stemcell). BOSH uses compilation VMs to achieve this. Compilation brings up the machine or VM, takes the source package, runs a packaging script, and then produces a compiled package. BOSH then saves these compiled packages and will then use the compiled packages to deploy the instance group machines. Compilation VMs were discussed earlier in "Compilation VMs" on page 187.

Summary

A BOSH release does the following:

- Encapsulates all your software in a self-contained way
- Includes all configuration and dependencies required to build and run your software in a reproducible way
- Has five release primitives, the most significant being *jobs*, *packages*, *src*, and *blobs*
- Can be versioned, packaged, and distributed

BOSH deploys software to the defined IaaS layer using a deployment manifest, one or more stemcells, and one or more releases. A BOSH deployment consists of a collection of one or more machines or VMs, built from stemcells and then layered and configured with specified release jobs obtained from software releases.

What you choose to actually deploy is not dictated by releases; you have the freedom to select which release jobs you would like to deploy and on which instance groups those jobs should reside. This choice is defined in the deployment manifest. Chapter 12 looks more closely at BOSH deployments and deployment manifests.

BOSH Deployments

This chapter provides a brief overview of BOSH deployments, including Cloud Foundry's deployment manifest. BOSH deploys software to infrastructure (often an IaaS layer) using a deployment manifest, one or more stemcells, and one or more releases.

As described in Chapter 11, releases exist to package of all your required artifacts. Releases are then deployed to one or more machines (often VMs) known as instance groups, via a deployment manifest. A deployment manifest describes how to install releases. It defines how the various processes (release jobs) that have been packaged by releases should be distributed and deployed to various instance groups.

There is no direct correlation of release contents and what process runs on an instance group. This correlation is explicitly defined in the deployment manifest. Releases are always IaaS-agnostic. A release coupled with a deployment manifest can also be IaaS-agnostic if written correctly. As of this writing, only stemcells remain explicitly IaaS format–specific. IaaS format–specific means that certain stemcells can be reused across the same IaaS format; for example, OpenStack stemcells can be reused for RackHD, and vSphere stemcells can be reused for vCloudDirector and VirtualBox. However, where the IaaS format differs, such as between GCP and AWS, separate stemcells that are specific to each IaaS format are required.

YAML Files

Both BOSH and Cloud Foundry make extensive use of YAML files. This includes the following:

- Manifests for creating a BOSH Director environment
- Release files that describe release jobs and related blobs
- Deployment manifests

- App deployment manifests
- Cloud configuration IaaS information

To read manifests, you need to understand basic YAML syntax. YAML is a human-readable data serialization standard for programming languages. It is generally considered easier for humans to read and write YAML versus other common data formats like JSON or XML.

You can edit YAML with a regular text editor. If you want to dig deeper into YAML, you can find further information at *http://yaml.org*.

Understanding YAML Syntax

BOSH deployment manifests are currently by far the most complex aspect of Cloud Foundry. The recent work on BOSH 2.0 has made great strides toward simplifying the deployment manifest. However, for cloud operators, understanding how manifests are constructed to relay correct information to BOSH is vital. This section uses a snippet from the Cloud Foundry deployment manifest to walk you through the salient points of the YAML structure widely used in deployment manifests.

Many YAML files make extensive use of lists. Lists can contain individual items or hashes. A hash is represented in a simple `key: value` form (the colon must be followed by a space). A simple hash could contain a key of "name," with the value "java_buildpack." Most lists in Cloud Foundry contain hashes. All members of a list are lines beginning at the same indentation level starting with a "- " (a - and a space):

```
# A list of buildpacks

    install_buildpacks:
    - name: java_buildpack
      package: buildpack_java
    - name: ruby_buildpack
      package: buildpack_ruby
    - name: nodejs_buildpack
      package: buildpack_nodejs
    - name: go_buildpack
      package: buildpack_go
    - name: python_buildpack
      package: buildpack_python
    - name: php_buildpack
      package: buildpack_php
```

Hash values can contain further hashes or even lists of hashes. The `install_build packs` element is itself a hash key that has a value containing a list of nested hashes. In this case, each nested hash is actually two nested hashes (name and package). Here's another more complex example:

```
# A list of resource pool hashes: each item is a hash representing a single
# resource pool, uniquely identified by the "name" key

resource_pools:
  - name: small_z1
    cloud_properties:
      instance_type: c3.large
      ephemeral_disk:
        size: 10_240
        type: gp2
      availability_zone:

  - name: small_z2
    cloud_properties:
      instance_type: c3.large
      ephemeral_disk:
        size: 10_240
        type: gp2
      availability_zone:
```

The `resource_pools` key has a value containing a list of two hashes: `small_z1` and `small_z2`. Let's explore the first hash element in the list:

```
  - name: small_z1
    cloud_properties:
      instance_type: c3.large
      ephemeral_disk:
        size: 10_240
        type: gp2
      availability_zone: (( meta.zones.z1 ))
```

This hash has two keys. The first key, `name`, maps to a unique value that identifies this resource pool as `small_z1`. The second key, `cloud_properties`, is another nested hash that contains metadata about the specific resource pool. With the exception of readability, the ordering of the `name` and `cloud_properties` keys is not important to BOSH. Let's explore the `cloud_properties` value:

```
      instance_type: c3.large
      ephemeral_disk:
        size: 10_240
        type: gp2
      availability_zone:
```

This nested hash has three keys: `instance_type`, `ephemeral_disk`, and `availability_zone`. The `ephemeral_disk` key has a value containing a further two nested hashes: `size` and `type`.

The remainder of this chapter explores the specifics of deployment manifests.

Deployment Manifests

As discussed, deployments are configured and created based on a YAML file called a deployment manifest (often referred to as simply a manifest). Deployment manifests provide a way to state, as code, an explicit combination of stemcells, release jobs, and operator-specified properties. BOSH deployments are deployed to a specific IaaS.

Cloud Configuration

IaaS-specific BOSH concerns are defined in the Director's cloud configuration, enabling BOSH deployments to be completely IaaS-agnostic. IaaS-specific concerns such as network information or resource pools (including VM type) are configured once per Director. Cloud configuration was discussed in "Cloud Configuration" on page 180.

Because all the IaaS configuration is now encapsulated in a separate cloud configuration YAML file, deployment manifests are significantly reduced, defining only configurations specific to the actual deployment. These configurations include the following:

1. Deployment name
2. Director universally unique identifier (UUID) (not required with BOSH 2.0)
3. Stemcells
4. Releases
5. Instance groups (VMs)
6. Properties
7. Updates

Director UUID and Deployment Name

The first name in the manifest is the deployment name. This name does not matter. The BOSH Director UUID is required to ensure that the Platform Operators install a deployment on the correct director. For example, imagine that you are targeted on your BOSH production environment, but you want to deploy a development release to your BOSH test environment. If you forget to retarget BOSH to the test environment, the fact that the deployment manifest specifies the BOSH test environment UUID will cause BOSH to prevent the release from being deployed to the production environment. The need for specifying UUID in the manifest has been deprecated with the BOSH CLI v2. The BOSH CLI v2 deals with the aforementioned issue by requiring users to explicitly specify the BOSH environment and deployment when deploying; for example:

```
$ bosh -e prod -d dep deploy dep-manifest.yml
```

Release Names

With respect to release names and version (in the deployment manifest releases section), this naming does matter. If you type bosh releases, you will see the releases uploaded to the Director. However, the name you specify at the release.name should match the name of the uploaded release. Any version number defined here dictates the specific release version. You can use the release version for tracking deployed software.

Stemcell

The stemcell is either picked automatically based on the OS name and version provided:

```
stemcells:
- alias: default
  os: ubuntu-trusty
  version: 3074
```

Or, you can specify an explicit stemcell name for an exact stemcell match:

```
stemcells:
- alias: default
  name: bosh-aws-xen-hvm-ubuntu-trusty-go_agent
  version: 3074
```

The preferred approach is to pick up the stemcell version based on OS and version because this allows the manifest to remain IaaS-agnostic. An error will be raised during a deploy if none of the stemcells that have been uploaded to the Director match the version defined in the deployment manifest.

Instance Groups

The deployment manifest can have one or more instance groups. Instance groups collectively provide the distributed system as a whole. An instance group is a logical unit containing the desired components (release jobs) from releases (such as a database service or a web UI app). Here are the aspects of an instance group:

- They are defined in the deployment manifest by the Platform Operator.
- Each is encapsulated on a separate VM.
- They can have *N* number of instances.
- They can be comprised of one or more release jobs from one or more releases.

- Each represents a discrete functionality (such as that of the Cloud Controller or the GoRouter).

A deployed instance group exists on N number of machines. Therefore, an instance group can have multiple deployed instances. Instance groups are based on a defined stemcell, and they execute either a long-running service or a short-running BOSH task known as an errand.[1] Errands are discussed further in "Errand" on page 216.

The operator who writes the deployment manifest decides which instance groups are required for a specific deployment. For example, by default a RabbitMQ deployment has an HAProxy instance group, broker instance group, and server instance group. For a Cloud Foundry deployment, there are numerous different instance groups.

By convention, the instance group name contains only a descriptive name. They can then be striped across different AZs through the AZ configuration described in "AZs" on page 187. The `network`, `vm_type`, and `persistent_disk_type` are defined in the cloud configuration manifest. You must also specify any additional instance group properties.

`Jobs` defines a list of release jobs required to be run on an instance group. Each instance group must be backed by the software from one or more BOSH releases. When defining an instance group, the deployment manifest author must specify which releases make up the component. For example, the `cf-deployment` manifest defines, among other things, a UAA instance group. The UAA instance group currently specifies five release jobs (`consul_agent`, `uaa`, `route_registrar`, `metron_agent`, and `statsd-injector`) obtained from four BOSH releases (`consul`, `uaa`, `routing`, and `loggregator`). Those four BOSH releases each contain packaged software relevant to the UAA:

```
- name: uaa
  ...
  jobs:
  - name: consul_agent
    release: consul
    properties:
    ...
  - name: uaa
    release: uaa
    properties:
    ...
  - name: route_registrar
    release: routing
    properties:
```

---

1 Note that BOSH errands are different from Cloud Foundry Tasks. Errands are finite tasks run by BOSH on a machine; Cloud Foundry Tasks are run by Diego in a container on a Cell machine.

```
    ...
  - name: metron_agent
    release: loggregator
    properties:
    ...
  - name: statsd-injector
    release: loggregator
    properties:
    ...
```

When you BOSH deploy a release (or releases), BOSH creates one or more instance group machines. The BOSH Director communicates with the agent on the instance group machine to execute the commands defined in a control script. The agent currently executes these commands by using that control script. The control script for Linux is currently Monit, an open source process supervision tool (see "Control scripts" on page 194).

The deployed instance group machine contains a directory tree starting at */var/vcap/* and BOSH places release resources (including compiled code), as defined by the deployment manifest, under that directory. BOSH also creates four subdirectories: *jobs*, *packages*, *src*, and *blobs*. These display on instance group machines as */var/vcap/ jobs*, */var/vcap/packages*, */var/vcap/src*, and */var/vcap/blobs*, respectively. These directories directly map to the release job directories that were discussed in "Anatomy of a BOSH Release" on page 192.

Instance groups define the machine's network, vm_type, and any required static IPs along with a persistent disk if required. Additionally, release jobs contain property placeholders, discussed in the section that follows. The deployment manifest author must provide any required property placeholder values.

Properties

During a BOSH deployment, the BOSH Director creates a new machine for an instance group, and places the release resources on that machine. During this process, BOSH begins by reviewing the release job's specification file to see what properties are required. The specification file contains default values that are set for the job's required properties. The properties section defines the properties that the release job requires, as defined by the release job in its specification file. Regardless of what properties are set in the manifest, they will be injected into the job's machine only if they are defined in the specification file.

Properties can currently be set at the job level, instance group level, and global level, as demonstrated here:

```
instance-groups:
  - name: postgres
    jobs:
      - properties:
```

```
    #job level (top priority)

  properties:
    #instance-group level - overrides global properties and overriden by job
    properties

properties:
  #global level
```

When BOSH evaluates the release job, `job level` properties take ultimate precedence. If no `job level` property exists, `instance-group` and `global` properties are used, with `instance-group` properties taking precedence. `instance-group` level and `global`–level properties are being phased out because they can pollute the manifest with complexity. For example, `global` level properties can be accidentally picked up if specified only at the global level and not at the job level. Ideally, the manifest should specify job property information as close to where it is needed, namely the job level. Because nothing gets merged into job-level properties, the properties definition schema remains clean.

BOSH links (discussed in Chapter 10) come into play when you define a property on one job, such as a password, and another job then requires that property. Instead of duplicating the property information across the two jobs (and risking repetition configuration errors), you can use BOSH links to provide this information, as shown in the following example:

```
instance-groups:
  - name: postgres
    jobs:
      - properties:
          #job level (top priority)
          password: ...

  - name: app
    consumes:
      conn: {from postgres}
```

This removes the need to repeat properties in multiple places. BOSH links do not replace properties; they simply aid the consumption of properties between jobs.

Update

The `update` section contains `canaries` and is important for production environments. Canary instances are instances that are updated before other instances. We use them as a fail-fast mechanism, because any update error in a canary instance will terminate the deployment.

Because only canaries are affected before the update stops, problem packages or release jobs are prevented from taking over all instance groups and derailing the entire deployment. The `update` section defines the number of canaries to use during an update, including the maximum number of canaries to be running at any period of time:

```
update:
  canaries: 1
  canary_watch_time: 30000-1200000
  update_watch_time: 5000-1200000
  max_in_flight: 5
  serial: false
```

In this example, `serial: false` means that BOSH will deploy all instance groups at the same time. `serial: true` means that BOSH will deploy a single instance group (the order is based on the order of the instance groups in the deployment manifest) and will not continue to the next instance group until the current `canary` has success-fully finished. `serial: true` is safer (and is the default) because sometimes dependencies exist between instance groups (i.e., the Cloud Controller cannot start if the Cloud Controller database has not been started).

Theoretically, a "well-constructed" release should support deploying jobs in parallel. For example, if the Cloud Controller cannot connect to the Cloud Controller database, the Cloud Controller process will initially fail. However, Monit will try to restart the Cloud Controller process again, some seconds later, until eventually it succeeds in connecting to the database.

You can define `canary` properties both globally and locally. If you specify `canary` properties in the global `update` hash, those properties are applied globally to all instance groups. You can further override or add `canary` properties in an `update` hash that is local to a specific instance group, as demonstrated here:

```
update:
  canaries: 1
  canary_watch_time: 30000-1200000
  max_in_flight: 5
  serial: false
  update_watch_time: 5000-1200000
instance_groups:
- name: consul
...
  update:
    max_in_flight: 1
    serial: true
```

Credentials

Credentials are commonplace in distributed systems. For example, username and password credentials are typically used to protect specific endpoints, such as access to a postgres database or a blobstore, and SSH keys serve as a means of identifying your-self to an SSH server.

BOSH is responsible for generating required credentials. Credential generation is backed by a generic API implementation known as `config-server`, and is currently implemented by a component known as `cred-hub`. The deployment manifest speci-fies the places where credentials are required using a double parentheses syntax `cred-name`. BOSH will then autogenerate and populate those required credentials. Currently, BOSH supports credential generation for the following:

- RSA key (used for the UAA signing key)
- SSH keys
- Certificate
- Password

BOSH achieves credential generation by using its `config-server` API. This API makes it possible for you to extend BOSH to generate different types of credentials without the need to modify the BOSH Director. With the introduction of the `config-server` API, it is now possible to implement automatic credential rotation for all software deployed by the Director. This strengthens Cloud Foundry's security posture significantly.

To use variables generated by BOSH, the manifest must specify where the variables should be interpolated:

```
properties:
  password: ((postgres_password))
```

BOSH generates actual values for these credentials and then inserts the real value in the `postgres_password` placeholder, just before configuration is sent to individual instances.

 BOSH create-env

When you run `$ bosh create-env ...` to create the Director, the CLI has limited ability to generate initial credentials because the Director is not available. The syntax for specifying credentials in the manifest and through the CLI is the same.

In the case of the Director, because it is built from a stemcell, it requires a password for the BOSH agent and SSH keys so that you can connect to the Director VM over SSH. However, the Director manifest also has a Director SSL certificate, blobstore password, and so on, all generated by the BOSH CLI. In the BOSH Director's BOSH release repository, you can inspect the bosh.yml deployment manifest and see place-holders through the deployment manifest for all the required passwords.

As of this writing, work is being done to allow BOSH to generate and manage as well as rotate the required credentials for all the releases that BOSH is responsible for deploying.

Summary

BOSH deploys software to the defined IaaS layer by using a deployment manifest, one or more stemcells, and one or more releases:

- A BOSH deployment consists of a collection of one or more specialized machines known as instance groups.
- An instance group is an individual component such as the GoRouter or Cell that resides on a dedicated machine.
- Instance groups are built from undifferentiated stemcells by layering and config-uring specified release jobs that are obtained from one or more BOSH releases.
- The various instance groups and their specified release jobs are defined by a deployment manifest and deployed by the BOSH Director.
- As implied by the name, each instance group can run several instances.

The Cloud Foundry distributed system as a whole comprises the sum of the deployed instance groups.

## CHAPTER 13

BOSH Components and Commands

For Platform Operators who would like a deeper understanding of how BOSH works, this chapter explores BOSH's internal components, including the individual components and terminology that comprise a BOSH environment. It also introduces some of the fundamental BOSH commands for getting started with BOSH deployments such as Cloud Foundry.

Figure 13-1 gets the ball rolling by providing a visual tour of the components that make up the BOSH ecosystem.

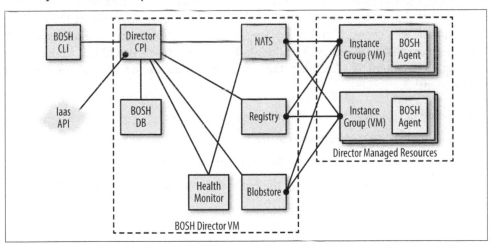

Figure 13-1. BOSH components

The BOSH Director

Deployments are managed by the BOSH Director, a centralized management and orchestration server. To deploy a BOSH release, the release is first uploaded to a BOSH Director along with the appropriate stemcell, and the deployment manifest is set. Upon deployment, the Director then causes the instance group machines (often VMs) requested in the manifest to be allocated and stored, forming a deployment. All interaction with the BOSH Director is through the BOSH CLI.

This is an overview of the process to create a deployment:

1. Create a deployment manifest referencing one or more releases.
2. Through the BOSH CLI, upload stemcells and releases used by the manifest to the BOSH Director.
3. Direct BOSH to the location of the deployment manifest.
4. Initiate a deployment by using the `bosh deploy` command to form a deployment managed by the Director.

A user (or CI/CD pipeline) continues to manage a BOSH deployment through changes to the deployment manifest. In addition to defining the initial deployment, the deployment manifest contains all required information for tracking, managing, and updating the release software layered onto the deployment's machines. After a deployment has been installed, the BOSH Director keeps track of all the associated machines and any attached persistent disks used by the deployment. If the deployment manifest is changed and redeployed, old machines are replaced and updated, but persistent disks are retained and reattached to the newer machines. Updating an existing deployment is effectively the same procedure as for that of the original deployment:

1. Update deployment manifest with necessary changes.
2. Upload any new stemcells or releases.
3. Direct BOSH to the location of the deployment manifest.
4. Initiate a deployment by using the `bosh deploy` command to apply changes to the deployment.

The Director creates actionable tasks:

- By translating commands sent by the Platform Operator through the BOSH CLI
- From scheduled processes like backups or snapshots

- By self-healing through reconciling expected machine state with actual machine state

The Director adds these tasks to the Task Queue. Worker processes then take tasks from the Task Queue to act on them.

Director Blobstore

The Director blobstore is the repository where BOSH stores the uploaded release artifacts and other content. The blobstore stores the source forms of releases and the compiled images of BOSH releases. An operator uploads a release using the BOSH CLI, and the Director inserts either the release tarball or release blobs into the blobstore. When you deploy a release, BOSH orchestrates the compilation of packages and stores the result in the blobstore.

Director Task, Queue, and Workers

A task is a basic unit of work performed by the BOSH Director. Tasks include BOSH commands such as bosh deploy and bosh run errand. You can monitor the task throughout its life cycle and use the bosh vms command to view its status and logs whenever required.

The Task Queue is an asynchronous queue used by the Director and workers to manage tasks. The workers then take tasks from the Task Queue and act upon them.

Director Database

The Director uses a database (currently MySQL) to store information about the desired state of a BOSH deployment. This database includes information about stemcells, releases, and deployments.

Director Registry

When the Director creates or updates a machine, it stores configuration information for the machine in a Registry so that it can be used during the bootstrapping of the machine. The Registry is not required on all IaaS offerings; for example, vSphere does not require it. The Registry is used only for an IaaS that does not allow the machine metadata to be modified after the machine has started (e.g., AWS and OpenStack).

BOSH Agent

An agent is included on every machine that BOSH deploys. The agent is a single process that runs continuously. It listens for instructions from the Director via messages (currently sent via NATS). The agent then executes instructions in response to the messages it receives from the Director.

The agent receives job specifications from the Director and uses them to assign a role or instance group to the machine. These specifications include which packages to install and how jobs should be configured to create the instance group VM. In essence, it is the agent that converts undifferentiated stemcells into the specialized components known as instance groups.

Errand

A BOSH errand is a short-lived BOSH job, defined in a deployment manifest, that the Platform Operator can run several times after a deploy has finished. Example errands include the CATS that you should run after every new Cloud Foundry deployment, and the Cloud Foundry service broker `broker-registrar` and `broker-deregistrar` errands that simplify registering service brokers in a Cloud Foundry deployment.

The Command Line Interface

The CLI is the primary operator interface to BOSH. An operator uses the CLI to interact with the BOSH Director. The BOSH Director then translates those commands and performs actions against the underlying cloud infrastructure. The CLI is typically installed on a machine or VM that can directly communicate with the Director's API; for example, an operator's laptop or a jump box in a data center. The BOSH CLI is what you use to run BOSH commands. For assistance with BOSH commands, you can run `$ bosh help --all` to view the help. We discuss BOSH CLI commands further in "Basic BOSH Commands" on page 221.

The Cloud Provider Interface

A CPI is an API that the Director uses to interact with an IaaS provider to create and manage networks, VMs, and disks. A CPI abstracts the cloud infrastructure from the rest of BOSH, allowing for portability of BOSH releases across different IaaS layers. You can read more about the CPI in "The Cloud Provider Interface" on page 172.

Health Monitor

The Health Monitor uses status and life cycle events received from BOSH Agents to monitor the health of machines. If the Health Monitor detects a problem with a machine, it can send an alert through a notification plug-in, or trigger the Resurrector. The Health Monitor works in the following way:

1. The Health Monitor pings the Director for a list of agents.
2. The Health Monitor listens for pings (currently via NATS) from worker agents.
3. The Health Monitor uses the CPI to contact nonresponding agents.

4. If no response is retrieved, it follows retry logic (it instructs the Director to run the bosh cck command).

Resurrector

If enabled, the Resurrector plug-in automatically re-creates machines identified by the Health Monitor as missing or unresponsive. It uses the same Director API that CLI uses.

Message Bus (NATS)

The Director and the agents communicate through a lightweight publish-subscribe messaging system called NATS. These messages have two purposes:

- To perform the provisioning of instructions to the VMs
- To inform the Health Monitor about changes in the health of monitored processes

You can also use NATS for cross-component communication.

Creating a New VM

To better understand how the BOSH components interact, let's explore what happens when a new machine or VM is created. Figure 13-2 depicts the process, and is followed by a description of each of the numbered stages in the figure.

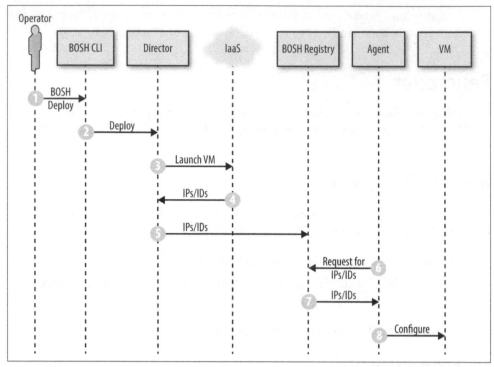

Figure 13-2. BOSH VM creation

1. Through the BOSH CLI, the Platform Operator takes an action such as deploying Cloud Foundry for the first time or scaling up an existing deployment. These specific actions require creating a new machine.

2. The BOSH CLI passes the deployment manifest to the Director. The Director then determines that one or more new machines are needed.

3. The Director uses the CPI to instruct the IaaS to create disks and machines. The CPI communicates with the IaaS and requests that it create a new machine using the defined stemcell image.

4. The IaaS provides the Director with information (IP addresses and IDs) that the BOSH agent requires to configure the VM.

5. The Director updates the BOSH registry with the configuration information for the machine.

6. The BOSH agent is started. The agent is responsible for all machine configuration. It requests the configuration information for the machine from the BOSH registry.

7. The registry responds with IP addresses and IDs.

8. The agent then uses the IP addresses and IDs to configure the machine. As the machine starts, an *init* script starts the BOSH agent. An init (short for initialization) process is the first process started when the system boots. The BOSH agent remains continually running on the machine. Ubuntu-based stemcells use Linux utilities to monitor the BOSH agent using a *runsv service* containing a run script that takes over the init jobs and manages the BOSH agent process. Bootstrapping the BOSH agent deals with all the standard Linux concerns such as creating the vcap user, starting the SSH daemon, and starting the Monit daemon. The BOSH agent also deals with creating disks and networking.

As part of the VM configuration in step 8, BOSH will create disks and set up networking for the VM.

Disk Creation

It is possible to define two different types of storage solutions: ephemeral and persistent disks. These are both in addition to the root machine disk. The distinction between ephemeral and persistent provides the flexibility to use more cost-effective storage for temporary storage requirements and persistent storage for long-lived data.

Within the machine, the BOSH agent checks for the presence of the root disk. By default, all stemcells have 3 GB of root disk (2.5 GB available after system use). The BOSH agent partitions a root filesystem on the root disk.

If an instance group is using an ephemeral disk, two partitions are created: one for *swap* and one for a *tmp* space under */var/vcap/data*. The creation of the disk depends on the IaaS and CPI implementation. For vSphere, the Director creates an ephemeral disk and attaches it to the machine. For AWS and OpenStack, it is the IaaS that creates the disk based on the instance type.

If there is no ephemeral disk, the BOSH agent uses the unused root disk space to create the *swap* and *tmp* partitions. Although the root partition is usually 3 GB, the real disk size is often greater, depending on the instance type, so often some unused space will remain.

Persistent disks are created after the machine has been created. If a persistent disk has been specified in the instance group, the CPI communicates with the IaaS to create a persistent disk and then attaches the persistent disk to the required machine. The CPI communicates with the BOSH agent to inform it about the new disk. The BOSH agent then looks for that disk, mounts it, and creates the */var/vcap/store* for persistent data.

Without the Platform Operator cross-checking, the instance group does not know if the release job requires a persistent disk. For example, you can deploy a Postgres release job without specifying in the deployment manifest that the resulting instance group needs a persistent disk. In that scenario, the release job's start scripts (not the agent) creates the */var/vcap/store* directory, which will reside on the ephemeral disk. Be aware that if the release job does require a persistent disk but no persistent disk was specified by the instance group, */var/vcap/store* will be mounted on the ephemeral disk.

If */var/vcap/store* is mounted on persistent storage, you will not lose your data if the VM is recycled. If */var/vcap/store* is mounted on ephemeral storage and the machine goes away, you will lose your data.

Let's consider three different Cloud Foundry jobs.

Instance groups using an ephemeral disk have a VM with two mounted filesystems; for example:

```
/ mounted on the local VM storage /dev/sda1
/var/vcap/data mounted on ephemeral disk  /dev/sdb2
```

Instance groups that specify a persistent disk will have a third filesystem; for example:

```
/var/vcap/store mounted on /dev/sdc1
```

You can also mount additional directories. One of the Cloud Foundry jobs is a blob-store for an Amazon S3 bucket in AWS. The Cloud Foundry Cloud Controller VM has an additional remote directory:

```
/var/vcap/nfs residing on the blobstore server under /var/vcap/store.
```

Networking Definition

There are three options for setting up networking for the VM:

1. Dynamic
2. Manual
3. VIP

If you have a choice, the recommended approach, as of this writing, is to use manual networks.

The BOSH CLI v2

There is a new v2 BOSH CLI written in Go. It is designed to be significantly faster and more stable than the original BOSH CLI that was written in Ruby. Consistency across different developer environments including Mac OS, Windows, and Linux is of primary importance.

All of the original CLI behavior remains, and most of the commands are the same, but the user experience (UX) has changed slightly, making a few of the older commands redundant. In addition, commands have become hyphenated; for example, `upload release` becomes `upload-release`.

The UX also enforces consistency. For example, you must always specify `-e <my-environment>` and `-d <my-deployment>`. For example, to set the deployment manifest:

```
$ bosh -e <my-director-env> -d <my-deployment> deploy <deployment-name.yml>
```

Specifying the deployment manifest in this manner means that when we invoke other commands such as `BOSH -e <env> cck`, you do not need to download manifests; you need only reference the deployment name. The only time you need a deployment manifest is when you deploy. This is a significant enhancement to overall usability. The `-d` argument is per-deployment context. Commands that are outside of a specific deployment context, such as the generic `cloud-config`, do not require the `-d` argument. Here's an example:

```
$ bosh -e <env> update-cloud-config ./cloud.yml
```

Another key difference between the v1 and v2 CLIs is that the new CLI combines `bosh-init` functionality with the CLI, as shown here:

```
$ bosh create-env ...
```

You can find more information on the BOSH v2 2.0 CLI at the BOSH website (*http://bosh.io/docs/cli-v2.html*).

Basic BOSH Commands

Knowledge of some basic BOSH commands is essential for rudimentary debugging. As discussed in "BOSH Top-Level Primitives" on page 175, a deployment requires three key items: a stemcell, release, and deployment manifest.

To view a list of available commands, use the following:

```
$ bosh -h
```

Before deploying, you will need to upload a release and stemcell by using the following commands:

```
$ bosh -e <env> upload-release <release-location>
$ bosh -e <env> upload-stemcell <stemcell-location>
```

A release file and a stemcell location can be a local file or a remote URI. These two commands upload these artifacts to BOSH's blobstore. In addition to uploading a precompiled release, you can upload a release by uploading a release manifest. When uploading just the manifest, BOSH fetches the release components from a blobstore defined in the release.

Before deploying, you can specify the Director IaaS properties through cloud configuration. To apply the cloud configuration to the BOSH Director, use the update-cloud-config command, as follows:

```
$ bosh -e <env> update-cloud-config ./cloud.yml
```

You can retrieve the current cloud configuration from the BOSH Director and save the output via stdout:

```
$ bosh -e <my-director-env> cloud-config > cloud.yml
```

The deployment manifest is not uploaded to BOSH; rather, it is named via the -d argument. After you have uploaded your stemcell and release, specify the deployment manifest and deploy via:

```
$ bosh -e <env> -d <my-dep> deploy <deployment-name>.yml
```

As mentioned in "Director Task, Queue, and Workers" on page 215, a task is a basic unit of work performed by the Director. You can view the currently running tasks by running the following:

```
$ bosh -e <env> tasks
```

You can monitor task status throughout its life cycle or retrieve the status of previously run tasks:

```
$ bosh -e <env> task <task-number>
```

You can retrieve the logs for any previously run or currently running task:

```
$ bosh -e <env> task <task-number> --debug
```

If you require more advanced troubleshooting, you can view all of the machines in the BOSH environment:

```
$ bosh -e <env> instances
```

And, you can use SSH to access a specific machine:

```
$ bosh -e <env> -d <my-dep> ssh <vm-name>
```

For troubleshooting instance groups, start with this:

```
$ bosh -e <env> -d <my-dep> cck
```

CCK (short for Cloud Check) scans for differences between the desired VM state, as stored in the Director database, and the actual state of the VMs. For each difference the scan detects, bosh cck offers possible repair and recreate options.

Summary

This chapter provided a basic overview of the BOSH components and essential BOSH commands. To recap:

- BOSH deployments are managed by the BOSH Director, a centralized management and orchestration server.
- The BOSH Director comprises a number of subcomponents.
- The BOSH Director manages the machines it deploys via a BOSH agent. The agent residing on BOSH-managed machines is provided by the stemcell.
- Knowledge of some basic BOSH commands is essential for deploying BOSH releases and for rudimentary debugging.

This chapter concludes our deep dive into the BOSH release-engineering tool chain. Now that you are familar with some basic BOSH commands, Chapter 14 focuses on the debugging and logging aspects of running Cloud Foundry.

Debugging Cloud Foundry

As a topic, debugging is nuanced and complex. Debugging any system is a skill. Due to the complexity of both the layered software stack and infrastructure underpinning Cloud Foundry as well as the Cloud Foundry distributed architecture itself, debugging Cloud Foundry is a huge topic. The topic of debugging the Cloud Foundry distributed system deserves an entire book devoted to the subject.

This chapter, although certainly not exhaustive, gives you an introduction to the basic tools and techniques used for debugging the platform. It focuses on some unique potential failure scenarios. With each scenario, I will walk you through the steps, tools, and rationale used to troubleshoot the issue and remedy the situation. The techniques used in these scenarios are valuable and applicable in helping you debug numerous failure scenarios.

The failure scenarios explored in this chapter were constructed with the help of Dan Higham, Principal Engineer and Service Lead at Pivotal. Dan spends his days troubleshooting Cloud Foundry issues on behalf of client companies, and he is an authority on the topic of platform debugging.

Cloud Foundry Acceptance Tests

To validate integrity, Cloud Foundry provides a suite of acceptance tests known as the Cloud Foundry Acceptance Tests, or CATS (*https://github.com/cloudfoundry/cf-acceptance-tests*). You should run these tests after an initial installation to verify that the integrity of the installation. After you deploy Cloud Foundry and it passes CATS, you are most of, if not all, the way there. For this reason, most of this chapter focuses on debugging techniques used to restore a failed instance group (a BOSH-deployed Cloud Foundry component).

Logging

Before you explore debugging-specific failure scenarios, you need to understand how logging works.

The logging system within Cloud Foundry is known as the Loggregator (a combination of log and aggregator). It is the inner voice of the system that informs the operator and developer as to what is happening. You use it to manage the performance, health, and scale of running apps and the platform itself. The Loggregator continually streams logging and metric information. The Loggregator's Firehose provides access to app logs, container metrics (memory, CPU, and disk-per-app instance), some component metrics, and component counter/HTTP events. It provides the same log stream you see when you run $ cf logs APP. The Firehose does not provide component logs. You retrieve component logs through an rsyslog drain.

App logs contain information that is often coerced into events; for example, an app start or app crash event. App logs are streamed to a central location via the Loggregator. The Loggregator system aggregates this information in a structured, usable form, via the Firehose.

App Logging Requirements

An app must conform to the logging guidelines of writing logging information to standard out and standard error. A guidance from 12-Factor App (*https://12factor.net*) is to never log to the local filesystem. Doing so could result in logs that can fill up the disk, causing apps to fail, or the logs might become irretrievable due to the use of an ephemeral disk.

Writing logs to stdout and stderror does not mean that application code needs to invoke System.out.println(); rather it is the log configuration that must support being dumped to stdout. Logging frameworks such as Log4j, slf4j, and many others allow for runtime injection of log outputs. A more robust approach to logging is to use a log drain.

If you want to forward app logs to a syslog endpoint, you can create a user-provided service by using the -l parameter, as shown here:

```
$ cf create-user-provided-service SERVICE-INSTANCE -l SYSLOG-URL
```

If apps log directly to syslog or other logging services, you must establish a Cloud Foundry security group accordingly to expose application access to the endpoint.

You can use the Firehose in different ways. Downstream sinks can use all of the output of the Firehose. If more specific uses are required, such as a requirement to monitor system internals or a requirement to analyze specific user behavior, you can apply a specific *nozzle* to the Firehose.

Nozzles are clients that access the Firehose. As such, they require administrator access to the Cloud Foundry instance. A nozzle needs to have the `doppler.firehose` OAuth scope to be able to connect to the Firehose. Multiple consumers can use a unique `subscription_id` to connect to the Firehose endpoint or a pool of consumer clients can use a common `subscription_id`. If each consumer uses a different `subscription_id`, each consumer with a unique `subscription_id` receives the entire stream and, therefore, all of the messages. If you have multiple consumers with the same `subscription_id`, each consumer will receive a portion of the messages. The portion is roughly the percentage based on the number of consumers with that `subscription_id`; however, the aim is that all data will be distributed evenly among that subscriber's client pool. By default, message delivery is "send once, best effort," therefore, if your consumer is slow at retrieving the messages, Cloud Foundry adds a warning message to the stream and then might drop some messages.

The Firehose does not contain any system component logs. In general, all the system logs are collected by the "syslog aggregator"—meaning that they are pulled out of the rsyslog server on the instance group components. Component/instance group logs need to be connected to a syslog endpoint via the `syslog_daemon` configuration in the Cloud Foundry deployment manifest. If you want only app logs, you can use either the WebSocket endpoint that has all logs for a given app by `$ tail cf logs app name`, or multiple syslog drains.

There is an open source nozzle: `firehose-to-syslog`. Using this nozzle, you can drain logs from the Firehose so that you no longer need to bind your app to a syslog drain. The Firehose-to-syslog applies `cf app name`, `space name`, and `org name` to all the log messages. In addition to applying to the entire Firehose, it adds info to logs (which has other implications).

If you require a Loggregator client library, it is worth checking out NOAA (*http://github.com/cloudfoundry/noaa*). For configuring system logging, you can review the Cloud Foundry docs (*http://bit.ly/2qs6jSr*).

All Cloud Foundry components use Steno logging. Steno is a lightweight, modular logging library written specifically to support Cloud Foundry. It is comprised of three main classes:

Loggers
> The main entry points that consume user input and create and forward structured records on to configured sinks.

Sinks

As the ultimate destination for log records, sinks transform structured records into a strings via formatters and then typically write the transformed string to another transport.

Formatters

These provide a mechanism for converting structured log records into strings.

You can find more information on Steno at the Cloud Foundry GitHub page (*https://github.com/cloudfoundry/steno#from-yaml-file*).

Typical Failure Scenarios

Typically, you will observe errors for three core reasons:

- Issues with configuration
- Issues with infrastructure
- Release job process failures

The rest of this chapter examines the challenges of these three areas by walking you through seven distinct failure scenarios.

Configuration Failures

The typical challenges you will face generally occur when you are deploying a software release. Deploying a release requires configuring properties via a manifest. If you handcraft a deployment manifest, you are likely to encounter configuration (or rather misconfiguration) issues. As discussed in Chapter 5, there are several ways of installing Cloud Foundry. Various tools exist, and currently they all involve a level of complexity. Having a good deployment manifest helps significantly to contend with this problem. However, during the process of constructing that manifest, it is possible to introduce configuration errors.

When dealing with configuration errors, many will be caught by BOSH when you attempt to deploy the misconfigured instance group. For example, if the misconfiguration is significant enough, specific release jobs might fail and BOSH will be unable to configure the specific instance group. When BOSH fails to install a specific instance group (such as a Diego Cell or the GoRouter), it should provide you with some information as to the nature of the failure; thus, this type of failure is relatively easy to resolve.

The real challenge comes when your Cloud Foundry deployment actually deploys successfully but does not behave as you anticipated. Subtle misconfigurations are more difficult to track down. For example, misconfigured credentials that block specific communication flows between two instance groups is challenging because the exhibited behavior (component "A" cannot talk to component "B") can be caused by a variety of reasons. Because of this, checking how a component is configured in the deployment manifest is an important first step in debugging spurious failure scenarios. If configuration is not the issue, the steps outlined in the failure scenarios that follow later in the chapter will help.

Infrastructure Failures

Another core reason for platform failure is infrastructure failure. You have only to look at the recent Amazon S3 outage (*http://tcrn.ch/2qsoNlN*) to see how catastrophic infrastructure outage can be.

Infrastructure failure could be due to anything from an individual process crash to a data center–wide SAN failure. Infrastructure failures are often difficult to troubleshoot because they reside in the depths of the software and infrastructure stack that underpins or supports the platform, such as the network, database, IaaS, and so on. Understanding how the system is structured and then following a logical set of steps, such as those outlined in "Scenario Two: Network Address Translation Instance Deleted (Network Failure)" on page 231, will certainly help.

In addition, it is always worth getting the relevant subject matter expert (SME) involved. If you have connectivity issues, have your network or load balancer SMEs involved. If you have an IaaS issue, ensure that your IaaS operator is involved. From experience, some infrastructure issues exhibit themselves as a platform problem, whereas in reality they are due to a complex infrastructure configuration issue; for example, misconfigured network maximum transmission unit (MTU) settings or high VCPU ready times. Collaboratively working through the issues with the relevant SME is the most pragmatic approach.

Release Job Process Failure

All BOSH release jobs have their processes managed by a monitoring service. For Linux, this is currently Monit. Monit is a powerful tool for dealing with sporadic or random process failures. If a process fails during a deployment, a quick remedy might be possible via connecting to the failed instance group and, as root user, restarting the process in the following way:

```
$ bosh -e <env> -d <dep> ssh <failing_instance_group>
$ sudo su
$ monit summary
$ monit restart <process>
```

When the failed process is running again, you can then try redeploying the failed instance group.

Scenario One: The App Is Not Reachable

After you have deployed Cloud Foundry, you might still experience some issues when pushing an app. This scenario explores how to troubleshoot Diego and a failing app instance.

For this scenario, I used a basic app called "show-headers" (*https://github.com/danhig ham/show-headers*). This is a basic Ruby application that shows the HTML request header information. This scenario assumes that you use an appropriate app that can respond to HTTP requests.

First, push the app, as follows:

```
$ cf push show-headers -n duncheaders
```

When you push an app to Cloud Foundry, upon successful completion of the staging and running tasks, Cloud Foundry should return information about the running app including the URLs that you can use to reach it:

```
urls: duncheaders.cfapps.io
```

By clicking this URL, you should then be able to reach your application endpoint. If, for some reason, going to this URL does not return a response from the app, the first thing to check is whether the route still exists.

The `$ cf routes` command lists all of the routes within the given space:

```
# $ cf routes

space      host          domain       path    apps
myspace    duncheaders   cfapps.io            show-headers-app
```

If your route does not exist, it might have been pruned from the GoRouter's route table. The reasons for pruning a route from the route table are varied. For example, the app might have crashed or there might be a network partition between the Cell running the app and NATS, eventually causing the route to be pruned.

Assuming that there is no problem with the route and the app is still running, the next step is to review logs via `$ cf logs` to see if the app is returning a response. The output of `$ cf logs` should give you a clear indication as to why you cannot reach the app. For example, it could be that an app has crashed and Diego cannot restart it because all Cells are already at capacity.

For basic issues such as a pruned route or a crashed app that Diego cannot restart, `$ cf routes` and `$ cf logs` are the most appropriate steps to begin the troubleshooting process. For a deeper context of output information, run the command `CF_TRACE=true` before the `cf cli` command, as demonstrated here:

```
$ CF_TRACE=true cf logs show-headers-app
```

This scenario has provided you with the steps required for diagnosing why you might not be able to reach a specific app. It is important to note that although a crashed app is an obvious cause, other issues, such as a pruned route, might actually be the issue.

Scenario Two: Network Address Translation Instance Deleted (Network Failure)

This scenario is intended to show you how to debug the platform when various CF CLI commands fail due to infrastructure issues. If you followed the AWS environment setup in Chapter 5, the installation used both public and private subnets.

 Public networks have an internet gateway (edge router) through which you can route traffic from the network to the internet. However, for a VM to make a connection to another node on the internet, the VMs require a public IP so that external nodes can route traffic back. But for VMs on a private network, the private IP is abstracted via NAT. The NAT VM has the public address and the NAT then handles the address translation before handing the traffic on to the internet gateway. Traffic can come into the private network via a load balancer, but internal VMs cannot forge a connection to an external node without using the NAT VM.

To force a failure within the infrastructure, I deleted the NAT instance for the private network. Most private networks will have some kind of NAT gateway so that apps can create a new connection with the outside world. The recommended way for setting up a VPC is with both a public and private subnet. The public subnet contains your jumpbox and management plane, and the private network contains your deployments.

If the NAT instance or NAT gateway goes offline, the components lose their ability to forge a new outbound connection because their internal network address cannot be translated to an externally reachable address. This results in various Cloud Foundry instance groups failing to communicate properly. Apps can still be reached because the inbound connection is from an external Cloud Foundry client calling into the load balancer that fronts the GoRouters. There is nothing in the incoming connection from a client to an application that requires NAT.

This test used the previous basic Ruby app (*https://github.com/danhigham/show-headers*). Here are the steps to repeat this exercise:

1. Use $ cf push to push the app.
2. Stop the AWS NAT instance on the private subnet.

3. Run a command that exercises the CAPI.

For exercising the API, you can create a new user and set the Org role as follows:

```
$ cf create-user user@myorg.com password
$ cf set-org-role user@myorg.com my-org PrgManager
```

The `$ set-org-role` command should then fail. The reason that this specific command fails is because the Cloud Controller is calling back into the UAA via the load balancer (to verify via the UAA database that the new user has adequate permissions to be assigned the `PrgManager` Org role).

Therefore, the Cloud Controller is trying to forge a new outbound connection, which fails because there is no NAT. A logical first debugging step would be to run the command `$ cf ssh show-headers` to connect to the container running the application. The SSH-Proxy establishes a "man-in-the-middle" connection between the GoRouter and the container and so also requires NAT to be working. Therefore, `$ cf ssh` also failed. At this point, it should be clear to an operator that because a number of CAPI commands are failing, there is something fundamentally wrong with the CF CLI.

So how should you debug CF CLI failures? To troubleshoot the `$ cf ssh` command, your first step is to view the logs on Diego's Brain partition by performing the following steps:

1. Using SSH, connect to your jumpbox:

   ```
   $ ssh -i ./aws-cert.pem jumpbox.com
   ```

2. Set the BOSH deployment to your `cf-deployment.yml`:

   ```
   $ bosh deployment cf-deployment.yml
   ```

3. Run `$ bosh ssh` and select the `diego-brain-partition` to view what state the Brain is in.

4. Once on the Brain, change to the log directory:

   ```
   $ cd /var/vcap/sys/log
   ```

5. Follow the logs via `$ tail -f *` (or just tail the `ssh_proxy` log).

6. Back in your workstation terminal, rerun the following:

   ```
   $ cf ssh my-app
   ```

7. Review the log output.

From the output of the log file that follows (taken from the Brain VM at */var/vcap/sys/log/ssh-proxy.stderr.log*), you can see a call to the UAA. As described earlier, this call to the UAA is to ensure that the user in question is a valid CF user, with correct permissions to connect to the app:

```
{"timestamp":"1468599989.856470823","source":"ssh-proxy","message":↵
"ssh-proxy.cf-authenticate.exchange-access-code-for-token.↵
request-failed","log_level":2,"data":{"error":"Post↵
 https://uaa.my-cf.com/oauth/token: dial tcp 52.50.20.6:443:↵
 i/o timeout","session":"63.1"}}
...
{"timestamp":"1468599996.759604692","source":"ssh-proxy","message":↵
"ssh-proxy.authentication-failed","log_level":2,"data":{"error":↵
"Authentication failed","user":↵
"cf:743e63b9-4343-4179-b0d8-8e67175b091f/0"}}
```

From here, because components such as the Cloud Controller or the Brain are unable to call out and back to other components such as the UAA, we can deduce the following:

- Either those target components are offline (something that is easy to check by using the command $ bosh ... cloud-check or by looking at the status of the VMs in your IaaS), or
- There is a networking issue causing traffic not to reach the final destination.

In this manufactured scenario, there is a networking issue due to NAT not being available. Networking and traffic routing issues can be caused by many things, such as your load balancer configuration, expired or invalid certificates, the MTU configuration, or invalid security group policies. When you identify a networking-related issue, if the cause is not obvious after rudimentary debugging, it is worth reaching out to your networking SME to help you troubleshoot further.

The key takeaway here is that networking- and infrastructure-related issues can manifest themselves in multiple and sometimes extremely complex ways. For example, in this scenario, anything within the private network that uses the NAT VM will fail. Therefore, the failure is manifested across multiple components and several CF CLI calls. This issue did not just affect apps calling to external services; it also affected internal processes hair-pinning back into the load balancer. Whenever you observe several components failing—often for seemingly unspecified or unrelated issues—it is often an indication of an underlying infrastructure or networking issue.

Networking Tooling

dig and nslookup are valuable tools for assessing how a specific URL resolves. dig resolves the URL by using the actual nameserver that holds the DNS record, such as in the following example:

```
;; ANSWER SECTION:
duncheaders.cfapps.io. 60 IN A 54.86.159.28
duncheaders.cfapps.io. 60 IN A 52.72.73.102
```

nslookup resolves the URL based on how your machine resolves addresses (e.g., resolve.conf):

```
Non-authoritative answer:
Name: duncheaders.cfapps.io
Address: 52.72.73.102
Name: duncheaders.cfapps.io
Address: 54.86.159.28
```

To connect directly to the SSH server (in place of using cf ssh), you can use netcat:

```
nc ssh.mycf.com 2222
```

Scenario Three: Security Group Misconfiguration That Blocks Ingress Traffic

As discussed in "Scenario Two: Network Address Translation Instance Deleted (Network Failure)" on page 231, networking issues can trip you up at any point. In that scenario, you explored a north-south network issue (north-south being the traffic entering and exiting the network). This scenario reviews east-west traffic (the traffic between components within a specific network).

AWS employs a construct of security groups. A security group is effectively a layer above the networking stack that is typically applied to a VM. It acts as a virtual firewall for your deployed instance groups or VMs, giving you the ability to control the subnet's inbound and outbound traffic. Security groups are vital for segregating east-west network traffic between different subnets. They are used to impose communication restrictions from the VM to other components. For example, a VM attached to a developer-centric security group might not be allowed access to a production database residing in a services subnet.

However, if you misconfigure security groups, the Cloud Foundry components might not be able to communicate with each other in the required way. In "Scenario Two: Network Address Translation Instance Deleted (Network Failure)" on page 231, we wanted to connect to a container via SSH. When you use SSH to connect to a container, you, as the SSH client, are trying to establish an SSH connection from your jumpbox residing on the management subnet to the ssh-proxy component residing in the private Cloud Foundry subnet. The load balancer typically resides in a public network (either the management network or its own dedicated subnet) and forwards traffic to the components in the private Cloud Foundry subnet. The load balancer and jumpbox typically reside in a public subnet because they require an externally routable IP and direct access and interaction by the Cloud Foundry users or operators.

The load balancer and management components should have an applied security group, configured with specific ingress rules. Table 14-1 lists those ingress firewall rules that control the traffic to your load balancer.

Table 14-1. AWS ELB security group used to define firewall rules to control load balancer ingress traffic

Type	Protocol	Port range	Source
ALL TCP	TCP (6)	ALL	10.0.16.0/24 #Allowing ingress from any component on private subnet
ALL UDP	UDP (17)	ALL	10.0.16.0/24 #Allowing ingress from any component on private subnet
SSH (22)	TCP (6)	22	0.0.0.0/0
HTTP (80)	TCP (6)	80	0.0.0.0/0
HTTPS (443)	TCP (6)	443	0.0.0.0/0
Custom TCP rule	TCP (6)	4443	0.0.0.0/0
HTTP* (8080)	TCP (6)	8080	0.0.0.0/0

After you have installed Cloud Foundry, you can alter the 0.0.0.0/0 source (allowing traffic from anywhere) to be more restrictive if you desire finer control over traffic reaching Cloud Foundry. The ELB security group governs external access to Cloud Foundry from apps such as the CF CLI and app URLs.

Egress Traffic

A point to note on egress traffic is that most networking teams I have worked with have no issue allowing all egress traffic to leave the network to anywhere. Ingress traffic, however, is more tightly regulated.

In addition, to achieve an SSH connection, the security group applied to the load balancer requires the following custom ingress TCP rule:

```
Port Range 2222 from source 0.0.0.0/0
```

However, setting this rule on the load balancer security group is not enough. When running cf ssh my-app, you will still encounter an error opening the SSH connection because the load balancer tries to pass on the ssh-connection to the ssh-proxy instance group. The ssh-proxy instance group resides in the Cloud Foundry subnet. Therefore, to allow the load balancer to connect to the GoRouter, you must add the load balancer security group (LBSG) to the ingress of the Cloud Foundry security group. The Cloud Foundry security group defines the security group policies for the Cloud Foundry components. Therefore, the security group in which the ssh-proxy resides requires the additional following custom TCP rule:

```
Port Range 2222 from source <LOAD-BALANCER-SECURITY GROUP>
```

Figure 14-1 shows the required traffic flow between the management subnet and the Cloud Foundry subnet.

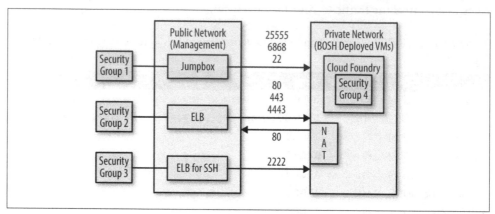

Figure 14-1. Security Group Configuration between the management subnet and the BOSH/Cloud Foundry subnet

This scenario highlights the importance of establishing the correct networking configuration to allow for the required east-west component traffic.

Scenario Four: Invoking High Memory Usage That Kills a Container

As discussed in "CGroups" on page 148, Cloud Foundry uses cgroups to constrain and limit container resources. Some resources, such as disk usage, will simply be capped on exhaustion. This means that you can reach the limit and the container and app will carry on running. However, even though your app is still running, because the disk limit cannot be exceeded, any further disk writes will fail. In essence, your app will still run, but it might not deliver the desired behavior.

Other resource violations, such as memory usage, will cause the container to fail. This is because the app behavior can be significantly and adversely affected by memory starvation, and therefore a safer action is to simply shut down the container and flag the issue. You can track the issue by invoking `$ cf events` and inspecting the log output.

It is possible to misconfigure the required memory limits for the container, or worse, you might have a bug in your app that exposes a memory leak over time. Both of these events can trigger the destruction of a container. The version of `downloader` `app` in Example 14-1 writes an Ubuntu disk image to a file and then tries to open it, reading the file into memory, resulting in a significant amount of memory usage beyond 1 GB.

Example 14-1. Write an Ubuntu disk image to a file

```
#downloader app`

require "open-uri"

run Proc.new { |env|

 `wget http://mirror.pnl.gov/releases/16.04/ubuntu-16.04-server-amd64.iso`

 file = File.open("ubuntu-16.04-server-amd64.iso", "rb")
 contents = file.read

 [200, {"Content-Type" => "text/html"}, [contents.length]]
}
```

On a terminal, use $ cf push to push the app and then, using the command-line tool watch, monitor app events via the $ cf events command:

```
$ cf push <downloader>
$ watch cf events <downloader>
```

Click the app URL to force the *iso* download and memory usage. You should see the out-of-memory error depicted in Figure 14-2.

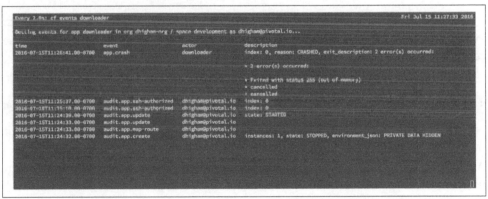

Figure 14-2. Out-of-memory error

For scenarios in which you have an unexpected memory leak or an out-of-memory event, the first step to debugging them is to open an SSH connection to the container by using the $ cf ssh command so that you can inspect what is happening:

```
$ cf ssh downloader
```

When you're inside the container, you can follow traditional out-of-memory debugging techniques such as running a profiling tool or triggering a memory heap dump. In this case, simply running $ top on the container to monitor memory usage and using $ wget to view the running process should be sufficient to indicate the issue.

However, you might have an additional challenge if you are running several app instances. If only one instance of the running app is crashing, you will need to target a specific container. The important question here is how you determine the specific container exhibiting the issue when running multiple app instances. For example, I have observed some rare cases in which an app fails only on a specific Cell. In these scenarios, to reveal what Cell hosts a specific container, I pushed Spring Music (*https://github.com/scottfrederick/spring-music*).

A typical user scenario is to push two different versions of the same app. Another scenario might be to troubleshoot a specific instance of a single app running multiple instances. In either scenario, the troubleshooting steps presented here are the same.

The first instance group you should inspect is the GoRouter. The GoRouter provides a list of the Cell IP addresses to which it forwards app traffic. From your jumpbox, run the $ bosh... vms command to discover the IP address of the GoRouter:

```
$ bosh -e <env> -d <deployment> vms

router is running on *.*.*.* ip address
```

The IP address of the GoRouter will be used later for querying the router status.

Next, use $ bosh... ssh to connect to the GoRouter:

```
$ bosh -e <env> -d <deployment> ssh <GoRouterVM>
```

When on the router, you can query the router status port. To do this, navigate to the *config* directory:

```
$ cd /var/vcap/jobs/gorouter/config
```

This directory contains the *gorouter.yml* file, which you can inspect by using the command-line tool more:

```
$ more gorouter.yml
```

At the top of this file, you can view the port number on which the GoRouter is running as well as the username and password for the status port:

```
---

status:
 port: 8080
 user: router_status
 pass: "edf0d4413ed727c6416e"
```

With this information you can use the curl command to reveal the GoRouter status port:

```
$ curl http://<user><pass>@<ROUTER IP ADDRESS>:8080/routes | python -m json.tool
```

The reason you looked up the GoRouter IP address earlier is because the GoRouter status does not run on the loopback address, so you need to run the `curl` command using the actual router IP address. For ease of reading the JSON output from the preceding command, you can use a JSON formatter known as JQ. When reviewing the output, you can clearly see the two cells hosting the Spring Music app:

```
1:48]
"spring-music-2-precentorial-abnormalcy.paas.high.am": [
    {
        "address": "10.0.16.27:60014",
        "ttl": 0
    }
],
"spring-music-dacryagogue-eyebright.paas.high.am": [
    {
        "address": "10.0.16.25:60024",
        "ttl": 0
    }
]
```

This JSON snippet reveals where your app instances are running, including the IP address of the two Cells (10.0.16.27 and 10.0.16.25) running your two app instances. The two ports (60014 and 60024) map to the containers running on the Cells. At this point, you know the Cells that are running your app instances, but you still need to correlate specific app instances with their respective containers. You can discover the containers that run your app by using a powerful tool known as Veritas.

Veritas (*https://github.com/pivotal-cf-experimental/veritas*) is a CLI for getting at Diego's truth. Follow the instructions on the Veritas GitHub page to use it. Veritas commands must include the location of the Diego BBS server. The BBS is not typically publicly routable, so you will need to run Veritas from a VM in the same subnet as the Diego Cells. On the private network, you can find the BBS at *https://bbs.service.cf.internal:8889*. Diego's internal DNS resolution (as of this writing, provided by Consul) will be able to resolve the BBS internal IP addresses.

Use $ `bosh ssh` to connect to one of the preceding Cells and then run the following:

```
$ pushd $HOME
  $ wget https://github.com/pivotal-cf-experimental/veritas \
  /releases/download/latest/veritas -O ./veritas
  $ chmod +x ./veritas

  $ echo "export PATH=$PATH:$PWD" > veritas.bash
  $ echo "export DROPSONDE_ORIGIN=veritas" >> veritas.bash
  $ echo "export DROPSONDE_DESTINATION=localhost:3457" >> veritas.bash
  $ ./veritas autodetect >> veritas.bash
  $ ./veritas completions >> veritas.bash

  $ source veritas.bash
$ popd
```

You will need to export the following environment variables to avoid having to specify them on every command invocation. For example, the following values configure these environment variables correctly on a BOSH-deployed Diego Cell VM:

```
$ export BBS_ENDPOINT=https://bbs.service.cf.internal:8889; \
$ export BBS_CERT_FILE=/var/vcap/jobs/rep/config/certs/bbs/client.crt; \
$ export BBS_KEY_FILE=/var/vcap/jobs/rep/config/certs/bbs/client.key
```

After running this once, you can simply source ~/veritas.bash when you log in to the Cell again. Now, you can simply run $ ./veritas dump-store to view all the IDs of the LRPs and the GUIDs for the processes running on the Cell. The output of this command queries the BBS database and therefore it will provide information for all Cells, as shown in Figure 14-3.

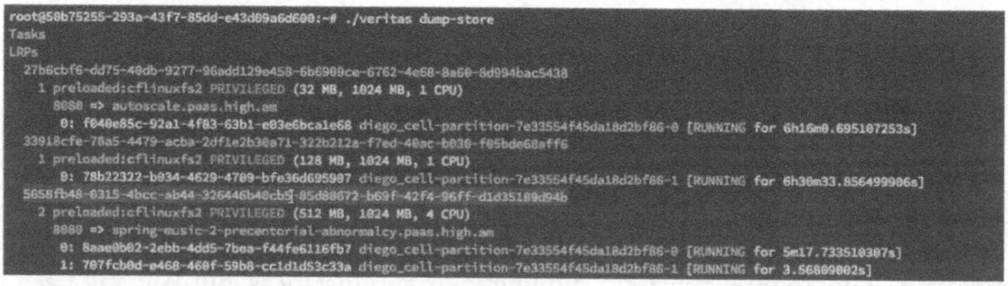

Figure 14-3. Veritas dump-store output

The first part of $ top GUID contains the app process GUID. The app GUID is the same across all instances, but the instance GUID is unique per instance. Because we scaled the spring-music-2 app to two instances, you can view two instances of the same app.

You can check the app GUID by running $ cf app springmusic-2 --guid (in this case, it is 5658fb48-0315-4bcc-ab44-326446b40cb5). By reviewing the output of $ ./veritas dump-store you can locate the specific app GUID and see exactly what Cell partition the app is running on. Finally, you can iterate through your instances via an SSH connection to the container with the CF CLI command:

```
$ cf shh app -i 0
$ cf shh app -i 1
...
```

After you're in the container, you can check what Cell you are on; the preceding command will show you the specific container ID in which you are running. There might be times when you do not want to use $ cf ssh because it does not allow root access. For cases in which you want to edit something that requires root permissions (e.g., resolve.conf), you need to go into the container via the Cell. Here's how to do that:

1. Use `$ bosh... ssh` to connect to the Cell based on the cell-partition as output from `./veritas dump-store`.

2. Run the following command:

   ```
   $ sudo su -
   ```

3. Change directory:

   ```
   $ cd /var/vcap/data/garden/depot
   ```

4. Review the list of containers running on the Cell:

   ```
   $ ls -lart
   ```

5. Grep the process list searching for the app ID and find the container by using the following:

   ```
   $ ps aux | grep <app-id>
   ```

This will show the specific container depot ID (e.g., lksdjlkahjs).

Then, you can change the directory into that container:

```
$ cd /var/vcap/data/garden/depot/lksdjlkahjs
$ ./bin/wsh
```

`$ ./bin/wsh` puts you into the container as root. Between the two approaches of discovering and logging on to a container, it is possible to locate all specific containers and Cells on which your apps are running. You can then either use `$ cf ssh` or `$ bosh ssh` to connect to the container to undertake any further debugging that might be required.

This scenario has provided you with the various steps and tools to first locate where your apps are running and then access the specific containers running your apps. These steps are crucial for app debugging for apps running within the platform.

Scenario Five: Route Collision

This scenario looks at the effects of a route collision due to the system and app domains being the same. Even though Cloud Foundry allows you to use the same domain for both system components and apps, it is strongly advised that you have different domains to separate these concerns. This was discussed in "Setting Up Domains and Certificates" on page 62. If both sys and app domains are the same, in theory, a developer could accidentally push an app with the same hostname as a system component, causing catastrophic routing complications.[1]

---

1 After this scenario was documented, certain domains and routes are now protected by CAPI to avoid this potential issue. Nonetheless, because this scenario provides valuable debugging steps, I decided to leave it in.

As of this writing, for simplicity, cf-deployment manifest generation scripts use only one domain for both system and apps. This is currently under review.

Creating this scenario allows us to demonstrate how you track down the specific Org and Space to which a route is mapped. This debugging process can be useful for other reasons; for example, discovering who else in your business is using a domain that you would like to use.

Components like the Cloud Controller register their `api` routes via the RouteRegistrar. We can then register the same `api` domain for our `show-headers` app, as follows:

```
$ cf push show-headers -n api
```

When a Cloud Foundry user registers a reserved hostname for his app (e.g., `api.mycf.com`), the GoRouter round-robins between the original Cloud Controller component and the new app. This scenario will typically be identified by getting more than one response for the same call. Curl the route information endpoint:

```
$ CF_TRACE=true curl http://api.mycf.com/v2/info
```

This shows the round-robin between two different calls: one to the Cloud Controller and one to the app:

```
MacBook-Pro:~ user$ curl http://api.mycf.com/v2/info
GATEWAY_INTERFACE: CGI/1.1↵
HTTP_ACCEPT: */*↵
HTTP_CONNECTION: close↵
HTTP_HOST: api.mycf.com↵
HTTP_USER_AGENT: curl/7.43.0↵
HTTP_VERSION: ↵
HTTP/1.1↵
HTTP_X_CF_APPLICATIONID: b4345d46-de57-4606-98fe-839212d52554↵
HTTP_X_CF_INSTANCEID: b455b4b6-946c-445f-5c69-18405f3212fb ↵
HTTP_X_FORWARDED_FOR: 50.53.67.65, 10.0.0.110↵
HTTP_X_FORWARDED_PORT: 80↵
HTTP_X_FORWARDED_PROTO: http↵
HTTP_X_REQUEST_START: 1468619218990↵
HTTP_X_VCAP_REQUEST_ID: f32aece5-d78a-4f88-714f-5c5e9f15a386↵
PATH_INFO: /v2/info↵
QUERY_STRING:
  ...

USER: vcap↵
VCAP_APPLICATION: {"application_id":"b4345d46-de57-4606-98fe-839212d52554",↵
"application_name":"show-headers","application_uris":["api.mycf.com"],↵
"application_version":↵
"9fea48ca-cb9c-4895-a31b-eb5c83b60841","host":"0.0.0.0",↵
```

```
"instance_id":"b455b4b6-946c-445f-5c69-18405f3212fb","instance_index":0,"limits"
:{"disk":1024,"fds":16384,"mem":1024},"name":"show-headers",
"port":8080,"space_id":"01094679-1d83-4063-ad03-e82b5df05eb1","space_name":
"test","uris":["api.paas.high.am"],"users":null,"version":
"9fea48ca-cb9c-4895-a31b-eb5c83b60841"}
VCAP_SERVICES: {}_: /home/vcap/app/vendor/bundle/ruby/2.2.0/bin/bundle
_ORIGINAL_GEM_PATH: /home/vcap/app/vendor/bundle/ruby/2.2.0:
```

```
MacBook-Pro:~ user$ curl http://api.mycf.com/v2/info
{"name":"","build":"","support":"https://support.pivotal.io", "version":0,
"description":"","authorization_endpoint": "https://login.api.mycf.com",
"token_endpoint":"https://uaa.api.mycf.com", "min_cli_version":"6.7.0",
 "min_recommended_cli_version":"6.11.2","api_version":"2.54.0",
"app_ssh_endpoint":"ssh.api.mycf.com:2222", "app_ssh_host_key_fingerprint":
"ac:2f:c7:96:9f:c3:0c:44:a3:15:bf:3a:8e:89:2c:8e",
 "app_ssh_oauth_client":"ssh-proxy", "logging_endpoint":
"wss://loggregator.api.mycf.com:4443", "doppler_logging_endpoint":
"wss://doppler.api.mycf.com:4443"}
```

From this point on, Cloud Foundry will not function properly because any request via the CF CLI will typically involve more than one call to the Cloud Controller, and therefore whenever you come across the rouge app, instead of CAPI, the request will fail.

So, after discovering this issue, the next step you need to take is to discover the offending app. Using Veritas as described in "Scenario Four: Invoking High Memory Usage That Kills a Container" on page 236, you can retrieve the app GUID associated with the route. If you happen to know the Space where the app is running, you can verify the app has the conflicting route by using $ cf apps to list all apps residing within that Space. However, in a larger deployment, it might be more difficult to track the specific app down by just going to the Spaces. Imagine an enterprise with several hundred Spaces. In this case, you can use Veritas to find the app associated with the conflicting route by doing the following:

1. Connect via SSH into the first Cell and follow the Veritas steps as described in "Scenario Four: Invoking High Memory Usage That Kills a Container" on page 236.

2. Using Veritas, find the app ID that is mapped to the offending route. Figure 14-4 shows an example of this.

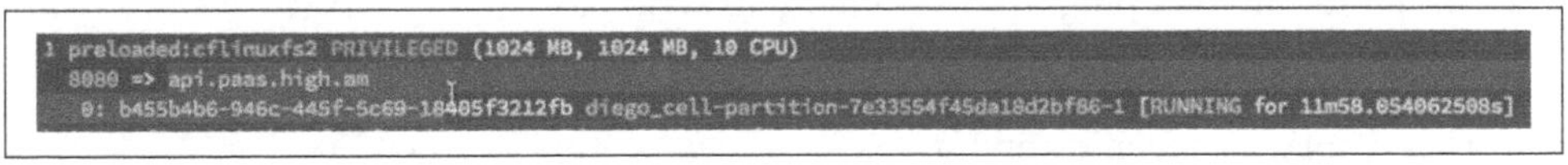

Figure 14-4. App ID mapped to the system route api.pass.high.am

If you simply kill the process by destroying the container, Cloud Foundry will restart the process. You will need to issue a curl request to delete the app (as cf admin):

```
$ cf curl -X DELETE /v2/app/<APP GUID>
```

Make sure that you explicitly address this command to the Cloud Controller. You might need to run it a couple of times in the scenario we described previously because the Cloud Controller route was mapped to both the Cloud Controller and a spurious app. From this point on, Cloud Foundry and the Cloud Controller should be back to working as designed.

It is often invaluable to be able to pull information from the Cloud Controller. The Cloud Foundry community has produced some basic scripts for pulling user information from the Cloud Controller, such as report.py (*http://bit.ly/2qJ4EnG*). However, for power users, Cloud Controller has its own dedicated console that you can use for power debugging. This tool is Interactive Ruby (IRB) for the Cloud Controller, and uses a Ruby library called pry ruby, a tool for interactive consoles. Here's how to access it:

1. Connect via SSH to the Cloud Controller.

2. Change the directory as follows:

    ```
    $ cd /var/vcap/jobs/cloud_controller_ng/bin
    ```

3. Run $ ./console.

This is not often referred to, because you can do significant damage to your Cloud Foundry installation if you use this tool incorrectly. The advantage of using interactive Ruby is that it supports data access through an exhaustive set of contexts. For example, typing VCAP::CloudController provides the context for the current scope. All models within that scope then output with a capital letter. From that scope, you can then do basic searches. Suppose that you want to repeat the previously described process of finding an app associated with a specific route. In this example, let's pick our previous show_headers route:

1. Run a query against the model as follows:

    ```
    $ Route.find.(:host => show-headers) # list all known active routes
    ```

    This displays a specific route ID.

2. Search for the mapping of this route ID to an app:

    ```
    $ RoutemMpping.find.(:rout_id => <ROUTE ID>)
    ```

    This displays a specific app ID.

3. Search for the actual app of this app ID:

    ```
    $ App.find(:id => <APP ID>)
    ```

This lists the app associated with the app ID that was mapped to the show-headers route.

4. Set this output to a local variable app:

```
$ app = App.find(:id => <APP ID>)+++
```

5. Search this variable for the methods, or a specific method, that can act on it:

```
$ app.methods.grep /delete/
```

6. Sure enough, the delete method exists. So calling that method on an app will delete the app. There is one caveat here: you can only delete the app after you first delete route mapping:

```
$ RoutemMpping.find.(:route_id => <ROUTE ID>).delete
```

Routing is a powerful capability with Cloud Foundry. This scenario has provided you with the required tools and steps for resolving any routing issues within the platform.

Scenario 6: Release Job Process Failures

As discussed in Chapter 11, BOSH releases are comprised of release jobs. The release jobs result in processes running on a machine based on how a specific instance group is configured by the deployment manifest. You can construct a specific instance group from several release jobs obtained from one or more BOSH releases. Under certain scenarios, a misconfiguration of the release job properties in the deployment manifest can result in the job process not starting properly. If the process fails, use Monit (or an equivalent process monitor), which will first try to restart the process. If the retries are unsuccessful, Monit will report the failure to the BOSH Director and the deployment will fail.

Another scenario might be that the process is configured perfectly, but for some reason, the process still did not start properly, or the process might have run and then crashed later on. In either case, it is a useful skill to diagnose the instance group component that is failing and then review any specific processes on that instance group that could be causing that failure. To demonstrate this scenario, we removed the rootfs file system from the Diego Cell, as illustrated in Figure 14-5.

```
- name: diego-cell
  templates:
   - name: rep
     release: diego
   - name: consul_agent
     release: cf
   - name: garden
     release: garden-linux
    - name: rootfses
      release: diego
   - name: metron_agent
     release: cf
  instances: 1
  resource_pool: cells
  networks:
   - name: default
     default: [dns, gateway]
```

Figure 14-5. Commenting-out Diego rootfs

If you do this and then redeploy Cloud Foundry, you will notice that the deployment of the Diego Cell instance group fails. To troubleshoot this, you can do the following:

1. Connect via SSH to the failing Cell machine using $ `bosh... ssh`.

2. Run $ `monit summary` to view any relevant log files.

Monit provides a view of all the running job processes. Using Monit we can start, restart, and stop processes. Here, we can see that the Cell's Rep process is not running:

```
root@3af8d775-12a1-4ac0-ad52-d679950554d6:~# monit summary
The Monit daemon 5.2.5 uptime: 10m

Process 'rep'                       not monitored
Process 'consul_agent'              running
Process 'garden'                    running
Process 'metron_agent'             running
System 'system_localhost'           running
```

Because we have identified an issue with the Cell's Rep, the next step is to inspect the Rep's log:

```
bosh_vm:/var/vcap/sys/log/rep $ tail -f *
```

When looking at the Rep's log, we can clearly see the issue causing the process and, therefore, the entire deployment to fail:

```
{"timestamp":"1471029528.793029070","source":"rep","message":↵
"rep.exited-with-failure", "log_level":2,"data":{"error":"Exit trace for group:↵
\ngarden_health_checker exited with error: repository_fetcher: stat file: lstat↵
/var/vcap/packages/rootfs_cflinuxfs2/rootfs:↵
no such file or directory\ncontainer-metrics-reporter↵
```

```
exited with nil\nhub-closer exited with nil\nmetrics-reporter exited with↵
nil\ndebug-server exited with nil\n"}}
```

We can see that the log complains that the Rep expects a certain file—/var/vcap/
packages/rootfs_cflinuxfs2/rootfs—and the process fails because no such file or
directory exists. Therefore, when we inspect the Cell instance group in the manifest,
we can quickly identify that the rootfs has been commented out. Adding these two
lines back into the manifest and redeploying Cloud Foundry fixes this issue:

```
release: garden-linux
#      - name: rootfses
#          release: diego
```

This scenario has explored a release job process failure. Although this might look like
a contrived issue, it is entirely reasonable to misconfigure a release job property
within your manifest. These types of misconfiguration result in failed processes and
therefore a failed deployment. Using the steps just described will help you pinpoint
the exact failure, allowing you to remedy the issue.

Scenario 7: Instance Group Failure

Every once in a while, the IaaS underpinning your platform might do something
undesirable, causing a specific VM to die. If BOSH does not bring this VM back for
some reason, your platform can experience issues.

VM Availability

Although BOSH can expertly and reliably bring VMs back, there
are cases where VM resurrection might not happen. An obvious
scenario is when the BOSH Resurrector is deliberately turned off.
A more subtle case might occur when you are using shared infrastructure. Between the VM failing and restarting, another VM
could be started by someone else using the IaaS. If the IaaS reaches
capacity from the new non-Cloud Foundry VM, all future VMs
(BOSH-managed and otherwise) will fail until extra capacity is
added. It is always best to run Cloud Foundry in a dedicated environment such as a set of dedicated vCenter Clusters or a dedicated
AWS VPC.

To demonstrate this scenario, we use $ bosh... ssh to connect to the NATS VM
and then run $ monit stop nats to stop the NATS process.

By using Monit to stop the process, it will not report the lack of a running process to
BOSH, because it has been told explicitly that the process should be stopped. If we
then look at the general state of the VMs by using $ bosh... vms, we can see that all
the instance groups that depend on NATS are failing, as depicted in Figure 14-6.

```
Director task 66

Task 66 done

+----------------------------------------------------------------------+---------+-----+---------+--------------+
| VM                                                                   | State   | AZ  | VM Type | IPs          |
+----------------------------------------------------------------------+---------+-----+---------+--------------+
| clock-global/0 (1419b167-dd27-48c7-970b-699f4dd0133d)                | running | n/a | common  | 10.0.16.14   |
| cloud-controller/0 (24bb6448-3326-44c8-b770-95aa7264df02)            | failing | n/a | common  | 10.0.16.13   |
| cloud-controller-worker/0 (c2dbf92a-7cd3-4490-8b02-baa34f471b61)     | running | n/a | common  | 10.0.16.15   |
| collector/0 (4b5bae4e-7dae-41ba-b4a7-2f1f5947e2c9)                   | running | n/a | common  | 10.0.16.16   |
| consul/0 (b2a1d8b3-690f-4e28-baed-44f3177b4f48)                      | running | n/a | common  | 10.0.16.4    |
| diego-brain/0 (4d7d2402-8cdb-4173-a876-99e89b0f9089)                 | running | n/a | common  | 10.0.16.18   |
| diego-cell/0 (a98866ea-2225-4b63-81b5-c813cc54ba5f)                  | running | n/a | cells   | 10.0.16.19   |
| diego-database/0 (874ed422-e2c9-41d4-893a-593803e2c274)              | running | n/a | database| 10.0.16.12   |
| doppler/0 (304cc2a4-8b77-49dc-bd1a-4a4dcf79231c)                     | running | n/a | common  | 10.0.16.22   |
| etcd/0 (dcfd19f0-405a-4a30-a8ef-717e98bcb576)                        | running | n/a | common  | 10.0.16.7    |
| haproxy/0 (37531fa4-4aca-4171-8a73-010a05c9a58d)                     | running | n/a | common  | 10.0.16.11   |
|                                                                      |         |     |         | 13.93.236.69 |
| loggregator-trafficcontroller/0 (6481e455-6fb3-4213-8eab-98e1e93f4d1d)| failing | n/a | common  | 10.0.16.23   |
| mysql/0 (b9701502-cce9-4782-ad64-9586b25c3d27)                       | running | n/a | database| 10.0.16.9    |
| mysql-proxy/0 (b7869102-e39c-49f3-98bd-3fe3cc3bc507)                 | running | n/a | common  | 10.0.16.10   |
| nats/0 (9b971450-1517-45fe-8c32-29334a95a3ff)                        | failing | n/a | common  | 10.0.16.5    |
| nfs/0 (d6dba1b5-bb0b-44d0-8f27-bf03a846199b)                         | running | n/a | common  | 10.0.16.8    |
| router/0 (195be1f5-4cbe-443a-8b86-f9ba7ec91b95)                      | failing | n/a | common  | 10.0.16.6    |
| uaa/0 (ab530bcb-e686-4934-915c-400af531df92)                         | failing | n/a | common  | 10.0.16.17   |
+----------------------------------------------------------------------+---------+-----+---------+--------------+

VMs total: 18
pivotal@myjumpboxd57hp2zsayoyy:~$ 
```

Figure 14-6. Instance groups failing due to failed NATS

A number of instance groups are now failing. This is because all of those components (Cloud Controller, Loggregator, router, and UAA) depend on NATS. Because we know that all those VMs depend on NATS and the NATS instance group has no further dependencies, it is tempting to jump straight onto the NATS VM for further debugging. However, in the interests of investigating a more thorough debugging path, let's assume that we do not know the root cause at this time.

You would most likely first detect errant behavior when you run a basic command against the Cloud Controller, such as $ cf apps. This returns a 503 - service unavailable error because the Cloud Controller process has failed. Therefore, a good starting point for troubleshooting would be to use $ bosh... ssh to connect to the Cloud Controller.

When you're on the VM, use $ sudo -su to become root and then run $ monit summary. This produces the output shown in Figure 14-7.

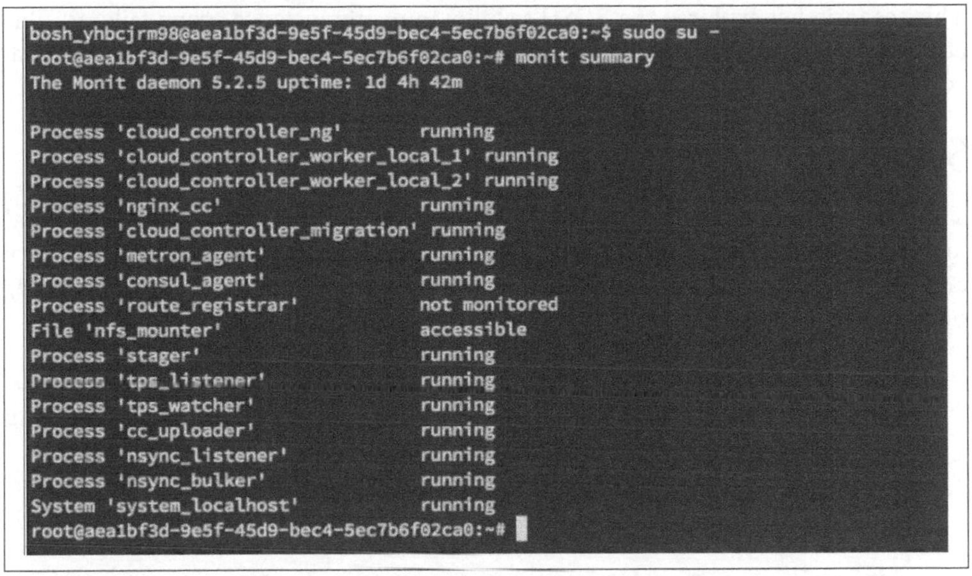

```
bosh_yhbcjrm98@aea1bf3d-9e5f-45d9-bec4-5ec7b6f02ca0:~$ sudo su -
root@aea1bf3d-9e5f-45d9-bec4-5ec7b6f02ca0:~# monit summary
The Monit daemon 5.2.5 uptime: 1d 4h 42m

Process 'cloud_controller_ng'          running
Process 'cloud_controller_worker_local_1' running
Process 'cloud_controller_worker_local_2' running
Process 'nginx_cc'                      running
Process 'cloud_controller_migration'   running
Process 'metron_agent'                  running
Process 'consul_agent'                  running
Process 'route_registrar'              not monitored
File 'nfs_mounter'                     accessible
Process 'stager'                        running
Process 'tps_listener'                  running
Process 'tps_watcher'                   running
Process 'cc_uploader'                   running
Process 'nsync_listener'                running
Process 'nsync_bulker'                  running
System 'system_localhost'               running
root@aea1bf3d-9e5f-45d9-bec4-5ec7b6f02ca0:~#
```

Figure 14-7. route_registrar process stopped due to a failed NATS

This shows us that the route registrar process is failing. The route registrar uses NATS to register app routes with the GoRouter, so this alone is a clear indication that something is probably wrong with NATS. However, to clarify this, we can further inspect the route registrar logs by looking under */var/vcap/sys/log/route_registrar*:

```
root@aea1bf3d-9e5f-45d9-bec4-5ec7b6f02ca0:/var/vcap/sys/log/route_registrar# ↵
tail -f *


{"timestamp":"1471030947.208235741","source":"Route Registrar",↵
"message":"Route Registrar.Exiting with error","log_level":3,"data":↵
{"error":"nats: No servers available for connection","trace":"goroutine 1
```

For the route_registrar.stdout.log, we can clearly identify the root cause of the failure residing with the NATS instance group by noticing the following:

```
"error":"nats: No servers available for connection"
```

The next step to resolve this issue would be to use $ bosh... ssh to connect to the NATS instance group and then run $ monit summary. As we saw earlier, this would show that the NATS process has stopped. Therefore, running $ monit start nats would restart the NATS process, and BOSH will subsequently restart all the other failing components on the other instance groups. This will restore Cloud Foundry to full health.

This scenario has explored the BOSH's ability to rectify instance group failures. This ability to bring back failing deployments is the reason I regard BOSH as the essential component underpinning the entire Cloud Foundry ecosystem.

Summary

This chapter introduced you to the fundamental troubleshooting, debugging, and logging techniques required for resolving various issues with both Cloud Foundry and the underlying infrastructure. Failures within Cloud Foundry typically occur for one of three core reasons:

- Issues with configuration; for example, misconfigured deployment manifests, component credentials, or misconfigured infrastructure (including networking and egress-ingress configuration between subnets)
- Issues with infrastructure failures or resource contention
- Release job process failures and specific app issues

Having an understanding of the flows of communication between the various components within the platform will really help you to pinpoint where to begin resolving and troubleshooting complex issues. This chapter provided you with a solid introduction to the essential tools and techniques required to get started. If you require further help, cf-dev (*http://bit.ly/2qJkxe5*) is an active community that can provide you with additional information and answers to specific Cloud Foundry questions.

## CHAPTER 15

User Account and Authentication Management

Role-based access control (RBAC) provides a mechanism for establishing who can access specific resources (be it an internal service or a user-facing app). The term "access" refers more broadly to the specific level of authorization a user might have, allowing her to perform a specific action such as to view or modify a resource.

Cloud Foundry RBAC defines two aspects: who can use the platform, and what those individuals can use it for. Cloud Foundry employs RBAC via a component known as the UAA service. The Cloud Foundry UAA is the central identity-management service for platform components, users, and apps.

The UAA has two key modes of operation:

- Secure the Cloud Foundry platform components and API endpoints; for example, the Cloud Controller and Doppler require clients like the Cloud Foundry CLI to use UAA access tokens when invoking the component's API

- Provide authentication and access control data for apps running on the platform that require access to internal services such as the Cloud Controller or any other external service that requires authentication

The UAA can manage the authentication of users internally, against the UAA's internal user-identity store. Alternatively, you can configure it to connect to external user stores through identity providers such as Lightweight Directory Access Protocol (LDAP), Security Assertion Markup Language (SAML), and OpenID Connect (OIDC). The UAA is based on the latest of security standards like OAuth2, OIDC, and the System for Cross-Domain Identity Management (SCIM).

There is a lot of online documentation on the UAA that covers how it works and how to use it. This chapter draws your attention to the high-level concepts and how best to interact with the UAA. Where appropriate, I provide links to online documentation for access to the latest status and information.

Background Information

Before working with the UAA, there is some additional background information you should be aware of, including an understanding of OAuth 2.0, the UAA documentation, and the UAA BOSH release.

OAuth 2.0

The UAA is an OAuth2 server that you can use for centralized identity management.[1]

OAuth 2.0 is an open authorization protocol designed to allow apps to access each other's data. It allows you to create two types of apps:

- One that reads users' data from other apps, commonly referred to as a client
- One that provides access to users' data to other apps, commonly referred to as a resource server, but also represented as a client in the UAA

For example, an app can access specific user data via access to another app; for example, Gmail. The original app achieves this access by asking a user to log in to the original app via Gmail. The user logs in to Gmail, and then is redirected back to the original app. Now the original app can access the user's data in Gmail, and call functions in Gmail on behalf of the user (e.g., querying contact addresses).

OAuth 2.0 relies on an authorization server to provide two factors of authentication and authorization. The user can be a person trying to authenticate and perform action via a client app that acts on the user's behalf or a client app simply acting on its own. For this reason, a client app is always required, but a real end user is optional.

OAuth2 token generation is via a REST API call and the token used is a JSON web token (JWT).

UAA Documentation

The UAA is primarily used within Cloud Foundry for securing the Cloud Controller API, and securing the Loggregator for end-user and client-app access. However, you

---

1 Before reading this chapter, an understanding of OAuth2 is required. There is an excellent presentation on OAuth 2.0 available on YouTube (*https://www.youtube.com/watch?v=u4BHKcZ2rxk*).

can use it for many other tasks that require access and authentication management; for example, securing the BOSH Director itself or for app access to a specific service.

For a more in-depth look at the UAA, I suggest you begin with the UAA overview (*http://docs.cloudfoundry.org/api/uaa/#overview*).

UAA Release

You can also deploy the UAA as a BOSH release. Like the other components of Cloud Foundry, it is a standalone repository that is pulled into cf-deployment. The current release is available on GitHub (*https://github.com/cloudfoundry/uaa-release*). The source code for the UAA can also be found at the Cloud Foundry GitHub (*https://github.com/cloudfoundry/uaa*).

Breaking out components from cf-release into their own release is a great strategy. It allows for components such as the UAA to be independently deployable and fosters a pattern of reuse. The fact that the UAA is packaged into its own independent release opens up a number of possibilities. For example, BOSH previously had just a single admin user. However, now that the UAA is packaged as an independent release, BOSH uses the UAA for its authentication and authorization. You now can manage BOSH user access via UAA. This provides the capability to plug in an external user store and potentially have multiple users with different roles for different deployments. At the very least, the UAA provides a solid audit trail for the different users accessing the BOSH Director.

UAA Responsibilities

As mentioned in Preface, the UAA has two key responsibilities within Cloud Foundry:

- Securing Cloud Foundry components and API endpoints
- Securing service access for apps

Securing Cloud Foundry Components and API Endpoints

You use the UAA to provide access tokens for Cloud Foundry platform components and API endpoints; for example, the Cloud Controller and Loggregator. All collaborators target a Cloud Foundry environment with their individual user account. Accounts are associated with role and grant types that govern what level and type of access the user has within that environment. Each UAA role grants permission to a specific resource that an app can target on behalf of the user.

For example, for the purposes of access decisions, user accounts are either "user" or "admin" types. These user types translate into granted authorities. Using the SCIM type field from the UAA's core schema, the granted authorities are either [uaa.user] or [uaa.admin,uaa.user], respectively. Resource servers then can choose to use this information as part of any access decision.

For a user accessing an app, the app will delegate to the UAA, and then the UAA can delegate this authentication to an external identity provider. Authorization takes place when the resource server evaluates the scopes, which we know as authorities, in the access token.

Securing Service Access for Apps

You can use the UAA to provide access tokens for any app running on the platform. You can configure any OAuth2-aware app to require authentication using the UAA.

In addition to getting an access token for Cloud Foundry apps running on the plat‐form, the UAA can also be used to authenticate and authorize apps that want to access an internal service such as the Cloud Controller, the Loggregator, or any other external service. For example, when using a cf command, such as cf create-org, we are invoking API endpoints on the Cloud Controller. If you run the command to cre‐ate a new Org with CF_TRACE=true prepended, you will see the specific API end‐points that are invoked, as shown in the following example:

```
$ CF_TRACE=true cf create-org new-org

REQUEST: [2016-12-07T09:48:44-08:00]
POST /v2/organizations HTTP/1.1

REQUEST: [2016-12-07T09:48:44-08:00]
GET /v2/config/feature_flags/set_roles_by_username HTTP/1.1

...
```

Another concrete example of securing apps is how Pivotal uses and runs the UAA as a multitenant identity service that is packaged as part of its single sign-on (SSO) Cloud Foundry service. Each tenant of that service can use the UAA for securing a group of OAuth-aware apps for access by end users.

App authentication and authorization can be against either the UAA's internal user-identity store or an external identity provider such as LDAP, SAML, or OIDC. For an external identity provider, apps can authenticate against the UAA and then the UAA can delegate this authentication and authorization to the external identity provider.

An access token is comprised of a set of claims. User claims are specific user informa‐tion that helps identify additional user attributes; access claims, like the scope claim, contain a list of authorities used to access and manipulate a specific resource. The ability to process claim information makes it possible to qualify authorization posi‐tions. Claims play a vital role, especially when it comes to app security, because all of the authorization positions (e.g., what services apps can access) are driven by claims. Claims can also be propagated from an external identity provider.

UAA Architecture and Configuration Within Cloud Foundry

The UAA setup within Cloud Foundry is fairly standard, and you should not need to deviate too much from the standard templates (assuming that you are following the standard deployment process as described by cf-deployment and by the Cloud Foundry documentation (*http://bit.ly/2pD9iaU*). Depending on your IaaS platform, you might need additional configuration. A key point is that you should always configure your own set of token keys and SAML certificates.

Instance Groups Governed by the UAA

BOSH-deployed instance groups that are UAA protected, such as the Cloud Controller, Doppler (part of the Loggregator), or Clock Global, will need to set specific UAA properties so that the instance group process can accept UAA requests and interact with the UAA. Typically, the properties required will include the following:

- URL (for accessing the UAA)
- JWT (a JSON web token that asserts some number of claims)
- Clients (a list of the clients with associated scopes and secrets)
- Login (the redirect to the login server)

See the cf-deployment manifest (*http://bit.ly/2pDm3Cm*) for some concrete examples of instance group UAA properties. The general structure (or set of properties) will be similar across instance groups that have their endpoints managed by the UAA; however, the UAA "clients" list will be instance group–specific.

UAA Instance Groups

The recommended approach is to deploy a cluster of UAA servers (a server being a single machine running a UAA instance). The cluster should consist of two UAA instances (or one instance per AZ) for high availability (HA) reasons. The instances should be split across different AZs.

bosh-bootloader will try to configure three AZs by default (assuming the IaaS you deploy to will support three distinct regions). cf-deployment will then deploy multiple instances of the UAA instance groups across the three AZs.

You can find an example of the UAA instance group in the cf-deployment manifest (*http://bit.ly/2pDm3Cm*).

UAA Database

The Cloud Foundry deployment requires a UAA database (UAADB). UAA uses a MySQL database or PostgreSQL. It is recommended that you use a highly available MySQL solution such as a Galera MariaDB cluster or the highly available RDS solution from AWS. The UAA can also run against the p-mysql service, when it is deployed as a separate release by BOSH. Your MySQL solution should provide both failover and HA because replicas of the data should be made on every node within the cluster. A Galera cluster is provided as the default deployment option for the UAA.

As discussed in Chapter 16, you should make backups of the UAADB regularly to be able to recover from any cluster outage or damage to the database. This is true for any critical datastore within Cloud Foundry, and this is discussed further in "Backup and Restore" on page 272.

You can configure all of the UAA connection parameters via the deployment manifest. The UAA specification file lists all of the UAADB configurations. You can review the #Database section for a list of the configurable properties at the Cloud Foundry GitHub page (*http://bit.ly/2pDo2GO*). However, you should not need to deviate from most of the defaults apart from the obvious connection base parameters such as IP.

For an example of the UAADB configuration properties, you can review the Cloud Foundry deployment manifest that you created during the steps in Chapter 5.

UAA Runtime Components

Tomcat is used as the runtime container for the core Java-based UAA web app. Setup of this environment is BOSH managed via the BOSH deployment of the UAA-release. As of this writing, this is based on Tomcat 8 and the latest OpenJDK build packaged by the Java buildpack. All of the JVM settings are configurable in the deployment manifest (e.g., `catalina_opts: "-Xmx768m"`); however, it is important to note that the defaults have been reported as consistently good and should not require tweaking.

UAA Logging and Metrics

The UAA system logs are written to the UAA component machine in a file named *uaa.log*. All of the audit events that are generated for the management and authentication operations are written to that log. As with all system components, you can stream the logs on a secure channel by a syslog forwarder to a syslog endpoint collector such as ELK or Splunk. The logs then can be correlated, and you can run reports for tasks such as audit compliance.

There is a document in GitHub that lists all the standard audit events (such as UAA requests and responses) that are logged. You can view this document at the Cloud Foundry GitHub page (*http://bit.ly/2pDxg63*).

UAA-Produced Metrics

The UAA-produced metrics are under revision. As of this writing, UAA metrics focus mainly on reporting authentication success and authentication failure events. You can view the current metrics at the Cloud Foundry documentation page (*http://bit.ly/2pDpHvT*).

The UAA also supports integration with NewRelic, and all the agent configuration parameters are exposed in the manifest. NewRelic integration activates automatically if a valid license is configured in the manifest.

Keys, Tokens, and Certificate Rotation

When a user logs on to Cloud Foundry, she is presented with a UAA token. The UAA token can be an opaque token or a JWT signed by an RSA key-pair. The signing keys can be rotated as required. At any given time, the UAA will use only one signing key, but can use multiple verification keys.

There is a separate certificate and private key when the UAA acts as a SAML service provider. For every SAML authentication request that the UAA makes, the UAA must sign those requests with its identity. Therefore, that SAML certificate and private key are also present in the UAA manifest configuration.

Tokens

Tokens must be auditable, irrefutable, and revocable. OAuth 2.0 tokens are REST-based and easy to implement for developers, and there is polyglot support in common and popular frameworks with almost 100 percent feature parity between languages. Tokens offer open standards with no vendor lock-in.

The token specification in use by the UAA is the JWT with the authentication and authorization protocol being OAuth 2.0. JWT is an open standard (RFC 7519) JSON object with a set of claims about current authentication. It is signed with an RSA private key for verification and acceptance. The JSON object becomes a string prepended by the signature algorithm. Both the JSON claims object and the token signature are base64 encoded.

The UAA uses two different tokens: access tokens and OIDC id_token-s.

- Access tokens are purposed for resource access to APIs such as the Cloud Controller or Doppler.

- OpenIDConnectID id_tokens are purposed for an app setting up a user session. This token captures information (identification) about the client that has already been authenticated against an external ID provider.

Grant types

A grant type is the way an access token can be requested. Cloud Foundry provides five different grant types:

client_credentials
> Client app requesting a token to represent a client only; no user credentials are involved.

password
> The client uses the user's credentials, passing them on to the UAA to generate a token.

implicit
> Similar to the password grant but without the requirement for a client password (secret).

authorization_code
> Relies on 302 redirects from the HTTP protocol. It is the most secure grant type because the client never sees the user's credentials.

authorization_code using token as authentication
> The OAuth token (*http://bit.ly/2pDC771*) itself is used for authentication.

User Import

One of the key tasks for the Platform Operator is to define the strategy for onboarding users. You can onboard them using one of four mechanisms:

- Internal user management in the UAA and credentials managed in the UAA
- External via LDAP—just-in-time provisioning
- External via SAML—just-in-time provisioning
- External via OIDC identity providers—just-in-time provisioning

Essentially, the Platform Operator will need to pick from among the aforementioned strategies. Internally managed users is a simple way to begin but ultimately most enterprises require an enterprise-wide userstore, both for security reasons and ease of use. For this reason, you can also manage users by using one of the three listed external identity providers.

With LDAP, OIDC, and SAML, the UAA manages a "just-in-time provisioning," provisioning users on the fly, as required. The best way to onboard users via LDAP or SAML is through the use of the UAA import tool, which you can find at *https://github.com/pivotalservices/uaaldapimport*. This import tool uses a set of APIs, namely the CC API and UAA API, to provision users with Org and Space access.

Additionally, you can bootstrap users via the manifest, but outside of bootstrapping, ultimately it is advisable to pick only one of the four strategies.

Roles and Scopes

The Cloud Foundry admin role and UAA scopes can be derived from the previously listed external group memberships (LDAP, SAML, etc.).

Scopes

OAuth employs the concept of scopes. Scopes are essentially permissions; they allow roles to be defined. Scopes are added as a named claim, called a scope, in the access token. Scopes label permissions in a token by using two different names:

scope
　　When the token represents a client acting on behalf of a user

authorities
　　When the token represents the client (app) itself

When a resource server receives a request containing a token, the server can make a decision based on the scope in the token. The resource must validate the token. There are several ways of doing this, which are discussed in the OAuth 2.0 specification.

Roles

A role grants a specific set of permissions to a resource that can be targeted by an app on behalf of the user. Within the context of Cloud Foundry, there are two different sets of roles used to define different permissions:

- Cloud Foundry defines a set of roles relating to Orgs and Spaces.
- The UAA has a set of roles based on the UAA scope that are different from Cloud Foundry roles. UAA roles (essentially scopes) include `cloudcontroller.admin`, `scim.read`, and `scim.write`. The scopes define the access permissions for a user, namely what services she can interact with and what she is allowed to do with that service.

The Cloud Foundry roles must clearly map to a set of UAA roles; for example, a Cloud Foundry *Space Auditor* has only read access, but a Cloud Foundry *Space Developer* can create new services.

You must set up Cloud Foundry roles via direct interaction with the Cloud Controller. For this reason, onboarding requires two separate API calls: calls to the UAA and calls to the Cloud Controller. Therefore, the aforementioned UAA-import tool makes bulk onboarding significantly easier.

You can map these requirements to a specification file. For more information on that, go to the Cloud Foundry UAA release GitHub repository (*http://bit.ly/2pDo2GO*).

Separation of role concerns

UAA permissions and scopes managed by the UAA should not be confused with the Cloud Foundry roles managed by the CAPI.

Cloud Controller roles and permissions

The Cloud Controller governs Orgs and Space roles and responsibilities for a user. These roles persist in the Cloud Controller database. These roles are managed by the CAPI through any client of the Cloud Controller—typically through the Cloud Foundry CLI.

UAA roles and permissions

UAA roles (OAuth scopes) are, essentially, defined roles that allow users access to, and control of, certain resources. For example, some Cloud Foundry users (e.g., a space developer) are responsible for Cloud Controller activities such as managing apps and services. These users would need the `cloudcontroller.admin` scope. This gives the user rights on the platform but not permission to manage users. UAA roles are stored in the UAADB.

Other Cloud Foundry users (i.e., the Platform Operator) are responsible for user management. For this ability, you need an admin user who is authorized to create other users. Such a user would need `scim.write` scope to manage other Cloud Foundry users.

Additionally, access to the Firehose requires a user with the `doppler.firehose` scope. The "cf" UAA client needs permission to grant this custom scope to platform users. The configuration of the UAA job in Cloud Foundry adds this scope by default.[2]

---

2 If your Cloud Foundry instance overrides the `properties.uaa.clients.cf` property in a stub, you need to add `doppler.firehose` to the scope list in the `properties.uaa.clients.cf.scope` property.

You can achieve this separation of duties by creating a new user and associating that user with the correct scope.

The UAA provides these out-of-the-box roles. However, there is no specific fine-grained permissions, such as the ability for this user to just manage services. There are plans to add finer-grained authorization and custom roles, but for most users, the out-of-the-box roles provide a sufficient level of granularity.

An important point to note is that you can bootstrap a predefined default set of CF users and UAA clients in the deployment manifest.

UAAC and the UAA API

UAA has a command-line utility user management tool called UAAC that can use the UAA API. It is a Ruby GEM, and you can perform OAuth client management and user management with it. Initially, most operators will not be required to use the UAAC tools, given that default UAA users are typically set up with the appropriate default scopes in the deployment manifest. If additional permissions for other Platform Operators are required—for example, access to Doppler—you can use the UAAC to access, inspect, and grant those permissions. There is a standard API document for the UAA API (*http://docs.cloudfoundry.org/api/uaa/*).

Summary

Cloud Foundry's UAA is the central identity-management service for both platform users and apps. The UAA is a perfect example of the benefits of designing Cloud Foundry as a composable distributed architecture because the UAA is its own independent release, and is not tightly coupled with any other component. This decomposition has allowed the UAA to be reused for other concerns such as managing BOSH authentication and authorization user access.

The overall flexibility of the UAA provides benefits for securing the platform components, apps running on the platform, and any backing services. The UAA also achieves seamless integration with other enterprise user management technologies, allowing for the adoption of a single company user management strategy for both Cloud Foundry and other technologies with your business.

## CHAPTER 16

Designing for Resilience, Planning for Disaster

Reliability, recoverability, timely error detection, and continuous operations are primary characteristics of any high-availability solution. Cloud Foundry, if used correctly, can become the central platform for your app development and deployment activities. As such, the resiliency of the platform is critical to your business continuity. Preparing for disaster and disruption to Cloud Foundry and the underlying stack is vital.

You can mitigate and handle failures in three key ways:

- Design for added resiliency and high availability
- Employ backup and restoration mechanisms
- Repeatedly run platform verification tests

This chapter provides you with an overview of Cloud Foundry's built-in resiliency capabilities. It then goes on to discuss how you can further expand resiliency. This chapter also provides you with an overview of some of the available techniques used for backing up and restoring Cloud Foundry.

High Availability Considerations

Resiliency and high availability go hand in hand. End users do not care how resilient your system is; they are concerned only about the availability of their app, service, or functionality. For example, when I am watching Netflix, the last thing on my mind is that Chaos Monkey (*https://github.com/Netflix/SimianArmy/wiki/Chaos-Monkey*) can take out a vital component. I care only about watching my movie. Operators employ resiliency in technical stacks to promote HA. HA is measured from the perception of the end user. End users experience frustration, resulting in a negative perception when the service they want to access is unavailable or unreliable in some fashion. Ultimately, this is what you are guarding against.

Being HA is the degree to which a component is available to a user upon demand. At its core, HA is primarily achieved simply through the redundant setup of each component such that any single point of failure is avoided.[1]

Establishing HA is a concern that applies to every layer of the technology stack. For example, when using replication of components to establish HA, you should see replication at every layer of the technology stack, be it multiple Top-of-Rack (ToR) switches for network availability to a VIP underpinned by a cluster of load balancers to allow for fast failover of your VIP. Establishing replication only for a single component will typically be insufficient. HA considerations span several components, and there are different levels of HA that you can attain, because failures can occur due to a variety of reasons. For example, performance failures due to higher than expected usage can create the same havoc as the failure of a critical component or a network outage.[2]

The different levels of HA are captured and reasoned over through the consideration of failure boundaries. For example, the lowest level of HA might be your data center itself. You then need to consider your physical infrastructure and networking layers followed by your IaaS clusters. You need to think about HA at every single layer. Designing for HA is essential if your system is required to be continuously operational. This means that your Cloud Foundry developer environments must also be production grade if you require developers to be constantly productive. As an example, I recently worked with a large retail company that estimated that (based on employee cost per minute) that five minutes of down time could be equated to $1 million in sunk costs.

The key question to ask when making your system resilient is how much HA is actually required and at what cost. The answer to this question historically has depended on the appetite for risk coupled with the ability to recover, contrasted against additional expenses incurred through replicating components.

Understanding the failure boundaries, whether in terms of network, host, cluster, region, or process, can help shape your HA strategy as it helps you assess specific risks contrasted against the costs involved in mitigating those risks. For example, there is a high probability that an individual process or machine can fail, and therefore it is a reasonable and cost-effective approach to run more than one process or

---

1 Cloud Foundry component and app redundancy is covered in "Instance group replication" on page 54.

2 HA that is achieved purely through additional redundancy can double the total cost of ownership compared to a non-HA system.

machine. Conversely, the risks of an entire data center going offline may be significantly small and the costs associated with replicating the data center versus the perceived risk may likely be too high. Understanding what can fail, the impact of those failures, and how much it would cost to mitigate those risks is an essential step in defining your HA strategy.

Within a distributed system such as Cloud Foundry, you must apply special focus to the intersection and interconnectivity of components so that every failure of an individual component can be bypassed without loss of the overall system functionality. Cloud Foundry takes a unique approach to providing HA by moving beyond just replication, although that strategy is still a key focus. Cloud Foundry, coupled with BOSH, promotes resiliency through self-healing. Self-healing is the ability to recover from app, process, and component failure through inbuilt error handling and correction.

Cloud Foundry addresses HA from the top down, beginning with app availability, and then moving through the system components to the infrastructure. This is a logical way to view HA. Generally speaking, the lower the layer affected, the higher the overall impact. Failures at the top of the stack, such as a failed process, are potentially more frequent but easier and less costly to rectify. Failures at the bottom of the stack, such as a SAN outage, are rare but can be catastrophic to the entire system and even the data center.

Data Center Availability

Before embarking on a Cloud Foundry HA strategy, there is an implicit assumption that your data center is set up correctly with an appropriate level of HA and resiliency for your hardware, storage, servers, networking, power, and so on.

Extending Cloud Foundry's Built-In Resiliency

In the previous section, I discussed the requirement for replicating both apps and the underlying components as a mechanism for establishing HA. Cloud Foundry moves beyond the simple strategy of replication by establishing resiliency and HA on your behalf. It achieves built-in resiliency in four key ways, referred to in the Cloud Foundry community as "the four levels of HA." An introduction to the four levels of HA were discussed in "Built-In Resilience and Fault Tolerance" on page 15. They include the following:

- Restarting failed system processes
- Recreating missing or unresponsive VMs

- Dynamic deployment of new app instances if an app crashes or becomes unresponsive
- App striping across AZs to enforce separation of the underlying infrastructure

Cloud Foundry does more of the resiliency heavy lifting for you by providing self-healing of apps, processes, and VMs. The four levels of HA provide resiliency within the boundaries of a single installation. However, if you experience wider data center failure due to underlying infrastructure issues such as a SAN outage or a load balancer VIP cluster becoming unreachable, a single Cloud Foundry deployment could become temporarily unusable.

Data center outages are extremely rare. However, if you require an additional level of resiliency to mitigate any potential data center failures, it is possible to run multiple deployments of Cloud Foundry in different data centers. Whether you run dual deployments of Cloud Foundry in active–active modes or active–passive modes, there are some important considerations of which you need to be mindful.

Resiliency Through Multiple Cloud Foundry Deployments

Consider the scenario of running two Cloud Foundry deployments across two different data centers; let's call them West and East. This could be a preproduction instance in one data center and a production instance in the other, or two production deployments running apps and services in an active–active fashion. This configuration gives you the ability to shut down an entire Cloud Foundry deployment and still keep your production apps running in the second deployment.

Because you have two data centers, there are at least five required default domains to cover both the system components and the app domain.

Conceptually, assuming you are not yet using a pipeline, here's what you have:

1. Developers can push myapp at "cf-west.com".
2. Developers can push myapp at "cf-east.com".
3. End-user clients access apps at "mycf.com" .
4. Developers and operators target the system domain `api.system.cf-west.com`.
5. Developers and operators target the system domain `api.system.cf-east.com`.

Clearly, the number of domains can further increase with additional environments (e.g., a production and development instance in each data center).

Traffic will typically first hit a global load balancer (e.g., F5's Global Traffic Manager [GTM]) that spans both deployments. Using the global load balancer, the end-user traffic can be balanced across both active–active environments based on, for example, geographic location or existing load in the data center. The global load balancer consults DNS and then routes the traffic to a local data center's load balancer after it decides which data center to route the traffic to.

All domains for all the Cloud Foundry deployments must be registered as a DNS record so that the global load balancer can route traffic to the correct location. Each Cloud Foundry deployment should have all five domains defined in its certificate. This allows the local load balancer to route traffic across to a different data center if, for some rare reason, the local load balancer is unable to connect to the local Cloud Foundry deployment.

With this approach, developers who need to target a specific Cloud Foundry installation can do so by using the local data center–centric domain. Ideally though, developers should not be burdened with the need to deploy to two environments. Instead, developers should simply check in their code commit and leave the deployment responsibility to a CI/CD pipeline.

Resiliency Through Pipelines

We discussed in "Why BOSH?" on page 170 the need for environmental consistency and reproducibility. This is even more pertinent when mirroring environments in two or more installations. BOSH provides environmental consistency by means of releases and stemcells, assuming that you have mirrored your deployment configuration correctly, with only instance-specific concerns such as domains, networks, and credentials unique to a specific installation.

However, neither Cloud Foundry nor BOSH will ensure that a developer will push an identical app in the same way, using the same buildpack and dependencies, to two different Cloud Foundry environments. Therefore, deploying an app to multiple production environments should not be a developer concern; it should be governed by a CI/CD pipeline such as concourse.ci. The pipeline should handle deploying the app artifact or Docker OCI image in exactly the same way to both environments, in a repeatable fashion.

Data Consistency Through Services

One of the biggest challenges with running any app layer technology in an active–active fashion across two data centers is the data layer underpinning the app. Many apps will have some requirement to persist data to a backing service such as a database. The backing data services must maintain consistency between the two data centers. This consistency concern is explained by the CAP theorem, which states that it is impossible for a distributed system to simultaneously provide consistency, availability, and partition tolerance guarantees; at any one time, a distributed system can ensure only two out of the three requirements.

Maintaining data consistency across different data centers increases the CAP theorem challenge because of increased latency when trying to propagate data changes across two separate locations. If you adopt a write-through model across your data centers, in which you return a confirmation of a successful write only after the write is completed, the end-user experience could be painfully slow. Latency is ultimately an availability issue, and any additional network latency or extra network hops will only compound this issue. If you adopt a write-behind model in which you immediately return a confirmation of a successful write and then try and propagate the change after the fact, you risk the two datastores falling out of synchronization, leaving inconsistent data.

The solution here is to use a local caching layer such as Geode (*http://geode.apache.org*) or Cassandra (*http://cassandra.apache.org*). Using a distributed data layer that ensures eventual consistency over a wide-area network (WAN) makes it possible for you to preserve changes locally, allowing a fast response (and HA) to the end user. In write-behind mode, these technologies can then propagate the write both to a local backing database and across a WAN to another grid in your other data center. After the data update is in the second data center, the second grid can also persist the changes locally. If a conflict does occur, technologies such as Geode employ various conflict resolution algorithms to ensure that the system is eventually consistent. Although no eventually consistent system is bulletproof, they provide a solid solution to the intrinsically challenging problem of data consistency across a WAN.

HA IaaS Configuration

Establishing the correct infrastructure configuration is essential for establishing HA. As discussed in "Infrastructure Failures" on page 229, if your infrastructure is either resource constrained or misconfigured, it can have catastrophic effects on the overall health of Cloud Foundry and the apps running on it. This section briefly describes the failure boundaries for AWS, and then explores the failure boundaries for vCenter in closer detail.

AWS Failure Boundaries

When considering HA, it is important to understand the failure boundaries. For example, AWS HA failure boundaries (along with their subsequent requirements) are fairly straightforward: Cloud Foundry AZs map directly to AWS AZs. As you can see in Figure 16-1, this configuration uses a VPC with three AZs: AZ1, AZ2, and AZ3. Each AZ has a private, dedicated subnet and the Cloud Foundry components will be striped across the three AZs.

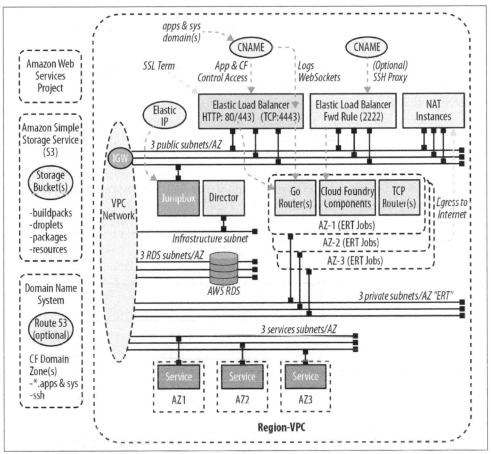

Figure 16-1. AWS Reference Architecture using three AZs to establish HA

Because AWS failure boundaries are so well defined by AZs and private, dedicated subnets that map one-to-one directly to Cloud Foundry AZs, this configuration is straighforward and does not require an in-depth analysis.

vCenter Failure Boundaries

This section explores the host configuration for a vCenter cluster. Establishing failure boundaries for on-premises IaaS is nuanced, and therefore, you are required to understand more about the underlying host configuration.

You can use vSphere HA in conjunction with the BOSH Resurrector, provided that the resurrection cadence is different. Using both capabilities can augment the HA strategy for instance groups in a powerful way. Ideally, for vCenter, a cluster should have a minimum of two hosts for resiliency, but preferably three. Even though the vSphere HA can bring back failed VMs, in a complete host failure situation, a single host ESXi cluster would render the cluster inoperable. For that reason, a minimum of two hosts per cluster (although three is preferable) ensures that you do not lose an entire AZ if a host server fails.

Therefore, sizing your infrastructure with three Cloud Foundry AZs and three hosts per cluster will result in a nine-host cluster. Some companies at this point become concerned that they are oversizing their IaaS. It is important to note that, within a cluster, you can still use the logical construct of resource pools for sharing infrastructure between different Cloud Foundry installations. For example, you can run a development installation, a production installation, and sandbox, all on the same set of clusters with isolation and AZs achieved through resource pool and cluster combinations. This nine-host cluster/resource pool configuration, supporting multiple Cloud Foundry foundations, is illustrated in Figure 16-2.

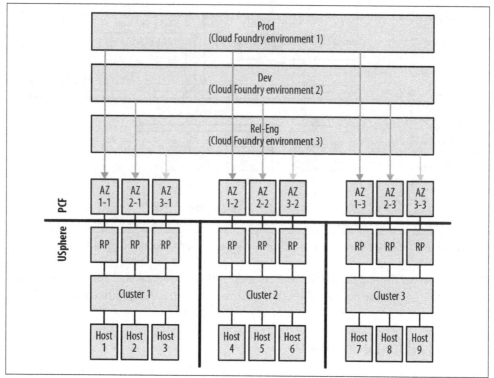

Figure 16-2. Using vSphere resource pools to allow multiple Cloud Foundry installations to use the same cluster sets

In line with the previous AWS example, Figure 16-3 presents a topology diagram for the vCenter scenario described, including a sensible networking definition.

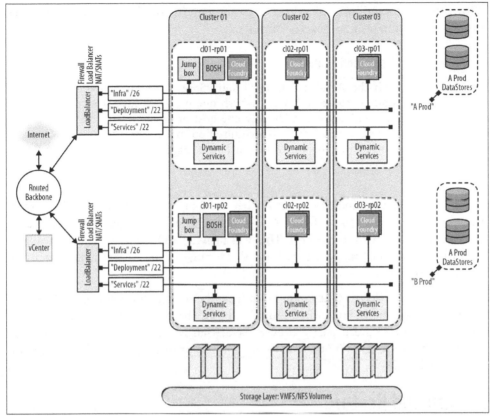

Figure 16-3. An HA Cloud Foundry architecture with two Cloud Foundry deployments spanning three vCenter clusters

When configuring your capacity for Cloud Foundry, you need to take into consideration the HA capabilities and effects of the underlying infrastructure. vSphere HA works in two ways. Primarily there is the reactive action of booting VMs that have lost a host on which to run. In addition, vSphere also employs a construct known as *admission control*.

Admission Control guards capacity and prevents new VMs from being powered on if it violates the capacity retention policy. This means that you can have a cluster of hosts that has plenty of spare capacity but will not boot additional VMs because Admission Control prevents you from eating into capacity you previously specified as reserved. You can disable Admission Control, but it is usually turned on. A typical configuration with both Admission Control and vSphere HA turned on often has each cluster establish one protected host. The default Admission Control policy is $n + 1$ host protection so that each cluster effectively loses a host's worth of capacity.

With this configuration, a nine-host environment (three clusters each with three hosts) will result in only six hosts of capacity.

Cluster Configuration

With the Admission Control and vSphere HA configuration, a two-host cluster will still establish one protected host. Therefore, this configuration yields only one host of capacity per cluster. If you are striving for a higher-utilization model, three hosts is the preferred option, provided that you have the need for total capacity.

As with other IaaS technologies, many other configurations are possible. For example, it is totally feasible to configure a three-host cluster with vSphere HA turned on and Admission Control turned off. This will provide 100 percent capacity available for VMs but if you lose an entire host, there can well be insufficient capacity to reboot the lost VMs.

The key takeaway here is that Cloud Foundry is a consolidation play (containers) on top of a consolidation play (virtualization). Do not cheat yourself at either layer. You need adequate HA and capacity at every layer (hardware, IaaS, Cloud Foundry) in order for the platform to function as desired and to protect your workload from failures at any layer.

Backup and Restore

From time to time, you might need to completely restore your environment. This could be due to any of these situations:

- Creating a carbon copy of an existing deployment to create a brand new environment
- Maintenance reasons such as swapping out or upgrading your networking, server, or storage layer
- Recovering from a data center–wide malicious attack that causes a catastrophic failure

There are several projects that exist to back up and restore Cloud Foundry. Here are a couple of them:

- cf-converger from Engineer Better (*http://bit.ly/2pG98jf*)
- cfops from Pivotal Services (*http://bit.ly/2pGsoNy*)

The latter is focused on Pivotal Cloud Foundry, but, with the exception of backing up Pivotal's Operations Manager configuration, most of the underlying principles (e.g., backing up the databases) apply to any Cloud Foundry installation.

To restore your environment, you first need to create a backup of the data layer. When thinking about Cloud Foundry from a disaster recovery perspective, you need to forget all of the moving parts—all the processes—and think about the distributed system as a set of persistent disks holding the following:

- The CCDB
- The UAA database
- The BBS
- The BOSH DB
- The blobstore or NFS server
- Configuration (all deployment manifests, including BOSH itself)
- Any other app-centric persistence layer (e.g., Pivotal Cloud Foundry uses an additional App Manager database)

The persistence layer *is Cloud Foundry* from a disaster recovery perspective; everything else—all of the running processes—can easily be wired back in.

Cloud Foundry Availability

Backing up Cloud Foundry will suspend Cloud Controller writes for the duration of the backup. This is important because you cannot simultaneously write to a database and keep the integrity of the database backup. Suspending the Cloud Controller writes (thus effectively taking CAPI offline) will cause your foundation to become read-only for the duration of the backup. App pushes and so on will not work during this time, but your existing apps will still be running and able to accept traffic.

Restoring BOSH

Bringing back BOSH is the first step to recovering any offline Cloud Foundry environment. Therefore, it is vital that you back up the original BOSH manifest (let's call it *bosh.yml*) and take regular snapshots of the BOSH DB or attached BOSH disk. With your *bosh.yml*, you can bring your original BOSH back, provided that you have a snapshot of the disk volume that contains the BOSH DB and blobstore, or you can use an external DB like MySQL on AWS-RDS and an external blobstore like Amazon S3. You must, however, bring BOSH back on the original IP as the BOSH worker nodes. Your BOSH-deployed machines hosting your deployments will have BOSH agents that are configured to communicate with BOSH on that original IP.

It's best to use an external database like clustered MySQL or AWS-RDS and an external blobstore like Amazon S3. However, if you use BOSH's internal database, there are some additional steps required to back up and restore BOSH's internal database and blobstore.

For illustrative purposes, when using AWS, you can use the following steps to back up BOSH's internal database and blobstore:

1. Using SSH, connect to BOSH: `$ ssh -i key vcap@boship`
2. Become root: `$ su -` (use your VM credentials)
3. Run `$ monit summary` to view all BOSH processes
4. Run `$ monit stop all` to cleanly stop all BOSH processes
5. Take a snapshot of the BOSH persistent disk volume

Here are the steps to restore BOSH's internal database and blobstore:

1. Using your original *bosh.yml* manifest, rebuild BOSH. This creates a new empty persistent disk.
2. Repeat steps 1 through 4 of the backup procedure. You will need to stop all processes before detaching the persistent disk.
3. Detach the persistent disk (deleting it).
4. Create a new volume from your disk volume snapshot, and then manually attach the new volume to the BOSH VM.
5. Start all processes again. BOSH will now have the same BOSH UUID (because it is stored in the database).

Bringing Back Cloud Foundry

After you have successfully restored BOSH, BOSH itself should successfully restore the Cloud Foundry deployment, assuming that you have used an external and reachable database and blobstore for the other components.

Validating Platform Integrity in Production

This section discusses how to validate the health and integrity of your production environment. After you have successfully deployed Cloud Foundry, you should run the smoke tests and CATS to ensure that your environment is working properly. You should also maintain a dedicated sandbox to try out any changes prior to altering any development or production environment.

Start with a Sandbox

If you run business-critical workloads on a production instance of Cloud Foundry, you should consider using a sandbox/staging environment prior to making any production platform changes. This approach gives you the ability to test any production apps in an isolated way before rolling out new platform changes (be it an infrastructure upgrade, stemcell change, Cloud Foundry release upgrade, buildpack change, or service upgrade) to production.

The sandbox environment should mirror the production environment as closely as possible. It should also contain a representation of the production apps and a mock up of the production services to ensure that you validate the health of the apps running on the platform.

Production Verification Testing

To test the behavior of your platform before making the production environment live, run the following:

- `cf-smoke-tests` to ensure that core Cloud Foundry functionality is working
- `cf-acceptance-tests` to test Cloud Foundry behavior and component integration in more detail
- Your own custom acceptance tests against the apps and services you have written, including any established or customized configuration, ensuring established app behavior does not break
- External monitoring against your deployed apps

An example set of app tests could include the following:

1. Use `cf push` to push the app.
2. Bind the app to a service(s).
3. Start the app.
4. Target the app on a restful endpoint and validate the response.
5. Target the app on a restful endpoint to write to a given data service.
6. Target the app on a restful endpoint to read a written value.
7. Generate and log a unique string to validate app logging.
8. Stop the app.
9. Delete the app.

This set of tests should be designed to exercise the app's core user-facing functionality, including the app's interaction with any backing services.

Running these sorts of tests against each Cloud Foundry instance on a CI server with a metrics dashboard is the desired approach for ease of repeatability. Not only do you get volume testing for free (e.g., you can easily fill up a buildpack cache that way), you can publish the dashboard URL to both your platform consumers (namely developers) and stakeholders (namely line of business owners) alike. Linking these tests to alerting/paging systems is also better than paging people due to IaaS-level failures.

After you make the environment live, it is still important to identify any unintended behavior changes. Therefore, the ongoing periodic running of platform validation tests in production is absolutely recommended. For example, it is possible that you may uncover a problem with the underlying infrastructure that can be noticed only by running your platform validation tests in production.

Summary

This chapter provided you with a core understanding of the issues, decision points, and built-in capabilities pertaining to platform resiliency.

The key consideration in ensuring that your platform is resilient is understanding the environmental failure boundaries. When you have established those boundaries and assessed your appetite for risk versus cost, you will be in a much better position to design your Cloud Foundry topology for the desired level of HA.

After you have provisioned your Cloud Foundry environment, it is essential to make regular backups. Backup and restore is not as complex as it might first appear; however, making regular backups and, in addition, frequently testing that you can successfully restore your Cloud Foundry environment, should be a part of your ongoing disaster recovery plan.

Consuming and reacting to system events and logging information will also help establish resiliency. Using a sandbox/staging environment prior to making any production platform changes provides an additional defense against introducing instability to the platform. Finally, you should continue to run your platform tests (smoke tests, platform and app verification tests, etc.) to ensure that your environment is working properly. If you do all of this, you will be in much better shape if unforeseen issues do arise.

## CHAPTER 17

Cloud Foundry Roadmap

As mentioned throughout the early chapters of this book, Cloud Foundry technology is exceptionally fast moving. Any review of the architecture is just a snapshot in time, and any future view of the technology is subject to refinement. However, keeping one eye on the Cloud Foundry roadmap helps to provide a perspective on the emerging trends that are shaping the IT industry. This chapter explores, at a high level, some of the recent and soon to emerge features, and some speculation as to where the architecture might evolve further.

Roadmap Topics

There is a wiki (*http://bit.ly/2pGBtFN*) dedicated to roadmap topics. Roadmaps are generally reflected in public Pivotal Tracker projects, with each core component having its own dedicated project.

v3 API

The third incarnation of the Cloud Foundry API (known as the v3 API) provides a richer set of building blocks with which you can orchestrate diverse and complex workflows.

Multiple Droplets per App

With the v2 API, a user (be it a developer or a CI/CD pipeline) can deploy a single droplet per app, as illustrated in Figure 17-1. There is a direct correlation of one app name and one app GUID being associated with one droplet.

Figure 17-1. Traditional app-to-droplet mapping

For each app, a user can request several running instances. Each app instance will use the same droplet and will be tagged by the same app GUID. A user can subsequently push, stage, and run a second version of the same app. From Cloud Foundry's perspective, the two running apps (version one and version two) are viewed as two completely independent apps because they have two different app names and therefore two different app GUIDs, as depicted in Figure 17-2. It does not matter if the two apps are binary identical; if they are pushed with different app names, they will have different droplets, and Cloud Foundry will treat them as different apps.

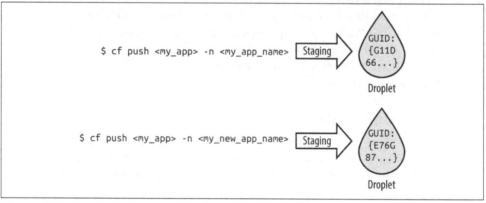

Figure 17-2. Traditional app-to-droplet mapping with different droplets generated from the same app artifact

With the v3 API, you can now push more than one version of your app, resulting in multiple droplets that are all regarded as the same app because they have the same app name and app GUID, as presented in Figure 17-3. This allows the user to manage the transition between the different droplet versions within Cloud Foundry in an orchestrated manner.

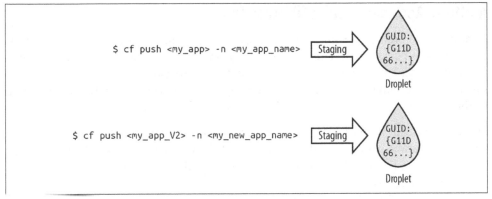

```
$ cf push <my_app> -n <my_app_name>          Staging      GUID:
                                                          {G11D
                                                           66...}
                                                          Droplet

$ cf push <my_app_V2> -n <my_new_app_name>   Staging      GUID:
                                                          {G11D
                                                           66...}
                                                          Droplet
```

Figure 17-3. Two app versions mapped to the same droplet version with identical GUIDs

Currently, when you restage your app with the v2 API, the app instance must be stopped because new files are uploaded and the app dependencies and artifacts are replaced during the buildpack compilation phase. With the v2 API, downtime is mitigated by pushing more than one instance and using rolling blue/green deployments. With the v3 API, downtime can be further mitigated by pushing the second version of the app alongside the first running app instance, without affecting the already running instance. After you have pushed it, you can restage the second version of your app, again with no impact to the current running app. When the new version of your app has finished staging and is successfully running, the user can then choose to instantaneously expose it in place of the original instance.

If you stage and run the new droplet and discover that it does not perform adequately, you can easily revert to the original droplet because it is still running. This workflow essentially allows for the native establishment of deployment patterns such as canaries and blue/green deployments within Cloud Foundry itself, as opposed to establishing these patterns via a pipeline or route service. Essentially, there are fewer steps required to achieve the necessary deployment patterns. For example, the mapping of routes between blue and green app versions could become a thing of the past if Cloud Foundry handles this as a native transition.

The approach of multiple droplets per app has additional implications for managing logs. With this v3 approach, if the new app is running successfully, because the same app GUID will be used for both the old and new apps, it becomes much easier to track the health of the app throughout its entire life cycle because all logs from all deployed app versions are aggregated into the same stream.

Multiple Apps per Droplet (Process Types)

In addition to multiple droplets per app, the v3 API plans to allow you to have multiple processes per droplet. This breaks away from the v2 model that allows for only one app process per droplet. Therefore, the direct correlation of one app name and one app GUID being associated with one droplet, as described earlier, will be a thing of the past.

With the v3 API, with one cf push and one stage, you can now have multiple processes (e.g., a web process, worker process, and Cron process) within the same droplet, as shown in Figure 17-4. There is no longer a need to have the separate cf pushes and three staging events.

After it has been pushed, each app instance contains all three processes, but only one process is active; there is still only one process running per container. The model allows for each process to be scaled independently; for example, you might want two web process instances, four worker process instances, and one Cron process instance. Each process can have its own defined resources; for example, my worker process might need double the memory of the web process. A benefit of collating processing with the same droplet is that all processes have the same app GUID, so they all can be tracked easily by the same stream in the aggregated log. When moving to a microservices architecture, this allows the monitoring of your big-A app (the overarching app that is comprised of smaller services) while still tracking the behavior of each individual service.

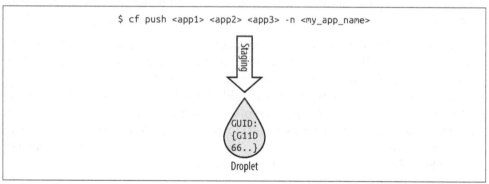

Figure 17-4. Multiple process-to-one-droplet mapping

Tasks

Tasks allow you to push your app code and then, instead of running your app as an LRP, run one-off commands. Tasks run at most only once; then, upon exit of the specified Task, the app will shut down and the container will be destroyed. If the Task produced a failed result, either Cloud Foundry or the user can detect the failure and then retry the Task.

Tasks are great for running one-off processes such as Cron-like jobs or database migrations. Additionally, you could build a service that repeatedly runs your task on, perhaps, a nightly basis.

If you were trying to orchestrate a database migration, the task workflow might be as follows:

1. Push your new app version alongside your existing app, as described above, but leave the new version staged but not running.
2. Invoke your database migration task.
3. Transition the droplet to run the new version of your app and bring your old app offline.

Tasks provide a huge amount of power for new workflows, especially around handling batch and computational workflows that involve data processing through patterns such as pipes and filters.

Diego Scheduling

Advanced features are being added to Diego's scheduling capability. Two key features under consideration include Cell rebalancing and a concept of boulder support to ensure appropriate app distribution.

Cell Rebalancing

Imagine the scenario in which the Cloud Foundry operator provisions two cells (let's call them Cell A and Cell B). If a Cloud Foundry user pushes two instances of her app, Diego will try and deploy an instance of the app to both Cells for resiliency reasons. Now, if because of some IaaS-related issue Cell B dies, Diego will notice the loss of the Cell and start a new instance of the app on Cell A. This is good for availability because both instances of the app are running and handling traffic. However, when Cell B comes back online, we now have the scenario in which both apps are still running on Cell A.

Leaving both apps running on Cell A is not good for resiliency. If Cell A fails, all instances of the app will need to be re-created simultaneously, causing app downtime until two new instances are recreated on Cell B.

As of this writing, work is underway to address this scenario so that apps can be gracefully and slowly migrated back to a resilient distribution across both Cells to avoid any app downtime if a specific Cell dies (see Figure 17-5). Rebalancing is typically a costly processing exercise for the Diego scheduler (the Diego Brain), and so the algorithm required for this work should be graceful and measured so as to be transparent to any end-user activity.

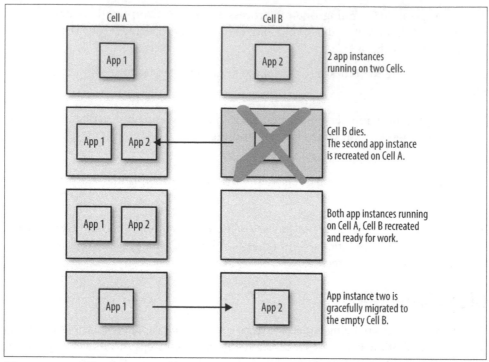

Figure 17-5. Cell rebalancing for a single app with two instances running across two Cells

Boulders

Consider a scenario in which there are six 32 GB Cells. Each Cell contains lots of pebble-sized apps (e.g., 512 MB to 2 GB); however, due to the number of apps deployed, every Cell has only a maximum of 6 GB of RAM remaining. When adding up all of the available RAM, in theory, there should be enough room for a larger than average app because there is 36 GB of unused RAM on aggregate across all Cells. However, if a user wants to push a boulder-sized app of say 10 GB, the cf push command will fail because there is no single Cell that can accommodate the new boulder-sized app. At this point, you are constrained to pushing apps that are less than 6 GB in size.

For this reason, work is currently being done to relocate some of the smaller pebble-sized apps, provided that they will not experience downtime, to create enough room on a single Cell to accommodate the boulder-sized 10 GB app.

Tracing

As of this writing, work is being done to respect and log an HTTP header trace ID. If an HTTP request/response header trace ID is respected and logged at the GoRouter, this would allow the app user to reason over the traffic flow. This is valuable both for the developer and for Cloud Foundry itself, especially when inspecting internal traffic response times. For example, if a call to the Cloud Controller is slow, inspecting the trace ID between the Cloud Foundry components will quickly show you where the bottleneck resides.

Containers

Container management is an essential component of Cloud Foundry. Regardless of whether you run a Docker Image, app, or Task, the Garden-managed container is where your workload runs. Work is specifically being added to containers with respect to network shaping, taking snapshots, networking, and additional traffic resiliency.

Network Shaping

Network shaping of egress and ingress traffic is an important capability that can be added to Garden. Developers can already add additional route services for traffic management tasks such as rate limiting. However, the Platform Operator might also want to impose some additional network quotas around development spaces. For example, if a developer pushes an app to a development space and then starts to route a high amount of traffic to that app, Garden could rate-limit the traffic to the app so as to avoid saturating the network in a way that could disable other, more important apps.

Container Snapshots

Container snapshots are a valuable feature for security reasons such as quarantine purposes. Snapshots of the container could also be a valuable technique for additional debugging.

Container-to-Container Networking

Container-to-container networking is an important topic, and there is work currently being undertaken to assign a single IP per container as opposed to using a local host NAT to reach an app. Current thinking on container-to-container traffic is to take advantage of an overlay network so that an app can communicate with itself or other apps residing in other containers without having to go via the GoRouter. Additional app-to-app traffic policies can then be established in order to specify that app A can communicate directly with app B on a defined port. You can achieve point-to-point routing by using an internal service discovery such as Consul or Eureka. Currently, when a user provisions a service, it is bound to a single space. For the maximum benefit of service discovery, your app or service needs to be exposed across multiple spaces, and work is being undertaken to allow for this.

You can read about the current thinking and proposal on this topic in "A Vision for the Future of Container Networking on Cloud Foundry" (*http://bit.ly/2pGRtrq*).

Traffic Resiliency

Currently, Cloud Foundry optimizes for consistency over availability. Therefore, the GoRouter begins pruning routes from the route table after two minutes if it has not received a heartbeat from the Route Emitter. This is because as time goes on, if the route is not pruned and there is still no heartbeat, there is an increased possibility that an intended app request might be routed to a dead app instance.

This preference for consistency above availability can cause unnecessary app downtime if a critical component event occurs. For example, consider a scenario in which all apps are running well, but for some reason the heartbeat messages are not being received by the GoRouter. In this scenario, it might be preferable to still allow users to reach the existing apps and not prune the routes because the apps are still running. However, Diego might be moving or starting new instances of apps, and some of the running instances might have failed, resulting in the container being destroyed. With no visibility of the health of the routes, you still require a way to ensure that packets are not directed to the wrong app.

You can place the GoRouter on an overlay network. This allows the GoRouter to indicate on the packet encapsulation what app a specific request was intended for. When the packet lands at a Cell host, if the Cell determines that the packet was not intended for the apps running on it, the Cell can reject that traffic. This mechanism allows the Cells to deal with and reject any bad routes in the event that the GoRouter's route table becomes temporarily stale. This approach makes it possible for Cloud Foundry to incorporate additional availability while maintaining consistency.

Buildpacks and Staging

Buildpacks are an essential step in the deployment flow when deploying app artifacts. There are a number of proposed enhancements in this area. Three critical changes include the use of multiple buildpacks (a parent buildpack that can pull in multiple child buildpacks), the introduction of post-staging policies, and the isolation of compilers from running apps.

Multibuildpacks

Buildpack aggregation is a valuable feature that allows you to combine several runtimes that might be required. For example, if your app is a PHP app but also requires a Perl module, you can pull in both PHP and Perl runtimes by using a multibuildpack. This alleviates the need for customizing the PHP buildpack to pull in a specific Perl library.

Post-Staging Policy or Step

An operator might want to define a post-staging policy or step. For example, after staging is complete, she might want to run a script to package-scan the droplet for compliance reasons, or to upload the droplet to a corporate repository such as artifactory. Therefore, the addition of this step provides additional control and governance over the created droplet artifact.

Compiler-Less Rootfs and Stemcells

If the rootfs and stemcell are compiler-less, all compilers will be excluded from the resulting container. This reduces the attack surface for all running apps. For example, because for many scenarios a compiler is required only during the staging process, Cloud Foundry could use a different rootfs for the staging containers. This is one approach, but in essence, the objective of making Cloud Foundry more secure by reducing the attach surface of running apps by removing compilers is extremely valuable.

Isolation Segments

The concept of placement pools has been around for a couple of years under the guise of several different names (placement pools, isolation zones, elastic clusters). The objective of isolation segments focuses on the specific isolation of select Cloud Foundry components (e.g., the Cells, GoRouter, and Loggregator) on to a dedicated subnet and set of underlying resources so as to provide a dedicated and isolated environment within a Cloud Foundry foundation, without the need to build an entirely new Cloud Foundry environment.

This feature is especially valuable for apps that are required to be run in a strictly isolated environment. An example of such a need would be a PCI- or HIPPA-certified environment. Alternatively, the Cells in the segregated environment might be configured to be more performant and are therefore more costly to run and should be reserved for specific apps with demanding memory and CPU characteristics. With isolation segments, you can establish a segregated environment with, for example, dedicated Cells, GoRouter, and Loggregator that share a pool containing the remaining Cloud Foundry components (such as the Cloud Controller and other Diego components).

When you deploy your app, you can ensure that it lands on a Cell within your isolation segments, and all traffic to that app will be routed by the specific isolation segment GoRouter. When you deploy an app with no segregation requirements, it will reside in the default non-isolated environment and will be accessed by the default GoRouter. This approach allows both segregated and non-segregated apps to reside within the same Cloud Foundry installation and therefore will reduce both your overall deployment footprint and ongoing maintenance costs because you can consolidate several environments.

Summary

This chapter has only scratched the surface on what might be coming next. The premise of Cloud Foundry remains the same: to remove as much of the undifferentiated heavy lifting as possible so that developers can focus on delivering business value iteratively with repeated velocity. However, the high-water mark of what Cloud Foundry can do for you is constantly evolving as new capabilities are always being added to the platform. The extent of new services and capabilities within Cloud Foundry is potentially limitless.

In addition, new app frameworks that run on, and can use Cloud Foundry, are emerging; for example, Spring Cloud Data Flow and Spring Cloud Services. Spring Cloud Data Flow is a project aimed to simplify development of big data apps. It contains stream and batch modules existing as Spring Boot–based stream and task microservices apps. These apps can be autonomously deployed units that can "natively" run in Cloud Foundry. Spring Cloud Data Flow offers a collection of patterns and best practices for microservices-based distributed streaming and batch-data pipelines. This opens Cloud Foundry to new types of workloads and becomes especially pertinent when dealing with Internet of Things–based traffic. In essence, it creates possibilities for Cloud Foundry not only to be the platform for running your apps, but an ideal platform to serve as the integration hub for the enterprise.

Established microservices patterns are also emerging through projects such as Spring Cloud Services, Spring Cloud Netflix, and Spring Cloud Config. Taking advantage of these battle-tested microservice patterns, and of the libraries that implement them, can now be as simple as including a few dependencies in your app build file and applying the appropriate annotation in your source code.

When you step back and review all the recent changes to IT that make technologies like Cloud Foundry possible, it is clear that the IT industry is experiencing phenomenally exciting times right now. I have learned an enormous amount through working on Cloud Foundry, and it is my hope that this book will facilitate your own journey with it.

Index

benefits of, xix, 2
deploying, 43, 266
    (see also environment setup)
documentation, 30
expanded uses for, 80
factors to consider when running, xvii, 40
GitHub repository, 40
installing, 67
    (see also installation)
modular distributed architecture, 29
online resources, xx
platform overview, 5
    (see also cloud-native platforms)
prerequisites to learning, xviii
recently released and future features,
    277-287
supplemental material, 1, 277
Cloud Provider Interfaces (CPIs), 48, 172, 216
cloud-based operating systems
benefits of, 8
fundamental capabilities needed for, 40
cloud-native applications, 13
cloud-native platforms
benefits of, 1
evolution of, 1
major concepts, 2
open, 5
opinionated, 4
prerequisites to learning, xx
structured vs. unstructured, 4
code examples, obtaining and using, 40
colocation requirements, 25
command line interface (CLI), 216, 221
command prompt ($), xxi
comments and questions, xxii
common vulnerabilities and exposures (CVEs),
    156
components
additional
    buildpacks and Docker images, 39
    infrastructure and Cloud Provider Inter-
      face, 40
    marketplace of on-demand services, 37
    stacks, 37
for application execution, 35
benefits of distributed systems, 29
Cloud Controller (CAPI), 33-35
load balancer and GoRouter, 31
messaging, 37

for metrics and logging, 36
overview of, 30
user management and UAA, 32
composable actions
actions included, 86
defined, 82
examples of, 85
relationship to Tasks and LRPs, 86
Concourse.ci, 35
configuration drift, 20
configuration failures, 228
Consul, 112
contact information, xxii
containers
advanced features, 283
benefits of, 3, 141, 154
challenges of, 154
container images, 142
container management, 81, 142
container users, 103
creating, 35
defined, 141
elements of, 142
high memory usage failures, 236-241
implementation in Cloud Foundry, 150-153
Linux containers, 144-150
orchestration of, 153
runtime architecture, 79
terminology, 142, 150
trusted containers, 148
context path routing, 124
context path-based routing, 26
continuous delivery pipelines, 35
Continuous Integration/Continuous Deploy-
    ment (CI/CD), 3, 267
Control Groups (CGroups), 148
control theory, 15
Converger process, 100
core concepts and capabilities
aggregated logging and metrics, 17
applications as units of deployment, 10
built-in resilience and fault tolerance, 15,
    265
cf push command for deployment, 11
cloud-based OS, 8
dealing with undifferentiated heavy lifting, 7
do more approach, 9
domains hosts and routes, 25
Organizations and Spaces, 23

infrastructure as code tools, 16, 172
infrastructure design
    BOSH CPIs, 48
    factors to consider, 49
    jumpbox VMs, 57
    resilience, 50
    setting up an AWS VPC, 55
    sizing and scoping, 50-55
infrastructure failures, 229
installation
    canonical approach, 66
    changing stacks, 73
    growing the platform, 73
    installing Cloud Foundry, 67-71
    key concerns and decisions, 65
    logical environment structure, 75
    pushing your first app, 77
    steps of, 43, 66
    validating platform integrity, 73-75, 274
instance groups, 84, 105, 205, 247-250, 255
integrations, 47
Interactive Ruby (IRB) tools, 244
Internet Gateway (edge routers), 231
internet security, three Rs of, 21
    (see also security)
IPSec, 130
isolation segments, 285

J

Java buildpacks (JBP), 160
jumpbox VMs, 57

K

keys, 257

L

Linux Container manager, 81, 144-150
  as high-level abstract concept, 144
  Control Groups (CGroups), 148
  core primitives and kernel features, 145
  data locality, 148
  disk quotas, 148
  filesystems, 148
  for Docker images, 81
  namespaces, 145
  security through namespaces, 146
  vs. traditional virtual machines, 144
  widespread use of, 142

load balancer
    choice of, 31
    configuring
        PROXY protocol, 130
        request header fields, 128, 283
        TLS termination and IPSec, 130
        WebSocket upgrades, 129
    dynamic approach, 15
    routing and, 126
    setup, 62
local caching layers, 268
logging
    aggregated streaming, 17
    components for, 36
    Diego workflow, 97
    process of, 226-228
    UAA logging, 256
Loggregator
    app log handling, 226
    benefits of, 17, 36
    duties of, 226
    Firehose, 226
    interaction with Diego, 83, 97
    nozzles, 227
Long Running Processes (LRPs)
    Cloud Foundry support for, 11
    defined, 80

M

marketplace of on-demand services, 37
memory
    high memory usage failures, 236-241
    overcommitting, 53
messages, capturing, 37
metrics
    aggregated streaming, 17
    components for, 36
    UAA-produced, 257
Metron agent, 36
microservices, 3
minimal change concept, 20

N

namespaces, 145-147
NATS messaging system
    purpose of, 217
    router implementation and, 131
Network Address Translation (NAT)., 231
network shaping, 283

sticky sessions, 133
TCPRouter, 134-136
uses for, 119
via load balancer and GoRouter, 31,
131-133
RunActions, 114
runC, 35, 81, 86, 150, 151
running containers, 150

S

SAML certificates, 257
sandbox environment, 46, 73, 275
(see also environment setup)
scaling
containers, 153
dynamic, 13
horizontal, 105
scheduling
advanced features, 281
benefits of, 82
defined, 82
scheduled processes, 84
scheduling algorithms, 105
scopes, 259
Secure Shell (SSH)-Proxy services, 106, 127
security
additional in Cloud Foundry, 21
advanced persistent threats (APTs), 20
app and dependency scanning, 158
BOSH management ports, 57
configuration drift and, 20
distributed system security, 19
jumpbox VMs, 57
minimal change concept, 20
networking security groups, 61
security group misconfiguration, 234
three Rs of enterprise security, 21
UAA management, 23, 251-261
self-healing feature, 12, 15
service broker, 38
service instances, 38
session affinity, 133
shared domains, 123
sizing and scoping, 50-55
Cells sizing, 53
instance group replication, 54
snowflake servers, 14
SOCKS5 protocol, 58
Spaces

benefits of, 23
logical environment structure, 75
Spring Cloud, 25
SSL certificates, 62
stacks
changing, 73
defined, 37
staging
advanced features, 284
buildpacks and, 39, 159-162
core concept of, 11
defined, 83
steps of, 114-117
workflow, 90
state machine, 107
static IPs, 59
stemcells, 176, 205, 285
Steno logging, 227
sticky sessions, 133
structured platforms, 4
subdomains, 123
subnets, 60
syslog aggregator, 227
(see also debugging)
system state
components for storing, 34
state machine, 107

T

Tasks
advanced features, 280
examples of, 80
life cycle, 111
TCPRouter, 80, 126, 134-136
teams (see platform-operations team)
testing
cf-acceptance-tests (CATS), 75, 274
production verification testing, 74, 275
three Rs of internet security, 21
time-to-live (TTL), 96
TLS decryption, 130
tokens, 257
TPS, 95-97
tracing, 283
Tracy, Derek, 244
troubleshooting (see debugging)
trusted containers, 148
Twelve-Factor contract, 13, 45, 226
typographical conventions, xx

About the Author

Duncan Winn has been working on Cloud Foundry for Pivotal since that company formed in 2013. Currently he works on Pivotal's Platform Architecture Team, helping companies to install and configure hardened Cloud Foundry environments and related services to get the most out of Cloud Foundry in an enterprise setting. Prior to moving to the United States, he was the EMEA Cloud Foundry developer advocate for Pivotal and ran Pivotal's Platform Architecture Team in London. He is actively involved in the Cloud Foundry community blogging, running meetups, and writing books.

Colophon

The animal on the cover of *Cloud Foundry: The Definitive Guide* is a black-winged kite (*Elanus caeruleus*).

It has distinctive long falcon-like wings with white, gray, and black plumage; its eyes are forward-facing with red irises. Its wings extend past its tail when perched, often on roadside wires. To balance itself, it jerks its tail up and down and adjusts its wings. This kite is recognizable for its habit of hovering over open grasslands. The kite doesn't migrate, but makes short distance movements based on weather.

Black-winged kites nest in loose platforms made of twigs. Females spend more energy constructing the nest than males, and lay 3–4 eggs in them during breeding season. Both parents incubate the eggs, but the male spends more time foraging for food, which includes grasshoppers, crickets, other large insects, lizards, and rodents.

Many of the animals on O'Reilly covers are endangered; all of them are important to the world. To learn more about how you can help, go to *animals.oreilly.com*.

The cover image is from *Lydekker's Royal Natural History*. The cover fonts are URW Typewriter and Guardian Sans. The text font is Adobe Minion Pro; the heading font is Adobe Myriad Condensed; and the code font is Dalton Maag's Ubuntu Mono.

Learn from experts.
Find the answers you need.

Sign up for a **10-day free trial** to get **unlimited access** to all of the content on Safari, including Learning Paths, interactive tutorials, and curated playlists that draw from thousands of ebooks and training videos on a wide range of topics, including data, design, DevOps, management, business—and much more.

Start your free trial at:
oreilly.com/safari

(No credit card required)